Listen
to the Land

Listen
to the Land

Selections from 25 Years of
Naturalist Writing in
The Des Moines Register

Larry A. Stone

Larry Stone

**Turkey River
Environmental Expressions
2004**

Printed in the United States of America.
Printed on recycled paper with 20% post-consumer waste content.

Published by: Turkey River Environmental Expressions
                23312 295th Street
                Elkader, IA 52043
                1.888.807.1828

ISBN 0-9729441-1-7

Other books by Larry A. Stone:

Sylvan T. Runkel: Citizen of the Natural World
2003 — coauthor Jon W. Stravers

Whitetail: Treasure, Trophy or Trouble — A History of Deer in Iowa
2003 — Iowa Department of Natural Resources

Iowa: Portrait of the Land
2000 — Iowa Department of Natural Resources

ACKNOWLEDGMENTS

Like a natural system, this book was shaped by countless members of a community. I'm indebted to my family: my parents for encouraging me to roam; my wife, Margaret, for her love and counsel; and my son, Andy, and daughter, Emily, for their companionship and patience.

Coe College professors Karl E. Goellner and the late Robert V. Drexler became not only teachers but also good friends and mentors. In grade school and high school, Helen Bates and Robert Scobee, especially, kindled excitement about learning.

Iowa naturalist Sylvan T. Runkel, who died in 1995, unselfishly shared his time and knowledge. A joint project, with Jon Stravers, to write Sylvan's biography, has reinforced our great respect for his strength of character and his dedication to teaching.

Finally, I'm grateful to the many, many people whose love of the outdoors brought us together. Here's a necessarily short list, with apologies for omissions:

Carl and Linda Kurtz, Don and Luella Reese, Don Muhm, Jean Prior, Gladys Black, Tom Kollings, Ries Tuttle, Frederic Leopold, Carolyn Benne, Ed and Virginia Crocker, Bill Leonard, Don Poggensee, Bill Horine, Nick and Linda Klepinger, John Garwood, Keith Kirkpatrick and the dedicated employees of Iowa's County Conservation Boards and the Iowa Department of Natural Resources.

But the real V.I.P.s of Iowa conservation are the individuals who still savor an autumn sunrise, delight in spring bird songs and live in harmony with this beautiful land.

DEDICATION

To Margaret, my bow paddler.

TABLE OF CONTENTS

PREFACE

For 25 years in Iowa, we have had what I think is one of the best nature writers and photographers of all time working and living among us.

My pal Larry Stone, the "outdoor writer" who was my colleague at the Des Moines Register, is indeed that good. But too many of us barely noticed Stone's work, underappreciated it or took it for granted. In short, we've treated this gentle soul's graceful, peaceful writing just about like most of us treat nature itself.

Mark my words, this book will be as much of a waker-upper as a March morning blizzard or that perfect, seductive, golden day in early October. When you see the best of Stone's work – about 100 of his favorite columns, stories and photos from a quarter-century at the Register – put together all in one place like this, you're going to become the same kind of major Larry Stone fan that I am.

Let me give you a brief Stone sampler.
– From November, 1989: "Randolph, Ia. – Chris Slutz curled a massive hand around the duck call, huffed deeply from his barrel chest – and played a love song to the shy hen mallard. 'Talk to me, sweetie,' he whispered."
– From January, 1995: "Read any good trees lately? Or snow drifts? Or leaves? Or dung piles?
   Mother Nature writes some mighty fine works, if we hunters, fishermen or naturalists will take the time to read them."
– From February, 1997, at the end of a cross-country skiing inspection of the pristine countryside following a big snowstorm: "You stop to relish the quiet hiss of the wind in the trees. But the gentle whoosh becomes a distant hum, then a rumble.
   The snowplow. Amber lights flashing, engine whining, blade clattering over the gravel, the huge truck unceremoniously sweeps the pretty snow into a heap in the ditch. The driver grins and waves, no doubt thinking he's 'rescued' you. Suddenly, you're back in touch with civilization.
   You can welcome the school bus, get important mail, go shopping, drive to yet another urgent meeting, smell the diesel fumes... Rescued? From what?"
– From June, 1997, on the sounds of nature being like a symphony on a summer evening: "First one gray tree frog uttered its bird-like 'twirr,' then another and another. Before long, the once-silent creek valley was filled with a background of frog music . . . Peaceful? Ahh, yes. But Quiet? Only until you really start to listen. . ."
   When you really start to read and listen to Larry Stone, you realize his voice is a call to real living, to balance in life, to respect for the great wonder that surrounds us – and to the fun of the hunt, the fishing expedition and the nature walk.

"There is more outdoor consciousness now, for sure," he said, when I asked how things have changed over his career.

"But an improved conservation ethic? I kind of wrestle over whether we've improved on that. I sometimes worry we haven't really gotten to the essence of the outdoor experience – that man is not the all-powerful, most important thing in nature, that humanity and the environment need to co-exist, that we're all a part of a natural community, right along with the snakes and bugs. But maybe sometimes I get too philosophical about it, too."

Stone is far too humble about all this. But it fits him to be that way. He is so much one of us, especially here in Iowa, that he starts squirming when somebody starts saying he is a very special and rare talent in our noisy, contemporary world of self-centeredness. Now 52, trim and an almost-scholarly looking man with a close-cropped mustache and beard, he traces his outdoor interests to his boyhood days on the farm of his parents, Warren and the late Virginia Stone, seven miles northeast of Indianola. There he learned a genuine, farm friendliness he still radiates today. And he loved the hunting, fishing and mushroom hunting with his father and grandfathers. In his high school years in Indianola, he began to be inspired by public TV's National Geographic wildlife specials by brothers John and Frank Craighead.

He went on to Coe College in Cedar Rapids to major in biology. Among the life-changing things that happened to him there, two especially important were, 1) he met Margaret Keith, a farm girl from Traer who he fell in love with, married and still counts as his best buddy today, and 2) his favorite biology professors Robert Drexler and Gene Goellner took the young Stone and a bunch of other students on field trips to northeast Iowa.

After graduating from Coe and getting married, Stone earned a University of Michigan master's degree in journalism, with an emphasis in natural resources. Margaret paid the bills by working as a medical technologist.

Then the Stones moved to Des Moines where he'd landed a farm reporting job with the Register. There was a chance, but no promises, he was told, that he would succeed the newspaper's legendary outdoor writer, Ries Tuttle, who was winding up a career of nearly 40 years. Stone got that job in 1972 and began traveling about 20,000 miles per year, all over Iowa, to do columns, stories and photos that appeared in the Sunday Register, as well as the daily Register and the late Des Moines Tribune. He has taken us along on canoe trips into Canada and across Iowa, into the eye-popping nature areas of the state and into the meeting rooms where major decisions on conservation and recreation were being made.

"In those first couple of years, Margaret and I lived in an apartment in Des Moines, but we were both from the farm and neither one of us was all that wild about living in the city," Larry said.

"One time she had her purse snatched when she was walking to a bus stop. Not long after that, one day I was grouchy at work and complained to Ed Heins, the managing editor who had hired me, about not liking living in the city. He said, 'Hell, you're never in the office anyway – go live wherever you want to.'" Shortly, the Stones had packed up and moved to their beloved northeast Iowa.

At first they plopped down $10,000 and bought "a little ol' house" in St. Olaf, a town of 140, and then started looking for an ideal spot for their "dream home." In 1992, they had it built on a hilltop southeast of Elkader where the Turkey River cuts through the big limestone hills. The arrangement worked well for both Stone and our bosses at the Register until 1997. He would travel the state, often writing his pieces on a laptop while Margaret drove their car.

"She became my 'right hand man,' chauffeur, copy editor, you name it," said Larry. Their children Andy, now adults with careers of their own, grew up and thrived in the small town, small-school atmosphere.

But in the spring of '97, Register editor Dennis Ryerson told Stone he wanted him to move back to central Iowa, work in the Des Moines office and focus more on central Iowa activities and people. Stone's decision was no big surprise to those of us who know him well. He opted to leave the Register and stay in northeast Iowa. "I can't imagine, I cannot even fathom, that I'd ever have been happy doing what Dennis wanted me to," Stone said. "So I left. I don't have any regrets or bitterness about it now. I had a lot of good years at the Register, and they gave me permission to use my columns in this book. I'm glad to be out on my own now."

His stories are appearing regularly in such publications as The Iowan magazine and the Iowa Natural Heritage Foundation magazine, and he coauthored a book on the late Iowa naturalist Sylvan Runkel, of Des Moines.

"I hope to continue a lot of the same type of writing that I've done," Stone told me, "to continue to spread a message of nature conservation and appreciation. That kind of makes me sound like an evangelist, I know, and I'm not sure whether that's good or bad. But nature is such a part of all of us that I want to help people realize how much it affects us. And I want to help them understand that you don't have to go to Yellowstone National Park to experience Nature. You can step out your own back door and do it right here."

– Chuck Offenburger

INTRODUCTION

Mom didn't much care for snakes. But, then again, how many mothers do?

My Mom was special, though. For all her trepidation about those wiggly reptiles, she could appreciate the antics of those in her family who felt otherwise. For example, whenever Dad found a bullsnake out in the field, he'd stick it inside his shirt and bring it back to turn loose under the corncrib. Good way to thin out those pesky rats and mice, he'd explain.

Before he released a snake, though, Dad would let it coil around his arm where we kids could admire its darting tongue and sparkling eyes and smooth scales and brown and yellow speckles. And, bless her, Mom would share our wonderment. Her message was unspoken, but clear: Each of Nature's creatures, in its own way, is a thing of beauty, worthy of our respect.

On the farm, that philosophy, and beauty, surrounded us daily. Meadowlarks warbled from the fenceposts, and we'd find their domed nests tucked in clumps of grass in the pasture. Brilliant-yellow goldfinches – "wild canaries," we called them – chattered from their perches on the barbed-wire fences. Turkey buzzards floated on summer thermals. Once in a while, somebody might even see a jackrabbit.

In the fall, big flocks of migrating ducks would stop briefly at the pond, or swing into the corn stubble for an evening meal. Occasionally, a red fox streaked across the road, fluffy tail floating.

Thorny-but-fragrant wild roses bloomed in the fencerows. Wild strawberries – red, juicy and sweet – ripened in the road ditches. We gobbled them with no fear of gravel dust or lead poisoning or pesticides. Later in the summer, we also picked raspberries. The goal may have been a batch of jelly, but most ended up in our stomachs, or in purple stains on our tongues, fingers or T-shirts. Jelly had to wait until the tangy wild grapes and wild plums of early fall.

At night, in those long-ago times without air conditioning or TV or soccer practice, we'd chase lightning bugs around the yard or sneak up on cicadas buzzing in the maple tree. You could even see the Milky Way, and more stars than anybody ever thought of counting. It was DARK back then, before every farmer thought he had to have a mercury-vapor security light.

And we took it all for granted. Even though we didn't realize it, farmers' children were the luckiest kids alive. Sure, you had to help with the chores and scoop manure. But those jobs also meant getting to watch the barn swallows build their mud nests under the eaves on the cattle shed – and laughing as the birds dive-bombed the cat.

The heat and sweat and chaff of baling hay were tempered by the breezy ride on top of the loaded hayrack, where we grabbed handfuls of mulberries off the branches that hung over the lane. Rounding up the cattle meant splashing across the creek and perhaps pausing to look for a frog or turtle or muskrat or fossil.

On the hottest days, we even got to loaf a little. Oh, Dad might wake us up early for a few hours of walking beans, but on a sticky afternoon we'd knock off and go swimming in the pond.

My town friends were envious. They'd jump at the chance to come to the farm, build dams in the creek or plink ground squirrels in the pasture with the .22 rifle. City kids couldn't imagine being able to walk to the pond to catch a bluegill, or that I could go rabbit hunting just by stepping out the door.

A hike to the grove of boxelders in the back pasture became a wilderness trek. We'd climb trees, throw horseweed spears, build dead-branch forts and roast hot dogs over smoky campfires. On the hottest days, we'd become spelunkers, wading through the mossy trickle that flowed through the big, concrete box culvert under our gravel road.

M

About the only thing I couldn't do was play baseball in the town Little League. But Dad fixed that. He sacrificed a couple of acres of his best bluegrass pasture to build a baseball diamond for my brothers and me and all the other farm kids for miles around. What's more, he coached that rag-tag team, with eager, 10-year-old faces changing annually, for the better part of two decades.

When I started driving (that is, got a license to drive something besides the tractor), I felt lucky to get permission to take the truck. Of course, the old Dodge was a far cry from the transportation today's kids have gotten used to. The lime green machine sported a stock rack, complete with brown, crusty smudges left by loose-boweled hogs or steers. This was, after all, a working pickup – not a recreational vehicle. Farmers had to be practical, Grandpa Homer reminded us.

To my dismay, Grandpa felt the same way about guns. With only a hint of sadness, he recalled the cherished Ithaca shotgun, a 16-gauge double barrel, that he had traded off because it was too fancy to use on the farm. He replaced the Ithaca with a single-shot 12-gauge Stevens; a plain, inexpensive gun that he didn't have to coddle. He couldn't have guessed that the double some-day would be a collector's item, while the old 12, even with all its sentimental value to the grand-kids, will always be just an old gun.

Still, Grandpa's stories have survived, even without the Ithaca. He sheepishly told of hunting rabbits from a horse-drawn bobsled. The well-trained team didn't mind the gunfire – but the muzzle blasts temporarily deafened the unfortunate animals.

Part of Grandpa's cottontail haven, a brushy slough, is still there, with clumps of big bluestem proving its link to the pioneer prairies. But the prairie chickens, which still boomed in one field when *his* father bought our farm, about 1920, vanished long ago. Great-grandpa Ira succeeded in taming the prairie and routing the chickens, as a good farmer of that era was expected to do. About all the native sod he left was a patch of slough grass in a waterway. I hated walking through the saw-toothed grass, which pioneers aptly named "ripgut." But Grandpa mowed it every year, then pitched it on top of the stack of hay bales to shed the water, just like a thatched roof.

Barns and black plastic kept hay drier, though, so even the slough grass and other prairie rem-nants eventually vanished in the face of "modern" farming. That's partly why I grew up culti-vating corn and walking beans and combining oats, instead of mowing prairie hay. And I hunt-ed pheasants, instead of prairie chickens. It took me several decades to realize that, just maybe, the change WASN'T progress.

My other Grandpa, Roy, was raised along the Missouri River, where he learned to fish with his hands and hunt ducks to help feed his family. The wild Missouri provided plenty of mallards and catfish – but the unruly river also brought floods and hard times for poor, bottomland farmers.

Thus, in the depths of the Great Depression, Grandpa packed up his wife and kids, including my Mom, and moved north. Times were tough in Iowa, too, but Grandpa found a job helping to install the pilings that eventually would channelize and tame his beloved/hated Missouri River. Years later, I learned the story of the once-wild Missouri, and of what a magnificent resource the "improve-ments" had destroyed. I didn't blame Grandpa, though; he probably was just grateful for a paycheck.

I couldn't comprehend or appreciate the hardships of my ancestors – but I loved those family stories almost as much as I savored my own freedom to roam in the pasture and along the creek. "Outdoors" wasn't just a place you went on the weekend: it was everything around me; it was where I lived and grew up.

Grandpa Roy and Grandpa Homer no doubt fueled my passion for hunting, too. After hearing their relatively tame tales of ducks and rabbits, I graduated to the more colorful yarns in

"Outdoor Life." Curled up with a magazine, I imagined myself stalking grizzlies in Alaska, tracking bighorn sheep in the Rockies or shooting a trophy whitetail in Minnesota.

Deer were beginning to thrive in Iowa, too, back in the early '60's. And it gradually dawned on me that I could hunt big game close to home. I re-read countless articles, sighted in my little 20-gauge, sharpened a cheap hunting knife and scouted the trails in our friend's woods. Time to prove my woodsman's skills!

Hindsight could argue that Lady Luck probably had more to do with it than skill – but I dropped my first buck with one shot. There probably wasn't a happier 16-year-old in all of Warren County – or all of Iowa – on the sunny Sunday afternoon when I tagged that deer.

The whole family admired the animal when I brought it home in the back of the pickup. There was no remorse – only curiosity – for the rare, beautiful creature. Farmers figured game animals were made to be hunted. Here was a resource that had been harvested; it would be used wisely.

With his years of practice butchering hogs and cattle on the farm, Grandpa Homer matter-of-factly showed me how to convert my deer to packages of venison. Together, we cut it up on a table in the garage. Later, Mom drew raves with her new venison recipes. Home-grown deer could be almost as good as farm-raised beef and pork, our family agreed.

Not much of that deer went to waste. I scraped, salted and stretched the hide, then hung it on the side of the shed. The skinny antlers paled beside those I'd seen in the hunting magazines, but with their base wrapped in red felt and fastened to a home-made plaque, they spruced up my bedroom wall.

Somehow, the whole deer hunting experience simply *felt good* – just like creek stomping and berry picking and working in the dirt out under the sky. Rural Iowa might as well be paradise. Wasn't this the way life was meant to be?

But, over the years, I gradually began to get uneasy about the subtle – and not so subtle – changes in those familiar surroundings. Was it when the county decided to widen and grade the dirt road, wiping out the plum thicket that always sheltered a covey of quail? Or did I feel the loss when a neighbor bulldozed a brushy pasture so he could plant more corn? I know I mourned when a nearby farmer sprayed for grasshoppers – and ended up killing off the bass in his pond with drift from the insecticide. I vaguely longed for clean water and vast forests and unspoiled scenery.

Two beloved Coe College professors helped focus that youthful idealism. Robert V. Drexler, a botanist with a passion for the northwoods canoe country, and Karl E. (Gene) Goellner, a field zoologist with an insatiable curiosity about wild critters, taught not only a love of learning but also a reverence for the natural world. Both men opened their homes and their hearts to a generation of students, including this lucky farm kid.

Goellner made us groan with his subtle jokes, awed us with his knowledge of birds and bird songs and led his classes on rattlesnake and salamander hunts. Always a true scientist, he also demanded that we know – at the very least – the difference between a tibia and a fibula.

Drexler expected his charges to learn the finer points of photosynthesis and plant taxonomy – and to share his appreciation for rare mosses, wild places and (before the word became popular) ecological relationships. Together, he and his students thrived at a northern Minnesota canoe-country field station, growing lean, sun-bronzed and shaggy-haired in a unique wilderness classroom.

With these two mentors, plus stints in journalism school, as an Earth Day organizer and as a forest researcher in the northern Rockies, I *should* have been an expert – on something. I was naive enough to think that was why The Des Moines Register picked me as their outdoor writer in 1972. I could tell people how to save the planet . . .

O

Right!

For a quarter century, I watched, wondered, wrote and photographed as we Iowans plowed up, seeded down, planted, paved over, clear-cut, blanket sprayed, dammed, dredged – and sometimes preserved – various parts of our state. We squabbled over dove hunting, deer hunting, tournament fishing, bottle and can deposits, park fees, bike trails, steel shot, hog lots, highway routes, wetland drainage, pollution rules and, of course, money.

Are we any smarter today? Perhaps. But, if so, why haven't we stopped squabbling? We can't even settle our past disagreements so we can move on to something new. Doves, deer, livestock confinements, highway projects, wetland protection and money for public land still spark rancorous debates.

We profess the need for clean air and clean water and wildlife habitat. Too often, however, we conveniently forget that our cars taint the air, our farm and lawn chemicals seep into rivers, and our passions for golf courses and shopping malls and highways hasten the destruction of natural areas.

Maybe we still don't "get it." We haven't accepted the fact that we're *all* citizens of this planet. Most of us are too busy fussing about our own pet projects and schemes and the latest techno-gadget to think how our consumptive lifestyles affect the environment. We're fiddling with the leaky faucet while our house is on fire.

I once knew a museum curator who agonized over the theft of some artifacts, while he showed no remorse about plowing a virgin prairie on his own farm. How could he mourn for some collector's trinket – yet not lament the conversion of an eons-old compass plant to yet another ear of corn?

Farmers get conservation awards – and taxpayer-funded financial incentives – for preserving their soil. Yet many landowners feel too pressured by neighbors' opinions or economics or tradition to fence cattle out of their woodlots, leave a plum thicket in a fencerow or even allow grassy cover to grow on a roadside. And then they try to blame hunters or the government for the lack of wildlife!

Government officials, in agencies assigned to manage our resources, sometimes fight for bureaucratic turf, rather than conservation principles. Environmental protection should be the foundation of our government, rather than an afterthought assigned to an underfunded department.

A few politicians brag about "green" votes, but most would rather promise tax cuts or pork barrel projects than address future environmental quality. And, sadly, voters rarely force candidates or public officials to debate conservation issues. Why can't conservation groups muster the support to make the environment an important election topic?

We claim to be environmentalists, as we plant trees, buy land, restore prairie and occasionally lobby legislators. But how many of us have changed our lifestyles to reduce consumption, drive less and think small? When we *do* speak of the environment, we tend to pay it lip service, offering only quick fixes to simple problems:

Want ducks? Plug a tile and build a marsh.

Like forests? Plant trees.

Prefer prairie? Seed some native grasses and flowers.

Oppose hunting? Take pictures instead.

Weeds in the cornfield, or the back yard? Spray them.

Too many chemicals? Ban them.

Too many people? Keep out the immigrants.

We've learned to package everything – even the outdoors and conservation – so we can stack it neatly on the shelf. We may even label it a problem or solution, or a destination.

P

We refuse to face the reality spelled out by native Iowan Aldo Leopold in his conservation classic, "A Sand County Almanac." To ensure the health of the planet, Leopold said, we must strive for a "land ethic." We must recognize that every living thing – plant or animal, large or small, human or bacterium – is a citizen of a natural community. We must treat each of those fellow citizens with respect. In the eyes of nature, we are equals. Conservation, Leopold said, is a state of harmony between men and the land.

"Harmony" implies cooperation among many individuals. Yet our society seems to be based on strife, confrontation and "me first." People want to dominate, conquer, manipulate and regulate. Nobody seems to think of coexistence.

What has happened to *respect* – for ourselves, our fellow humans, our Earth?

We try to include environmental education in our schools, but too often it becomes just another requirement shoe-horned into an overworked teacher's schedule. Faced with resource management disputes – over agricultural pollution, urban sprawl, deer populations or park use – we instinctively clamor for more laws.

Perhaps what we should be seeking is an *attitude* rather than a curriculum or a code book. Respect for the land, and the resolve to use its resources sustainably, may come more from a spiritual closeness to Nature than from lawyers or lectures that preach conservation. And we may best develop that respect – even reverence – for the earth from a lifetime of exploring and appreciating its marvels.

Some doomsayers might argue that we'll only mend our ways in the face of environmental disaster – if then. But I'm enough of an optimist to believe people are wiser than that. We inherently know that breathing air pollution and drinking chemicals aren't good for you; that preserving forests and prairies is better than building yet another shopping mall; that small is beautiful.

We have a long way to go to achieve Leopold's ideal of harmony – but some of us, at least, are on that path. Our salvation may lie with those people who understand that the outdoors isn't just a place to visit, or a topic of conversation, or a newspaper reporter's beat. It's our home.

Hundreds – thousands – of visionary Iowans know that. Most are not celebrities or politicians or VIPs. I've been privileged to meet a sampling of these ordinary – yet *extra*ordinary – folks, who are dedicated to saving our natural heritage. We all owe a debt of gratitude to the teachers who connect students to the earth, the farmers who think first of the health of their land and the business people who measure success not just in dollars but in their contribution to the natural community. Our heroes and heroines should be the logger who loves squirrels, the fisherman who cherishes prairie, a politician who savors wilderness, the hunter who watches warblers or the botanist who photographs snakes. Young or old, rich or poor, these men and women share a common bond. They look upon our world with what Rachel Carson called a "sense of wonder."

When they see a milkweed, they stop to smell its blossom or to look for a monarch butterfly, rather than instinctively reach for the herbicide. They're content to step lightly on the land, whether they're building on its surface, harvesting its crops or savoring its beauty. They know the difference between "needs" and "wants." (Transportation is a need. A gas-guzzling, hill-climbing, loud-mufflered, smoke-spewing four-wheeler is a "want.") They learn from mistakes of the past, when more was better, and work toward a brighter, sustainable future.

Those Iowans are a part of the outdoors – and the outdoors is a part of their soul. These stories of hope are dedicated to them – and to their grandchildren.

Q

CHAPTER 1

ALMANAC

From January's snow to February's cold to the first geese of March, each day, month and season unveils another side of Nature. We Iowans enjoy the privilege of smelling April's wildflowers, grumbling at August heat, relishing October colors and dodging November blizzards. Each new blossom, insect, bird song, constellation or farm field pattern creates a different mood, as we strive to experience the glories of the outdoors.

We can learn from the natural world, too, if we only heed the signs that Nature paints for us, and read the maps her creatures draw.

Stories in the snow

Nature's tales are told in the tracks

Read any good trees lately? Or snowdrifts? Or leaves? Or dung piles?

Mother Nature writes some mighty fine works, if we hunters, fishermen or naturalists will take the time to read them.

For example, remember the big buck that eluded you all fall?

He's a mystery fan. Can you figure out where he hid throughout the hunting season?

Now, you can almost hear his haughty chuckles, as he ambles across the ridge at twilight. Apart from the rest of the herd, his brown hulk looms half-again larger than the does and fawns.

At dawn, you find their tracks along the deserted roadside, where the deer must have delighted in prancing under starlight. Were they *trying* to torment you?

Maybe you can follow those tracks into the woods, maybe learn their secrets.

Good luck – the careful buck cleverly superimposes his footprints on dozens of others in the well-worn trail.

You wander off the path, and find the forest has plenty of other tales to tell.

A winged basswood seed lying on the snow suggests why your neighbor's honey is so clear and sweet: his bees favor basswood flowers.

And could that basswood be a den tree? The soft wood rots easily, leaving hollows for raccoons, squirrels and woodpeckers.

A parade of squirrel tracks leading to the gnarled trunk confirms your hunch.

Here and there, foraging turkeys have rumpled the soft, white blanket that had covered a once-smooth mat of leaves. The disheveled sites pinpoint the locations of the oak trees that produced the biggest and sweetest crops of acorns.

At the forest edge, bits of bark and splinters of wood hint at the epicurean delights lurking overhead in the dead elm. A diligent but messy downy woodpecker chiseled the tree to feast on juicy insect larvae.

The downy's giant cousin is even messier. A pileated woodpecker has ripped fist-size chunks from a rotting oak, littering the ground with hunks of wood.

The snow moves in front of you, as a meadow vole pops up in a flurry of white. Will the tiny rodent survive the winter – or become an hors d'oeuvre for a coyote's dinner?

The song-dogs *must* be hungry. All that late-night howling and revelry surely have to burn a lot of calories.

A patch of brown shows through the snow under a south-facing cedar tree. You think once more of deer.

A closer look finds a mat of grass and a nearby pile of pelleted deer droppings. A white-tail may have napped here on a cold, sunny afternoon.

But did he *have* to eat a bedtime snack of your white pines?

The evergreens have pale wounds on the tips of their branches, where deer nipped off the tender, new growth. What's more, they've pruned dogwoods, sumac and—to your chagrin—even your prized apple trees.

The buck is getting bolder.

2

Ahead he's left even more clues: the wrist-sized sapling with its bark scarred and peeled away by his September antler-polishing; the chewed maple branch hanging over the scrape, under which he pawed a scent post during the rut.

You ponder the snow, with its maze of tracks. Then, on a whim, you plunge down over the bluff to a secluded swale along the river bank.

Ahh, could this be the hide-away – the refuge where the cagey white-tails went to avoid woods full of hunters?

Deer tracks – and more tracks – weave through the clumps of canarygrass and stacks of logs left by the flood.

One trail leads from the river, where cakes of ice clink as they float by. Would the deer willingly take a frigid plunge? The answer is written in the snow, pocked by water droplets where the animal tried to drip-dry.

When you look back across the river from whence the deer came, it all starts to make sense. Just beyond the tree-lined bank is a corn field. To a hungry but water-proof deer, a meal of corn is well worth a quick dip in the river.

Food, shelter, a harem: It's no longer any mystery why that buck is here.

You wish him well – at least until *next* year!

January 8, 1995

Surviving Nature's beauty

Dawn comes late.

Swirling clouds of snow reduce the breakfast-bound deer to phantom shapes on the wind-swept hillside.

A hungry tree sparrow dances in a mound of white that buries the bird-feeding tray.

When you heed the bird's unspoken plea and fill the feeder, the goldfinches descend en masse. Even the ground-loving juncos join the feast, after a futile search belly-deep in the drifts below.

All morning, birds swarm to the feeder; house finches, nuthatches, chickadees, titmice, cardinals, red-bellied and downy woodpeckers. Snow flies as they alight on the porch railing to wait in line, then squabble over the best spot on the seed tray.

The storm has whetted the larger birds' appetites, as well.

A dozen crows – more practical than particular – find easy pickings behind the neighbor's manure spreader. The birds aren't fussy: corn is corn.

Other critters cope in their own ways.

A lone eagle circles the bluff, apparently putting more stock in a fleeting patch of blue than in the leaden clouds.

A red-tailed hawk hunkers in the lee of the woods, one eye cocked for a wayward mouse, but mostly content to wait out the blow.

You chuckle smugly at the plight of the fat squirrel, struggling to hop through the snow for its daily assault on the sunflower seed feeder. Ol' bushytail has to work a little harder for his stolen snack.

At midday, the storm abates. The fresh, clean snowscape beckons irresistibly. You snap on the skis.

But even with the slick sticks on your feet, it's a chore to travel through the foot-deep mantle. No wonder the squirrel had trouble.

It's said that the Eskimos have dozens of words for snow. Now you see why.

This snow grabs your skis and squeaks with the sound of a hand rubbing an inflated balloon. There's no comparison to the fine slick powder that fell on the trail during last month's sub-zero cold.

Nature, the artist, uses each kind of snow in a slightly different way. These flakes are like whipped cream, spread over the rough edges that humans have left on the landscape. The bluebird house wears a round, white dollop for a cap. What will the winter residents – the family of deer mice – think of the new roof ornament?

A creamy coating camouflages the rusting cupola on the old barn. Like frosting on holiday cookies, the snow sugarcoats fence posts, barbed wire and highway signs.

Even the woods have been transformed. The sticky, white snow clinging to stark, slate-colored tree trunks creates an optical illusion; a surreal maze. Is it white on black, or black on white; three-dimensional or single plane?

The damp breeze wiggles the branches, jarring loose marshmallow blobs that pock the surface below, creating a miniature moonscape on the once-smooth mantle.

Across the valley, through the lingering flurries, the trees, bluffs, hills and ravines merge into a myriad of grays.

You stop to relish the quiet hiss of the wind in the trees. But the gentle whoosh becomes a distant hum, then a rumble.

The snowplow. Amber lights flashing, engine whining, blade clattering over the gravel, the huge truck unceremoniously sweeps the pretty snow into a heap in the ditch.

The driver grins and waves, no doubt thinking how he's "rescued" you.

Suddenly, you're back in touch with civilization.

You can welcome the school bus, get important mail, go shopping, drive to yet another urgent meeting, smell the diesel fumes . . .

Rescued? From what?

February 9, 1997

Make way for spring,
Iowa winter is fading fast

"One swallow does not make a summer, but one skein of geese, cleaving the murk of a March thaw, is the spring."

– Aldo Leopold in "A Sand County Almanac."

They were just dark spots against fading twilight, skimming the tree-tops along the river bluff, playing hide-and-seek with the lengthening shadows.

But something made me look again, then catch my breath with excitement.

Geese! The first flock of the season! Two dozen Canadas, headed north.

Snow still lingered in the fencerows and swales, and a chill breeze swept the ridges. But with geese on the move, I knew winter was on the wane. This was not a false alarm. It was the real thing.

"A cardinal, whistling to a spring thaw but later finding himself mistaken, can retrieve his error by resuming his spring silence," Leopold wrote.

"But a migrating goose, staking 200 miles of black night on the chance of finding a hole in a lake, has no easy chance for retreat," Leopold continued. "His arrival carries the conviction of a prophet who has burned his bridges."

Oh, subtler signs have foretold spring's coming since early January. But we're slow to notice the sun's gradual ascent in the southern sky, and the minute or two of daylight we gain as the sun rises earlier and sets later each day.

Solar energy can't be denied, however. Every tree, every weed, every rock or dirt clod poking through the snow absorbs the sunlight, and gradually melts away the winter.

Bitter cold may grip the night, even into March. But rarely is the day so frigid that the sun can't start the icicles dripping.

The longer days trigger a new energy in plants and animals alike. The male goldfinch bravely dons tufts of new, bright-yellow feathers, flaunting them at the winter he's finally beaten.

Maple buds swell and redden. And the sap creeps upward to feed the awakening tree. The clear, faintly sweet liquid drips from a broken branch.

From the top of that maple, the now-confident cardinal greets the dawn with his rowsing "Cheer, cheer!"

A great horned owl prowls the dusk, ghost-like. The owls already have laid their eggs, and soon there will be young to feed.

Perhaps the owl will choose a rabbit supper, and the owlets will recycle my raspberry canes, which the cottontails nibbled last winter.

Or maybe the winged hunter will find a meadow vole, vulnerable now to predators after its network of snow tunnels collapsed. In the dead grass, the criss-crossing pathways map the winter wanderings of the little mammals.

Or perhaps the owl will feast on white-footed mice. Does the owl know what I know: that the mice have been winter tenants in my bluebird houses?

With the bluebirds due back any day, I'll soon evict the mice. Will they find a new home – or become appetizers for owls?

With the hills still brown and bare, I look for any spot of color to brighten the winter-weary landscape. A meadowlark, yellow breast aglow, perches on a roadside fence. He's silent yet, waiting for a clearer verdict before he serenades the spring. But at least he's moved back north.

In the woods, hardy mosses show pale-green against the musty dead leaves, patches of dirty snow and brown rotting logs. I look in vain for the first spring beauty or bloodroot. No blossoms yet – but they'll surely pop up before the month is out.

A stately white pine looms against a timbered ridge. But what's that bright speck near its crown?

With binoculars, I spy a red-tailed hawk; no, *two* red-tails perched on a dead limb, their rusty tails and brown-speckled backs glinting in the sun.

It *must* be spring. Why else would the raptors, which normally prefer more breathing room, be perched cozily together?

I want it to be spring – but still there's a lingering doubt. What about the ice-locked river backwaters, or the 2-foot drifts behind the grove, or the purple finches still gorging themselves at my feeder?

But then I remember the geese – and I smile.

If the geese think it's spring, who's a mere human to argue?

March 6, 1988

The sweet smell of spring

If there's any doubt that spring is here, step outside and take a whiff.

On a warm day in late winter, you may hear a cardinal or see a robin or yearn to follow a north-bound thread of geese – but the air still will smell like winter. The season's accumulation of grime on the landscape tinges the breeze with a musty, stale scent of dead vegetation and dirty snow.

Spring doesn't officially make its entrance until the first showers have washed away this residue, soaked up the waiting earth and triggered a burst of growth from long-dormant plants.

After the inaugural rains, the outdoors smells of sweet, rich soil – the nourishing earth that sustains us all.

Robins and grackles eagerly begin probing lawns for worms and grubs lured to the surface by the warmth and dampness.

Creeks that rushed through March with a load of muddy, frigid snowmelt now have slowed their pace and carry warmer, clearer, sweeter-smelling water.

The streams gurgle through valleys tinted pink by the bursting maple buds and delicately perfumed by the first shy wildflowers.

Hepaticas reach upward with their hairy stems, donning white or pink or purple or blue flowers. The bright bouquets rise in contrast to last year's liver-shaped leaves lying dead and crumpled at their feet.

The grass-like leaves and tiny buds of the spring beauty poke hesitantly from beneath the oak leaves. From these modest beginnings will blossom a flower worthy of the name "spring beauty," with pastel pink stripes accenting the miniature white petals.

Other signs of spring in the forest may be more subtle: the white spear of a May apple jabbing through the soil under a dead leaf; the deliberate swelling of a hickory bud; the increasing activity of insects and other tiny critters that make their homes in the duff; the sprouting of fruiting bodies, just millimeters high, on little clumps of moss.

Turkey vultures are drawn northward by thermals rising from the warming ground, and they glide for hours in search of carrion.

Red-tailed hawks speed up their frenzied nesting rituals in anticipation of the soon-to-hatch brood of fuzzy-headed little hawks.

Cock pheasants strut and crow boldly in the early-morning sun, coaxing hens to join their harems.

The liquid warble of a meadowlark floats from the pasture fencepost, celebrating the reappearance of the grass from beneath the winter's snows.

Nature's season of renewal is here – you can hear, feel and *smell* it in the air.

April 12, 1978

Nature gives meaning to spring's fresh feeling

Smell the sweetness of the wild plums, or the clean, earthy dampness left by a passing shower.

Savor the fresh greens of the cottonwoods, elms and maples.

Feel the excitement of the woods-rattling gobble of a lusty tom turkey.

Marvel at the dazzling yellow of the goldfinches against the rain-washed gray sky. The birds' golden glow is matched only by the new blossom of a dandelion on a sunny day.

Every year, right about now, Iowa outdoor-lovers experience sensory overload.

We go to sleep to the echoes of whip-poor-wills, and awake to the incessant whistles of field sparrows.

The soft first light of dawn accents the just emerging yellow-green leaves on gooseberries, wild cherries and elms. The warmer brown of young oak leaves softens the dark, sturdy branches.

In the lush pastures, the emerald grass is dotted with new-born calves – and pesky gopher mounds.

Wild babies, too, are beginning to appear. Rabbits want their young to be ready to feast on the first lettuce leaves in your garden.

The young owls must be able to hunt while the baby rabbits are easy prey.

Fuzzy yellow goslings explore the pond bank, while the doting goose and haughty gander guard their brood.

Fawns need warmer weather, so it may be a few more days before they totter out of the woods behind their sleek mothers.

For now, however, the scruffy deer – a majestic gray in winter and a rich tan in summer – are comically in between. Their rough, uneven coats turn a motley beige until the seasonal transition is complete.

But his bedraggled appearance doesn't faze the arrogant buck. Although his growing antlers are just velvety nubbins, he kicks and spars to drive away the yearlings.

When the warm winds sweep up from the south, a blizzard of raptors ride the air currents. Turkey vultures, eagles and red-tails soar on the thermals. Broad-wings, sharp-shinned and Cooper's hawks flap to gain speed, then flash past at eye level as you watch in awe from the bluff top.

If they're on time, the orioles and hummingbirds should be arriving any day now. And, of course, the first mosquitoes of the year won't be far behind.

After two days of rain, the great blue heron stalks the flooded creek backwaters in search of a wayward carp.

If you're a farmer, you might cuss the temperamental weather that can leave puddles standing in some fields, while dust blows across nearby ridge tops.

Even those whose livelihoods aren't so dependent on the weather may share the apprehension, wondering if the tulips will freeze or if the bird bath will become an avian skating rink.

You watch each thunderstorm, expecting a warm rain – but begrudgingly prepared for a burst of snow.

You hope the next Canadian front won't be *too* cold for the day-old bluebirds. Yet, at the same time, you fear a blast of southwestern air that could wither your newly planted pine seedlings.

But there's too much to do – and too little time – to fret.

With luck, there could be a feast of fresh crappies for supper tonight. And how about a side dish of mushrooms, or asparagus, or both?

The rose-breasted grosbeak is calling, cotton-ball clouds are drifting over the hills, the river is dancing with delight.

It's May!

May 11, 1997

When the sun sets, nature strikes up its symphony

On a perfect June evening, nature's sounds can be heard
if you start to listen.

"Red sun at night, sailor's delight."

The pink-orange ball sinking into the haze on the western tree line foretold another perfect June evening.

A dying breeze teased and tickled the trees. They whispered with delight, shyly waving their new cloaks of young, growing leaves.

The array of green foliage engulfed the forest, and perfumed the cooling air. Can a late-spring woodland really *smell* green?

No question about the hay field, though. The scent of just-mowed alfalfa flowed under the fence, through the valley and across the road. What a treat for harried drivers to inhale the soothing aroma of fresh hay, rather than dust and diesel fumes.

Well-rested from a lazy afternoon, the bird choristers broke into a joyous twilight songfest. The indigo bunting jabbered from a utility line. A bluebird chortled softly in the fencerow mulberry tree.

Shrill whistles revealed the cardinal's perch high in the dead oak, where the bird's distinctive red glowed even brighter in the setting sun.

Red also means food, if you're a hummingbird. A tiny ruby-throat's wings purred, as it darted from blossom to blossom on the columbine, probing deeply with its needle-like bill for a few drops of nectar for a bedtime snack.

As daylight faded, each bird hurried to complete one last verse. Song sparrows buzzed and twanged, peewees chirred plaintively, the catbird babbled its full repertoire, red-wings scolded passers-by, robins caroled.

Off through the woods, a barred owl tuned up its whoos – and a tom turkey on its night roost gobbled a grouchy response.

Even before the birds had finished, the amphibians chimed in.

First one gray tree frog uttered its bird-like "twirr," then another . . . and another.

Before long, the once-silent creek valley was filled with a background of frog music.

Then came the toads, slicing through the darkness with their high-pitched, monotone trill.

The crickets, which had been chirping all day, struggled to compete with the vociferous newcomers. The musicians seemed to be dueling in the darkness: Twirr, trill, chirp . . . twirr, trill, chirp.

Could the whip-poor-will settle the vocal contest, merely by blurting out its name? The tireless bird was bound to try. Over and over, it called from the woods' edge, as if repeating itself would end the debate.

But the exercise only succeeded in awaking more whip-poor-wills, which contributed volume, if not originality, to the noisy dialogue.

By now, the crescent moon shimmered overhead – bright enough to light a dim path along he old logging road.

Although stepping softly, two hikers startled a deer, which snorted in surprise to find humans invading its territory.

A smaller mammal – raccoon? skunk? opossum? – shuffled away through the darkness.

Tinier creatures – mice? shrews? insects? – rustled ever-so-softly in the forest litter.

A rattled "sizzz" traced the clumsy flight of a June bug through the unseen tree leaves.

Over the pasture, the first fireflies of the season flickered and flashed and danced.

Then – hmmmmmmm, slap.

It's mosquito season, too.

Stars began to prick the darkening sky. A bat fluttered past, its ghostly silhouette bringing life to the celestial display.

Abruptly, a farm dog yapped in the distance. The neighbor's old pickup, with its holey muffler, rumbled along the gravel road.

A flashing light raced through the stars, followed later by the blast of jet engines. The roar faded as quickly as it had come, as the aircraft sped cargo and passengers to urgent appointments.

Civilized sounds gave way again to nature's music. Twirr, trill, chirp . . . twirr, trill, chirp.

Peaceful? Ahhh, yes . . .

But quiet?

Only until you really start to listen . . .

June 15, 1997

Nature leaves hints: Summer has arrived

Smoky-blue haze smothers trees on the skyline.

The close, cool, clammy night air already is heating up in the first orange rays of sun.

You catch a sweet whiff of elderberry blossoms, steeped in the aroma of lush grass and spiced with a trace of the neighbor's hog lot.

Summer has come to Iowa.

Patches of black-eyed Susans turn hillsides to gold.

Monarchs, swallowtails and great-spangled fritillaries dart in the morning sun. The butterflies sip nectar from blooming clover, coneflowers, Queen Anne's lace and wild roses.

An indigo bunting chatters tirelessly from the utility wire – but his song is a solo performance. The spring choristers—robin, cardinal, field sparrow, and oriole – seldom chime in. They've grown shy after the peak of the breeding season, and they're too busy feeding young to bother with songs.

Goldfinches still gossip around the feeder, though. Their reproduction rush must await the first crop of thistle down, which every goldfinch knows is the *ultimate* nest material.

The red-bellied woodpecker also is a regular at the feeder. He stuffs his beak with seeds to feed his spoiled youngster that begs and squeals from the elm branch.

Other doting wildlife parents are teaching their offspring about survival. Spotted fawns follow a sleek doe. They melt in and out of the forest edge, flicking insects with their ears and tails.

Half-grown raccoons raid the compost pile and sniff the garden with their mother. As usual, the sweet corn crop will be in jeopardy.

Rabbits of all sizes lurk in the roadside grass, tempting fate as they learn about the perils of motor vehicles, hawks and farm dogs.

In the mid-day heat, a snapping turtle lumbers across the highway, perhaps headed back to the creek after laying her eggs in a sandy bank. Most cars swerve and whiz by, but one battered pickup stops, and the grinning driver hoists the critter by its tail. Turtle soup for supper?

By late afternoon, the sticky, calm air affirms the weather forecasters' prediction: a chance of scattered thunderstorms.

Fly rod in hand and eye to the sky, you head for a favorite pond. Might be a good time for a lunker – if those storms scatter elsewhere.

Ankle-deep in the cool water, you're lulled by the tick-tick-ticking of the cricket frogs and the evening song of a melodious catbird.

Suddenly, your fly rod becomes a maestro's baton. You persuade a portly bluegill to join the orchestra with a crashing, splashing attack on your orange-tailed clint-bug.

The bullfrog chorus booms its approval. Two mourning doves streak across the glowing sunset in an aerial salute to your piscatorial prowess.

With a final lunge and a shower of pond water, the big 'gill brings you to your senses.

You look around, surprised. Darkness has swallowed the trees, leaving only black shapes against a gray sky. The pond is a black pool, shimmering ever so slightly as fish dimple the surface.

Fireflies twinkle in the pasture, writing their love letters in flashes of light. . .

The crescent moon hangs in the west. Tree frogs are trilling. Even the mosquitoes are humming . . . .

July 9, 1995

Dawn to dusk,
the day is nature's poem

A "solitary" stroller finds plenty of company
on his daylong hike through Iowa's late-summer countryside.

White plumes of fog waft up the valley, shimmering briefly in the sunrise before they fade into a blue veil over the distant hills.

The damp leaves and dewy grass glow yellow-green in the haze.

You're up early to beat the heat – and you find lots of company.

Goldfinches probe the heads of sunflowers that sprouted from last winter's spilled bird seed.

A sassy crow boasts of his stature in the bird world, drawing an immediate challenge from his bossy cronies.

The hummingbird family buzzes at the feeder, awaiting breakfast. One young hummer spots you, hovers at arm's length and stares inquisitively. You sense the unspoken message: "The feeder is empty! Get with it!"

Chuckling, you head to the kitchen to brew the birds' sugar-water treat – and a glass of juice for yourself.

Back outside, other birds begin their late-summer chatter. They've abandoned those urgent, early spring love songs in favor of small talk.

A white-breasted nuthatch jabbers about his foraging in the furrowed bark of the big white oak.

The field sparrow quietly restates his claim to the corner of the old pasture.

In the woods, a turkey yelps her delight at the season's first acorns.

A catbird, secure in the elderberry tangle, mews a very unbirdlike greeting to passers-by.

You stop to look, and find a wren, a cardinal and a pewee sharing the thicket with the catbird. With nesting season over, territorial disputes can be put aside. Perhaps the birds have agreed to share the bounty of the ripening elderberries, or of the insects attracted to them.

The storm-wracked pin oak also has become a bird cafe. A chickadee, a nuthatch, another catbird and a migrating blue-gray gnatcatcher all take a turn searching the flaking bark for grubs or other tidbits.

On the far hill, you catch a flash of movement. Stealing from the shadowy forest, the old buck is sampling your neighbor's corn crop. Red coat shining, he sports a massive, velvet rack.

The deer pauses in a patch of sunlight, his body framed with his antlers. Through the binoculars, you count 10 points, dream of fall—and ponder whether you would pull the trigger if he crossed your sights.

You resume your walk, and feel the sun's rapidly growing power. Its heat also has aroused the bees. They swarm on the delicate blue blossoms of chicory, the splashy yellow patches of black-eyed Susan and the minty-smelling clumps of lavender bergamot.

In the shade, dew still spangles the spider webs, but the roadside ragweed is dry enough to spew a cloud of pollen when you bump it.

Allergy sufferers can take heart from the Virginia creeper, however. Its red leaves already hail the not-too-distant approach of autumn.

Nature's maturing crops of walnuts, acorns and dogwood berries likewise hint of the changing season.

The first trickles of birds also have begun to drift south. Shorebirds dot the mud flats. Warblers – now more quiet and drab than on their spring visit – flit in the woodlands.

The first wandering nighthawks float over hay fields in the late afternoon.

Toward dusk, the twin fawns boldly prance along the prairie edge, curiously sampling the different flavors of grass. They're big enough to venture away from their mother – but young enough to retain their spotted coats.

As darkness calms the breeze, the night serenade begins.

Katydids chatter, crickets chirp, locusts hum and other insects buzz mysteriously.

Down by the river, the barred owl asks the age-old question: "Who-cooks-for-you?"

On the next ridge, an adolescent coyote chorus is tuning up. You laugh at their off-key yips, yowls, squeals and wails. You wonder if the young rabbits and mice hear the howls – and whether their reaction is something other than amusement.

But the song-dogs soon fall silent, leaving you to muse at the moonlight shimmering on white plumes of fog that waft up the valley . . .

August 29, 1993

15

Fall is like a Disney movie

Birds dart among bright leaves as whole world sings

Bright yellow, dull brown.

Blue sky, leaden clouds.

Hot afternoon, frosty night.

That's fall – when Mother Nature can't make up her mind.

One male goldfinch at the feeder still wears his lemony summer jacket. But the next bird is mottled with the olive-drab patches that will become its winter coat.

Gobbling sunflower seeds to fortify themselves for the season's first Arctic blast, the birds are almost too busy to notice the marauding Cooper's hawk.

But the young raptor, probably a migrant, comes up empty-taloned in its swoop past the feeder. The goldfinches scatter, while the hawk perches briefly on a hackberry branch to nurse its injured pride and empty stomach.

Other birds quickly forget the commotion. A flock of cedar waxwings darts from tree to tree, whistling softly as if nothing happened.

A green-and-yellow blur dances through the leaves. A watcher understands why the bird book has the page for "confusing fall warblers!"

The fading greens and subtle yellows also gild the woodlands. Elm, cottonwood and walnut leaves flicker like candle flames.

Already, some treetops are growing bare. Each rain shower and wind gust drops another flurry of leaves that swirl and drift along the gravel road.

More yellows tint the right-of-way and nearby prairie remnants. Unmowed sites gleam with the muted gold of goldenrods, the bold saffron of Maximilian sunflowers, the flaxen pastel of common foxtail.

Sunlight filters through the withering leaves of Solomon's seal, silhouetting the dangling, dark-blue berries.

A patch of butter-and-eggs blooms brightly in a clump of dead, brown bromegrass, like breakfast goodies on a slice of whole-wheat toast.

Contrasting splashes of New England aster glow deep-purple against the mosaic of yellows. The hardy flowers should linger well into fall, offering one last sip of nectar to the creamy sulphur butterflies and diligent honeybees.

Other critters also feel the urge to prepare for winter. But foraging squirrels may have to work harder this season, because the oaks and walnuts have produced few nuts.

Flocks of turkeys also seem to be roaming farther from the woods. Unable to fill their crops with acorns, they feast in the neighbor's corn field or stalk insects in his still-green alfalfa.

The deer go where they please: to the garden to devour the Swiss chard, under the apple tree to chew on the windfalls, down the corn rows for the main course.

The twin fawns have lost their spots, although they're still just three-fourths grown, and spend most of their time with their mother.

A few bucks still carry tatters of velvet, but most have shined and polished their racks – at the expense of many a sapling.

16

That big 10-pointer is getting more wary – or maybe he's just harder to see since he shed his tawny summer coat. In his winter garb, the buck blends ever-so-nicely with a maze of tree trunks.

The deer must sense the coming hunting season. Or at least he knows the bowhunters are about, scouting trails, choosing stands, studying sign. The battle of wits is about to begin.

Waterfowlers, too, are restless. The night-time honks of a flock of Canada geese send shivers along a listener's spine. Whether the geese are local nesters or migrants from the Arctic, they sing of autumn.

It's a delightful melody about crisp mornings, red sumac, soaring hawks, apple cider, harvest moons, a hunter's quest.

Join the chorus.

September 24, 1995

October dabs into fall palette of hues

October is the take-your-breath away dazzle of a maple hillside burning red-orange in the morning sun; the nip of a breeze that hints of winter; the ringing chorus of southbound geese; the sweet tang of fresh-pressed apple cider; the pungency of damp leaves moldering their way back to Mother Earth.

There's so much for our senses to absorb that it's a wonder we don't overdose on October.

Hike on the ridge at dawn as the sky glows crimson behind a wisp of lavender clouds. In the valley, a whipped-cream ribbon of fog slithers along the river. A squadron of wood ducks parts the mist, zipping along the tree line.

The rising sun first tints the Virginia creeper atop the dead elm, flashing like a beacon on the red leaves. The color lures you to explore this woodland and to marvel at nature's redecorating in her once-green woods.

To native Americans, October is the month of the "leaf-falling moon," when trees and shrubs fling their summer garments to the winds. Walnut trees already stand like dark skeletons, waving their coarse branches against the sky. Last summer's leaflets – miniature solar collectors – lie abandoned on the forest floor.

But the maples still sport orange cloaks, in sharp contrast to the still-green robes of their oak neighbors and the deep-purple of the scattered ash trees.

The wild grapes gradually are losing their yellow foliage, revealing the secret of last summer's bumper crop.

Robins and cedar waxwings soon will make quick work of those purple prizes.

The elm along the lane also has solved a mystery, dropping its leafy veil to uncover the oriole nest that was hidden all summer in the greenery.

The forest floor becomes a kaleidoscope of red maple, yellow aspen and tan basswood leaves. They blow in disarray, nestling up to still-green ferns, wedging in cracks in brown rocks, dotting the clear waters of a limestone pool in the creek bed. They've served their purpose; now the leaves are dead and discarded.

But in many ways, fall means rebirth as well as death. The white-tail buck's thrashings on the maple sapling show he's thinking of the breeding season – and of the next generation.

The woolly bear caterpillars are searching for a sheltering log pile or other winter home. Their choice is vital; those that survive until spring will form cocoons and emerge as Isabella moths.

Snakes' Rocky Refuges

Snakes have a similar survival mission. Lethargic in the cooling weather, they seek rocky refuges below the frost line where they can hibernate until spring.

Other animals' fall duties are as important. Monarch butterflies must migrate to Mexico, where they winter by the millions in a mountain haven.

Many birds, too, fly south to warmer, more hospitable climes. Red-tailed hawks sweep down from the north with the cold fronts, riding the winds and thermals to happier hunting grounds. Yellow-bellied sapsuckers pay a brief, semi-annual visit to sip tree juices and refuel for migration. Tiny warblers, so bright and bubbly in the spring, also pass through Iowa in fall – but without their flashy plumage or cheery songs.

It's a busy time, with all nature's winter preparations.

Foretaste of Winter

October nights, with frost and sharp winds and occasional spits of snow, may foretell those frigid days to come. But it's hard to take those warnings too seriously when the afternoon sun revives the memories of summer, beating luxuriously on the south-facing tree crotch where a fat, lazy fox squirrel curls up for a nap.

Fall's colors are as varied as her moods. Brome grass in the road ditches withers a lifeless, dusty gray; fields of corn and soybeans ripen to pale, dirty browns; frosted meadows hang wilted and olive-drab.

And yet there is no deeper, richer green than an autumn moss clump on the north face of a limestone bluff; no brighter red than a bunch of jack-in-the-pulpit berries ripening on their short stalk; no sunnier yellow than a lemony cottonwood dancing against the crisp blue of an October morning.

Contrasts: That's an Iowa October. A shirt-sleeved afternoon, brightened by purple asters nodding along the roadside, yields to a crisp evening with waves of geese slipping into the sunset. Then, abruptly, a fierce north wind drives sleet pellets against the rattling window pane.

Dull and gaudy; cold and hot; gloom and sun. Beautiful, zesty, capricious.

Ah. October!

October 13, 1985

Taking a walk through the November forest

Driven by a northeast wind, droplets of mist spatter against the window.

A bedraggled chickadee darts to the swaying feeder, grabs a sunflower seed and flits to a sheltering cedar for breakfast.

Dawn has broken, but gray still shrouds the fields and distant trees.

"Windy, with a chance of rain changing to snow," groans the radio weatherman.

Do you *really* want to forsake the warm kitchen, with the aroma of toast and strawberry jam, for the gloom that's waiting outdoors?

With a sigh, you pull on your thermals, then a wool shirt and another pair of socks. You had planned all week for this outing – but what happened to Indian Summer?

Along the lane, bare maple branches wave their skeleton fingers in the wind. White oak leaves, ripped loose by gusts, swirl away through the trees.

But in the lee of the ridge, the wind has lost some of its teeth.

The deer sense that, of course. Two does flick their white tails, then prance away, gray shapes melting into gray plum thickets.

In the November forest, it seems *everything* is a shade of gray.

But what's that smudge of orange in the branches of the dead elm? You spot a cluster of bittersweet, with pale hulls peeled back from the flaming berries. They're pretty enough to eat – if you're a cedar waxwing.

Spots of creamy-white stand out on the gray-brown slopes of the ravine: puffballs. Drought or not, the fall mushrooms are right on schedule.

A deer trail – gouged black by sharp hooves in the duff – accents the subtle but distinct hues in the leafy carpet.

Rusty-brown red oak leaves, pale-orange maples, beige basswoods, milk-chocolate aspens and still-pink sumacs lie fading on the forest floor.

Wistfully, you recall the brilliant colors just a month ago.

You sigh, then inhale – and sniff the pungence of damp, decaying leaves. It's a smell of death, yet not of finality. The rotting leaves will renew the soil and nourish new seeds, new trees, new leaves.

But a jittery cottontail rabbit has no patience for such idle musings. His top priority is keeping his own hide intact. Bursting from behind a log, he streaks away through a blackberry tangle.

The screech owl in the broken oak snag isn't so shy. Ear tufts erect, eyes unblinking, the little owl stares as you stare back.

The storm-wracked oak may be dead, but in its trunk, owl life goes on.

The trail leads back to the breezy ridge top, but you cross down to the river valley, where the gale is muted.

On the moist slope, you savor another autumn pleasure: greening rocks. Soft, lush mosses will sheathe the limestone boulders all winter.

You stop to listen. The river gurgles as it slithers over riffles and around logs.

And what's that far-off whistle? A tiny bird singing from the breezy treetops?

But you search too high. The songsters – golden-crowned kinglets – are whispering from gooseberry bushes an arm's length away.

The dainty, greenish birds, with yellow-orange caps, striped heads and bold wing bars, ignore you. They're too busy hunting for just the right buds.

At the base of a leaning oak, you ponder a spot of white-wash. Looking up, you get your answer: Tucked beside the trunk is a ball of feathers that can only be a sleeping barred owl.

Shifting for a better view, you snap a twig. The owl's dark brown eyes pop open and it peers down in surprise. Then, in a flash, it turns and flaps silently away through the trees.

The bare wood on a basswood sapling gleams in the dark forest. A sparring buck has shredded the bark.

A sound makes you look up. Polished antlers held low, the big buck is slinking away. He had been watching – and finally had enough of this intrusion.

A cardinal also protests your presence, with a "chink, chink" from his maple perch by the river bank.

But the three gray squirrels chasing each other through the oak branches don't notice – or perhaps don't worry about – the human in their midst.

You grin at their antics and near misses as they leap from tree to tree.

Motionless, you watch the playful critters until a shiver breaks the spell.

The mist has turned to flurries: specks of white drifting, whirling.

You hurry on – then chuckle at man's yen for comforts. The squirrels, the owl, the deer – even the tiny chickadee – brave all that Nature dishes out. Yet you – a mighty human – head for shelter from a lowly snowflake.

November 20, 1988

Our Gift to Nature: Preservation

"'Tis more blessed to give than to receive," we're fond of saying – but how many of us apply this motto in our relationships with Mother Nature?

During this season, when we're showering gifts on everyone from Great-Uncle Charlie to the boss's secretary, perhaps we should consider how much we GET from Nature – and how little we GIVE in return.

Iowans are especially fortunate to have precious land resources. Nature has been laying down these topsoil riches for tens of thousands of years, giving us a huge – though not unlimited – store of wealth on which to draw. Our state's prosperity is deeply rooted to the soil – and the health of our people reflects the health of the land.

Earth is finite, but Nature has evolved systems of renewing and recycling her resources, to maintain a host of natural communities.

The spring flood, which man may consider a nuisance, is Nature's way of replenishing flood-plain topsoil, scouring clogged stream beds and recharging dry aquifers and wetlands.

Forest or prairie fires – though they seem destructive – are needed to renew the vigor and health of the vegetation.

Wildlife numbers likewise ebb and flow with centuries of natural change, but always balance out. A disease that kills a forest will bring insects to feed on dead trees – and birds will come to feast on the bugs.

An exploding population of hungry rabbits may mean a disaster for young shrubs but a bonanza for foxes and owls.

The "web of life" that Nature weaves with these intricate cycles is a thing of wonder and of beauty.

But we needn't comprehend the complexities of biology to appreciate Nature. All we have to do is look at a flaming sunrise, or a dew-kissed spider web, or a bustling chickadee, or even a fertile cornfield.

Yet all too often these bountiful gifts are taken for granted. Or, worse yet, we destroy them in our search for progress or prosperity.

Why shouldn't man give back something to the earth from which he has received so much?

Instead of laying bare the rich topsoil, we should cherish and protect it, so it may nourish another century's people.

Our gifts to Nature should be shelter belts, contoured fields and soil husbandry, not barren farms where eroded soil spills across the snowdrifts like blood around a wound.

Instead of gouging rivers into canals, to carry our legacy of silt, sewage and flood, we should manage our activities to complement Nature's drainage systems.

Why not hold the water briefly on the land, to seep into the soil, fill our wells and feed our crops, instead of rushing it away to choke the rivers and flood our downstream neighbors?

Instead of tiling the marshes, we should recognize their priceless roles in water storage, pollutant absorption and fish and wildlife habitat.

Perhaps our gift to Nature should be to still our busy hands – to stop our incessant destruction of her handiwork.

Instead of bulldozing woodlands and fencerows, we should plant trees and build windbreaks.

Why not cultivate forests and harvest the surplus that Nature provides rather than lay waste Earth's timber resources?

We have thrived on Nature's generosity – and we can continue to do so if we recognize her limitations and control our greed.

In the spirit of giving, let us resolve to repay Mother Nature for the gifts that make our lives possible, and to work with her, not against her, to keep our environment healthy and productive.

What did you give YOUR mother this Christmas?

December 25, 1977

Des Moines River

© The Des Moines Register

CHAPTER 2

RIVERS

To learn about the land and its people, explore its rivers.

Is there corn to the edge of the bank, or does the stream wind through a cathedral of trees? Does the water sparkle and dance through the riffles, or ooze along like spilled chocolate milk?

Walk, or paddle, the waterfront of a river town. Is it littered with the discards of our throw-away society – or vibrant and active with people drawn to its magic?

Do valley residents speak reverently of a prized natural resource – or plot ways to defeat a hated enemy?

Physically and philosophically, Iowa's rivers have helped shape her character.

Canoeing is great in ol' Raccoon's historic valley

SCRANTON, IA – History flows deeply through the Raccoon River valley.

In 1735 – some 40 years before the conception of the United States – the 'Coon made news when French army captain Joseph de Noyelles fought with the Sauk and Fox Indians near the river's mouth at the present site of Des Moines.

This "first and only battle between Indians and white men on Iowa soil," was the culmination of a march by the French from Detroit, where the Indians allegedly killed a French officer, according to Iowa historian William J. Peterson, in his book "Iowa – The Rivers of Her Valleys." De Noyelles intended to punish the Indians for the alleged murder of a French officer — but the battle ended in a draw.

Bill Wright, 74, of Scranton also recalls legends of Indian wars fought along the river near Horseshoe Bend, north of here.

Much folklore surrounds the aptly named river bend, and the imposing hill guarding its north bank. The site once was rich in Indian artifacts, giving rise to stories of Indian ceremonies and campsites there.

Settlers near Horseshoe Bend hastily built a fort for protection from Indians after the Spirit Lake Massacre of 1857, Wright said, but they had no occasion to use it, since the natives were friendly. Wright farmed near the site, and visited the old fort before it burned several years ago.

Youths in the Horseshoe Bend area also played on a huge oak tree where, legend had it, horse thieves were hanged in pioneer days, Wright said.

Leon Morland, 80, of Jefferson grew up near the river, and several members of his family farmed near Horseshoe Bend. Around the turn of the century, Morland and his young playmates often searched for gold that supposedly was buried there.

A few years later, Morland did find a treasure – a pearl in a river clam he'd caught for fish bait. He made the gem into an engagement ring for his future wife, Gladys.

Jim Andrew's ties to the river go back to his great-grandfather, who surveyed land in Greene County in 1851 and settled there in 1873.

Andrew, who farms near Jefferson, still owns land surveyed by his ancestor 125 years ago, and has cultivated a keen interest in other Greene County and Raccoon River history.

He's historian for the Greene County bicentennial commission, and has helped install monuments at a number of historic sites in the county.

The area around Squirrel Hollow county park south of Jefferson is rich in river history, Andrew said.

A small valley near there is named Rustler's Cove, for the cattle thieves who hid there with stolen stock in 1882.

Truman Davis, the county's first settler in 1849, is buried on a hill overlooking the river near there.

The old military road, which followed the river much of the way from Fort Des Moines to Sioux City in the mid-1800s, intersected a road to Fort Dodge at a huge cottonwood tree (now gone) near there.

West of Jefferson, at the McMahon Access, was the "old Fleck Bottom." Indians once wintered here to escape the severe weather of the open prairies. Later, about the turn of the century, the site was known as the Illinois Picnic Grounds, for the huge reunions of transplanted Illinoians who met there annually.

Darwin Thede, who now is the pioneer farmer at the Living History Farms near Des Moines, has explored the 'Coon for most of his 38 years. He found a number of buffalo skulls and Indian artifacts in the valley around his former home near Glidden.

On his first river trip, Thede rowed a 16-foot wooden boat down the river from Glidden to Des Moines to attend the Iowa State Fair. The boat "weighed a ton when it was dry and about three tons when it was wet," he recalled.

"I've never worked so hard in all my life."

He recommended the river for canoe travel, however, and we found his advice accurate.

In a short float through the Horseshoe Bend area, we enjoyed a variety of river conditions, from steep clay banks to rocky riffles to snag-choked channels. The rolling country has kept intensive agriculture back from the banks, so the valley appears heavily timbered from the water.

The 'Coon has done well to withstand man's heavy-handed advances. Let's hope it continues to make history – and flows with equal vigor on the nation's 300th birthday.

August 1, 1976

Nishnabotna – Iowa's river of 'good canoe'

SHENANDOAH, IA – Modern maps call it "Nishnabotna," southwest Iowans call it "Nish" or "Nishna," early explorers named it Ichinipokine, Neeshba, Nichenanbatonnis or anything else they pleased. The Indian translation of the name translates to "crossed in a canoe," or "good canoe" or place where canoes are made.

We like the Indian version since we did cross the river in our canoe and found it enjoyable. Herman Mayer, 74, of Shenandoah, shares the fondness for the "canoe" name, since he and his son Charles have an old dugout canoe they found half-buried in the silt along the river nearly 30 years ago.

The craft no doubt was paddled by an unknown native, as he navigated the tree-lined river while hunting or fishing. A few modern boaters still follow the river – but the trees are more scarce now, and the adjoining prairies grow corn, instead of bluestem. And the channelized stream flows relatively straight, between levees bulldozed on its banks.

Unlike the Indians – who probably depended on the river for food, water and transportation – some modern Iowans have almost forgotten the stream that shaped this prosperous valley.

"I don't recall anyone here ever asking about the river. . .," apologized a Chamber of Commerce receptionist, who searched her files in vain for river history.

But Shenandoah owes its name to the river, which formed the valley that reminded the town's founders of the Shenandoah Valley of Virginia.

The river also helped form the fertile soil upon which the area's agricultural and nursery economies are based.

One person who still appreciates the river is Conservation Officer Don Priebe of Shenandoah. We floated part of the East Nishnabotna, between Coburg and Riverton, with Don and conservation officer Dave Moore of Bedford while they patrolled for bank lines, illegal dumping, and spring fishermen.

We saw no other boats, and only two parties of fishermen. The Nish (as Don calls it) is a pretty good catfishing stream, Don said, but few people use boats on it. Most wade or fish from the bank.

The valley once was a prime waterfowl nesting area, Don said, since ducks were attracted to the bayous and potholes left by the wandering stream. Most of those wetlands are farmed now, he explained, but we still saw several species of ducks and geese.

Herman Mayer of Shenandoah remembers the river as it once was, with "75-pound catfish," prairie chickens in the valley, and waterfowl galore in the wetlands.

His grandfather homesteaded at Manti – the forerunner of Shenandoah – in the mid-1800's.

One of Herman's older brothers worked on the dredge boat that channeled the river in the early 1900's – but Herman thinks that channeling was a mistake. He vividly remembers the words of an old railroad man who watched sadly as the river was dredged.

"The good Lord put those bends in the river for a purpose," the old man said. "Boys, you may live to see the day when they regret they ever straightened it."

Adolph (Zeb) Mortimore, 72, has lived in Riverton all his life – and has watched the Nishnabotna rise to within yards of his home.

He recalled his parents spoke of conflicts over use of the river valley long before the river was straightened. Early farmers tried to farm the bottoms, he said, but the Indians only laughed at their efforts and predicted failure.

"The Indian said, 'Where there once was water, there'll be water again,'" Zeb said. They knew farmers who planted on the floodplain would be flooded out frequently. Man's manipulation of the river has enabled him to farm more of the valley, Zeb conceded, but it's still impossible to protect the valley completely.

"This old Nishna River has got a mortgage on low ground," Zeb said, "and when it takes a notion to foreclose, it just does it!"

April 11, 1976

Geologic 'footprints' still remain

Glaciers trudged through Iowa thousands of years ago,
leaving marks revealed by the rushing waters of the Des Moines River.

BOONE, IA – Just awhile back, in geologic time, there was *another* river.

About 300 million years ago, a many-channeled, braided waterway flowed southwesterly through a lush, tropical environment that now is central Iowa.

To be sure, Earth has changed a bit in the ensuing eons, but the bed of that primeval river is still visible where younger streams have cut down to the old, solidified sandbars.

The Des Moines River has gouged into this bedrock at Dolliver State Park and Woodman Hollow State Preserve, near Lehigh; Lake Red Rock, near Knoxville and the Saylorville Lake spillway near Polk City.

But nowhere is that clash more evident than at Ledges State Park, near Boone, where Davis Creek, Pea's Creek and the Des Moines River have carved through the ancient sandstone.

Jean Prior, senior research geologist for the Iowa Department of Natural Resources, said the cliffs and ledges that give the park its name are remnants of sediments along the earlier river.

The sands were deposited over millions of years, Prior said.

Layers Cemented Together

Over the eons, the sandbars formed many layers, which eventually were cemented together by minerals percolating through them.

But some minerals, such as calcium carbonate, make better "cement" than others, such as iron. Thus, when torrents of water from melting glaciers, followed by 10,000 years of slower runoff, scoured the sandstone, the layers eroded at different rates. The result was the sculptured canyons known today as "Ledges."

Last year's floods, which eroded parts of the Ledges Park canyons and left several feet of sediment along the creeks, were a textbook example of geological forces at work, Prior said.

"Once again, there's been a tremendous event associated with a river that caused this massive accumulation of water-deposited material," she said.

Unless there is an earthquake or volcanic eruption, earth-building processes usually aren't that dramatic, Prior said.

"But here we had our own version of a geologic process that was very apparent to everyone, and few people were *not* affected in one way or another."

Other landforms in the valley may not be as striking as Ledges, but they still reveal much about the Des Moines River, Prior said. "I like to think of geology as the broad framework that explains a lot of the other details of a place," she said.

In northwestern Iowa and southwestern Minnesota, the Des Moines River valley is quite young. The landscape is dotted with potholes left by glaciers that retreated less than 10,000 years ago. Wildlife abounds in the marshes, while crops thrive on drained wetlands.

Sometimes, the river flows along piles of rock, gravel and earth, or "moraines," left at the edge of the ice sheet. Cattle graze on slopes too steep or rocky to plow.

Glaciers also shaped the valley south of Des Moines, Prior said, but there the ice has been gone

29

much longer. In southeast Iowa, the Des Moines River winds through rolling hills more than 500,000 years old. The terrain is capped with sand and sediment blown from as far away as the Missouri River Valley.

Slopes are steeper and the soils are not as fertile. Hills along the valley often grow grass or trees instead of row crops.

As it nears the Mississippi River, the Des Moines cuts again into bed rock. The limestone was formed beneath seas that covered Iowa about 360 million years ago, Prior said.

Lacey-Keosauqua State Park near Keosauqua, Shimek State Forest near Croton and several county parks capitalize on rugged, scenic terrain.

In central and southeastern Iowa, the river valley also contains coal beds that developed in tropical swamps 300 million years ago. Many of the early settlements were lured by coal resources, as well as by the river.

Wherever you look, geology has shaped the Des Moines River and its people, Prior concluded. The footprints are indelible.

September 5, 1994

Lake swallowed a piece of history

RED ROCK, IA – History buffs prowl the hilltop cemetery.

And the red sandstone cliffs intrigue motorists on Iowa Highway 14's Mile Long Bridge.

Aside from that, however, Red Rock is no more. The feisty town on the banks of the Des Moines River drowned beneath Lake Red Rock when the big reservoir was filled in 1969.

Dragoons noted the unusual rock formations during their trek up the river from Keokuk in 1835.

But even before that, a huge sycamore tree at the site was a meeting place for American Indians.

"Red Rock Line"

The town was founded in 1843, after a treaty in 1842 created the "Red Rock Line." The boundary was the western limit of white settlement for three years, until the Sauk and Fox relinquished their lands.

At midnight on Oct. 10, 1845, settlers rushed westward across the Red Rock Line to claim the new territory.

At first, Red Rock was the home of unscrupulous traders – including Henry Lott, whose later misdeeds led to the Spirit Lake Massacre.

But after most of the traders followed the Indians west, the town settled down, said Pella historian Harriet Heusinkveld, in her book, "Saga of the Des Moines River Greenbelt."

Soon, Red Rock had sawmills, a flour mill, two general stores, a hotel and a doctor. Then came a school, church and post office.

The town even was considered as a site for the state capital, which was moved from Iowa City to Des Moines in 1855.

But a series of devastating floods, beginning in 1851, stifled Red Rock's growth. The town also lost out to nearby Coalport when steamboat companies sought a river landing.

Rail lines also spurned Red Rock in 1867 and 1887.

The little town hung on, said Dorothy Templeton of Knoxville, who farmed near the site with her late husband, Hugh. Some of her children attended country school there. But after three more floods in 1947, the community's fate was sealed. The U.S. Army Corps of Engineers, determined to tame the Des Moines River, made plans to submerge the town under Lake Red Rock.

Mourning Towns

Gladys Black, 85, of Pleasantville, lamented the demise of Red Rock and other river towns.

An area north of Pleasantville still is known as the Pinchey Bottoms, although the town disappeared a few years after the river changed course and moved two miles away in 1900. The burg's real name was Oradell, but the reputation of a penny-pinching grocer gave it a nickname that never died.

Cordova, just downstream from Red Rock, also was flooded by the Red Rock Dam. The nearby villages of Fifield and Percy had withered away even before the dam closed.

The shipping center of Coalport was doomed by a 1903 channel flood that left it three-fourths of a mile from the river. Its legacy is the Coal Ridge Baptist Church, on a hill south of the reservoir.

Black, who may be Iowa's best-known ornithologist, now studies birds on the shores of Lake Red Rock. Water and wildlife cover the nearly forgotten town sites.

Black has identified more than 300 bird species around the lake, but she mourns for the old valley.

"I don't think God will ever forgive us for ruining that river," she said.

September 9, 1994

'Little bit of heaven' along river

What a river!

Drop by drop, she comes to life in the marshes, lakes and creeks of Minnesota.

By the time she enters Iowa north of Estherville, she's a playful adolescent who swirls through log jams, tickles the bellies of Canada geese and tempts fishermen.

And before she reaches the Mississippi, in another 400 miles, the Des Moines River has become a proud river in a valley of proud people.

That's the message we got on our three-week trip down the river.

Their River

Call it pride, affection or Iowa stubbornness: The people in the valley are tied to *their* river. It's a force that has shaped the land and their lives.

As we canoed beside farm fields, under bridges, past industrial plants – down below the level of the usual highway traveler – we saw a unique part of the state.

Verne Downard of Keosauqua called it his "little bit of heaven."

Frank Ulrich of Mallard shrugged off the fact that he gets a crop from his bottomland only two years out of every five.

Madeline McLeland of Douds laughed about the 1993 flood that lapped at the back door of her cafe.

Craig and Shirley Lanman of Eldon moved back into their river bank home last fall, despite having water up to the eaves a few months earlier.

Mark Edwards of Madrid calls it a "sacred place," both to Native Americans and modern naturalists.

And Claude Carr of Fort Dodge dreams of having his ashes spread over his favorite fishing hole.

How is it that a river can seduce people so?

We found some examples.

Maybe it's the pink sunrise shimmering on the riffles at Eddyville.

How about the mink scampering the bank near Fort Dodge?

Try the tales of big flathead catfish near Croton.

What about the view from Yellow Banks Park near Des Moines?

Can you appreciate the musty, muddy, pungent smells of catfish bait, wet leaves and dead fish?

Or maybe it's just the soothing sound of water gurgling over every gravel bar and around each fallen snag.

We also savored a moonlight paddle near Argyle, exhilarating rapids at Humboldt, buffalo bones near Graettinger and fossils near Madrid.

And the wildlife: great blue herons, pelicans, ospreys, eagles, beaver, killdeers, kingfishers or wood ducks brightened nearly every mile of the trip.

But there are blemishes, too. Corn planted too close to the bank topples into an eroded bend. Broken appliances, worn-out farm machinery and old tires lie half-submerged in abandoned junk heaps. Manure from hillside hog lots may trickle into the water. Cabins on the bank have leaky septic systems.

Last year's floods left some scars, as well.

Especially in Mahaska and Wapello counties, dozens of summer homes were damaged or washed away.

Huge cottonwoods were toppled along many stretches of riverbank. High water cut some new channels and swept tons of sand onto bottomland fields.

But many people have begrudgingly accepted the floods as a part of the river. On the Manning Hotel in Keosauqua or on the old tree at the village of Rochester or on any handy bridge, they just paint another line to mark the latest high-water mark.

Over the ages, rivers flood and wander across broad flood plains. It's happened before and it will happen again. People would just prefer to have that natural geological phenomenon happen in some *other* century.

We may dam and straighten and shackle and bridge – but the river isn't tamed, not really.

We can borrow her water to drink or flush or irrigate. We may use it to float our boats or supply our factories or attract ducks to hunt. We steal her gravel for our roads and her sand for our concrete.

But the river's mystique is still there. Flowing endlessly, there seems to be no beginning, no end. She's *alive*.

She can be moody, too, we found.

She's hostile in the wind, somber in the rain. Depression may set in where the channel has been straightened. She laughs with delight over rapids, but grows restless when confined behind dams.

She writhes in agony over an oil slick.

An Eddyville fisherman summed it up as he sat in his boat, sipping a cup of coffee while watching the sunrise:

"Any day is a nice day on the river."

Discussing our trip down the Des Moines, people keep asking: Another year, another river?

Our answer: Who knows?

But why wait?

Paddle a mile or two or 10 or 20. Don't rush. Prowl a sandbar. Hike the hills. Admire the fall colors. Visit a park.

Talk, and listen, to river rats – those not-so-ordinary people who live and work and play on the river.

And one more thing: Think about that old river the next time you drink a glass of water or drive over a bridge – or flush.

NOTE OF THANKS

To all those Iowans who fed, sheltered, shuttled, befriended, encouraged, educated, entertained, greeted, tolerated and paddled with us: THANKS! We couldn't have done it without you!

September 18, 1994

Wolf Creek canoeing - bit of Iowa 'wilderness'

The watery ribbon snaked under the tree canopy, waltzing along to a symphony of bird songs. The music even caught our canoe paddles, as they swung and dipped and rippled the surface.

A tangle of vegetation pushed to the very brink of the stream banks, leaving the winding channel as the only path through the wilderness-like valley. Even that route occasionally was blocked by fallen trees or logjams.

No bridges or power lines or developments penetrated the wild corridor. Scarcely a beer can littered the shore line.

A great horned owl swooped from its perch, indignant over the intrusion. A female wood duck herded nearly a dozen young into hiding along the bank, then fluttered ahead to draw attention away from her brood.

At one bend, we surprised a family of Canada geese resting in a backwater. The parents honked defiantly as they formed a flotilla with the gander in front, the goose behind and the four goslings between. They swam ahead of our canoe until the gander left his family on a sand bar and set off down the creek as a diversion. He honked and splashed and false-charged for several minutes before taking to the air. He swept back over us to rejoin his mate and offspring.

The scene could have been in remote wilderness. We almost had the feeling our paddles were parting uncharted waters.

Instead, we floated through the heart of some of Iowa's richest farmland, within shouting distance of bustling feedlots and busy farmsteads and manicured fields of corn and soybeans.

Dick Keith of Burlington and I had discovered this "wilderness" on Wolf Creek near Traer. But the stream is not particularly unique in Iowa.

There are dozens – perhaps hundreds – of small rivers and creeks that can float a canoe. Most are ignored by recreationists because the water levels are unpredictable and the streams don't boast the spectacular scenery, strong current or good fishing of well-known canoeing waters.

For seclusion or good wildlife watching, these out-of-the-way streams are dreams come true. It's easy to "get lost" on a stretch of creek that might not see another boat all summer.

There are some drawbacks, of course. We had to drag the canoe around several obstructions in the narrow channel, and the steep, muddy creek banks made launching and landing difficult.

While we encountered no fences, barbed wired strung across the creek is a hazard on many waters.

The bed and banks of nearly all small streams belong to private individuals, so canoeists should ask permission to launch, land or camp.

Some streams may be vanishing. They've been straightened (often illegally!) or cut by roads and power lines or denuded of their adjacent timber.

The biggest obstacle to small-river floating is the water level. By early summer, many of these waters have dropped to wading depth. You must paddle them in the spring, or soon after a rain. Try to check the creek depth at several places before launching to float an unknown stretch.

Don't undertake too long a trip, either. You may eat up more time than you think negotiating logjams, fences or winding channels.

I also have floated parts of the Chariton River, the North Skunk and a small Des Moines River tributary below Lake Red Rock. The upper reaches of the Raccoon also might suit paddlers.

Half the fun of floating these waters is to find your own place to go. Take a second look at those creeks you cross when driving Iowa's back roads. Talk to farmers and fishermen and hunters to get ideas on new waters to explore.

And when you do find your own "mini-wilderness" worming through Iowa's intensely developed landscape, keep the news to yourself. No use spoiling a good thing.

June 6, 1979

Floods show that nature won't be controlled

It hurts. My stomach still knots when I see the destruction wrought by June 15 floods that pounded several northeast Iowa communities, including my hometown of St. Olaf.

Homes were ravaged; family mementoes lost; spirits tried. With tears in their eyes, people carry mud-clogged and water-soaked possessions to the trash heap. Furniture, books, clothing, home-canned garden produce: almost anything that absorbs water or is perishable has to go. Red Cross workers even advise against eating vegetables from a flooded garden.

We who live on higher ground – the lucky ones– can't bring back the lost or ruined treasures, so we try to help with the drudgery of clean-up. We can bucket out the silty glop that once was Iowa topsoil. We can try to offer a kind word or to make a joke to lighten heavy hearts. And we remember.

Sirens in the Dark
Awakened about 1:30 a.m. by cracks of lightning, shrieking sirens – and then the distant, ominous roar of rushing water – people watched helplessly as the usually placid Roberts Creek swelled to 700 times its normal volume.

The stream churned into town, roiled down Main Street, surged into homes. Powerful waters floated a large building from its foundation, then dumped the structure unceremoniously atop a road.

The water moved trucks, cars, rocks, trees, fences, livestock.

Our canoe – formerly just a pleasure craft – was pressed into service as a rescue boat to carry several people to dry ground, as water rose to their doorsteps.

We waited hopefully for news of a valiant – yes, heroic – rescue attempt. A man had been caught in the rising water as he tried to drive a friend's cattle away from the flood. Would the sheriff and volunteer firefighters, wading and boating through the darkness, reach him in time?

Hugs, tears of joy and audible sighs of relief rippled through the crowd, when our neighbor – tired and wet but unhurt – was hauled to shore after two hours in a fragile treetop.

A little after dawn, the water gradually began to recede. In its wake were washed-out bridges and roads, eroded valleys, crumpled buildings, shattered lives.

Crops had been literally scoured from the ground. Tons of rock and gravel were dumped on once-fertile fields.

No one could recall such destruction. The town's unofficial historian, a man of 82, knew of only one or two times when the water had even approached this year's level.

"I never would have imagined, . . ." every one said.

But as much as I ache for my friends and neighbors, I hope they'll agree, in retrospect, that we should have known.

After all, Nature has been sculpting these valleys for millennia. How did we think those scenic limestone cliffs were carved away? Where did we suppose those rich bottomland silt deposits came from?

Rivers and streams are drainage ways. They may run quietly within their banks for years, decades, centuries. But there is no guarantee the waters will always be so gentle. When we build our houses, businesses and fields where water is meant to flow, should we be surprised when it does?

Nature Sets the Course.

Perhaps we've grown complacent. It's too easy to forget, to ignore the gurgling stream, to challenge the law of averages.

Sure, we can blame road builders, whose embankments push the flood toward us, or farmers, whose bare fields hasten run-off into the already swollen stream.

We can lament the plowing or filling of sponge-like wetlands, which might have absorbed some of the excess flow.

We can plead for government help to build levees to protect us from "next time."

We can fight – and maybe even win – for awhile.

But when we lose, we must concede defeat to a greater power.

These are the forces that have shaped our very planet.

We battle them at our peril.

July 2, 1991

Fayette County

© Larry Stone

CHAPTER 3

PRAIRIE

Do we celebrate the wonders of Iowa prairies – or mourn their loss?

No living person can know the splendor that must have been, when ocean-like expanses of grass and flowers rolled to the horizon across three-quarters of the state. Iowa pioneers found, and conquered, an entire ecosystem in the space of an eye-blink. Lured by the richest of black, productive soil, they carved the wilderness into a patchwork of fields that now help feed the world.

Our few remaining relicts, preserved by visionaries, only hint at the former majesty of the tallgrass prairie. But, undaunted, new generations of dreamers are replanting their heritage. One day, we trust, the restored plots may emulate the vast tracts that were plowed and lost.

A trip back in time along Highway 69

Prairie grass . . . and visions of bison and sun-bronzed pioneers

A century and a half passed before my eyes recently, when I visited a central Iowa museum.

In the span of a few minutes, I re-lived an almost forgotten era — and touched the very roots of our state's heritage.

The "museum" was a lonely stretch of U.S. Highway 69 south of Ames, where a patch of compass plants triggered my trip back in time.

In those tall, yellow flowers with deeply-lobed leaves I visualized a sea of head-high stems, waving across the rolling plain.

Bison grazed in small herds on the horizon and prairie chickens loafed on the knolls. The sky swarmed with waterfowl above a pothole left from a glacier's retreat 10,000 years before.

The expanse was dotted with color from yellow sunflowers, purple blazing stars and green rattlesnake masters poking their heads between the clumps of prairie grass.

In the highway beside me I imagined a procession of sun-bronzed pioneers, heading their wagons across the treeless expanse in search of a friendly oak grove in which to settle. They shook their heads at the grassland under their feet, lamenting that the soil must be so poor it couldn't even grow trees.

My sturdy compass plant knew better, but the only advice it offered was to spread its flat leaves along a north-south axis as a guidepost to the weary travelers.

I wondered, as cars buzzed by on the modern highway, how many settlers chose the wooded hills and stream banks for their homesteads before a late-comer finally discovered that the prairie grassland really hid the richest soil of all.

That discovery was to spell the end of my imagined prairie paradise, since the fertile plains almost begged to be plowed and cropped and tamed into the world's finest farm ground.

The prairie could stand the trampling and grazing of wandering bison herds, and periodic charring by a prairie fire — but it could not stand the bite of a plow or the constant trimming by farmers' cattle or mowing machines.

Prairie relicts — like the compass plant clinging to an unkempt roadside — are all that remain of the vast grasslands that awed early explorers.

The sea of waving stems has given way to a single clump of bluestem jutting from a steep road ditch, or a bunch of Indian grass hugging a weathered gravestone to escape the cemetery maintenance crews.

A few railroad rights-of-way are kinder to the prairie, perhaps because they share a bond of having outlived their usefulness in a space-age society.

Will prairies, like the railroads, experience a revival as a few die-hards discover that these systems are not out-moded after all?

Will there still be compass plants and bluestem and blazing stars a hundred years from now?

I cannot answer, or perhaps I don't want to.

I only want to share my compass plant history book with the hurried travelers, to help them turn its imaginary pages, and to see their heritage in its flower and its guiding leaves.

I sense that the compass plant is yet trying to point the way, urging us to cling to our remaining prairie archives.

September 7, 1975

Anderson Prairie: Enthusiasts call it 'one of the jewels of Iowa'

ESTHERVILLE, IA – Wandering the ridges and prowling the swales, Bob Moats explored the spring morning.

What better place to celebrate the season than Anderson Prairie, a 200-acre state preserve northwest of Estherville?

"This is one of the jewels of Iowa, no question," Moats said. "Here you can get the prairie vista, feel the openness, feel the sky . . . .On those hills, you can just about visualize the bison."

Meadowlarks sang and fluttered across the grassland. A cock pheasant crowed, not knowing or caring that he'd invaded the ancestral haunts of the prairie chickens.

In a wet meadow, chorus frogs croaked a serenade.

Three deer, startled by human intruders, burst from a thicket and stole away down a ravine.

Scattered bur oaks marched up a hillside to form a savanna, where chickadees and nuthatches scolded from the gnarled, old trees.

"This is about as far as you can get yourself from a road in this county," said Moats, who is a conservation officer for the Iowa Department of Natural Resources.

To the east, a ribbon of trees traces the Des Moines River's course along the toe of a gravelly mountain dumped by glaciers 13,000 years ago. More glacial hills and valleys roll away to the west. To the north, another 240 acres of state and county land reinforce the image of open space.

Moats led the way to a broad hilltop – "up where the buffalo wind can bite us," he said with a grin.

Wind is part of the prairie, he said. The breezes help pollinate prairie plants, blow away the mosquitoes and ripple the long prairie grasses like waves on the ocean.

Tucked down among the dead grass out of the wind, Moats found a lavender pasque flower. On a dry hillside, he admired the rare wild parsley, or biscuitroot – the first plant on the prairie to bloom in the spring.

Those flowers were just a hint of things to come, Moats said.

More flowers bloom each week, he said, until the prairie glows with a mosaic of colors in late summer.

Anderson Prairie is even more diverse than some other prairies, thanks to its mix of dry hills and wet swales, said John Pearson, a botanist for the Iowa Department of Natural Resources. The tract includes more than 200 native species.

The prairie was preserved because the rugged land was too steep or rocky to plow, Pearson said. The grasslands were used for hay or pasture until the state bought the parcel in 1980.

About 60 acres of the prairie are in excellent shape, Pearson said. Biologists are attempting to restore other parts of the area that were damaged by heavy grazing and seeding of bromegrass.

The site has a colorful history, too, Moats said. He followed the still-visible ruts of a century-old wagon trail. He told of finding 600-year-old Indian campsites. He pointed across the Des Moines River to the site of Emmet Grove, the first post office in Emmet County.

Moats recalled his awe when he first discovered the prairie in the late 1970s. He was overwhelmed by the flowers, the terrain, the feeling, the heritage, the beauty.

"It kind of took me by storm," he said. And he still hasn't recovered.

June 1, 1993

Plenty of history in Iowa prairies

COLLEGE SPRINGS, IA – Grove Cemetery doesn't look like a museum.

From the dusty gravel road, it seems to be just another neglected graveyard, with a few headstones, some unmowed grass and the traditional pine tree on the hill.

But take a closer look. There's a lot of history among the tall clumps of big bluestem.

Here lies Daniel Dow, 1771-1860, who was a water boy in the Revolutionary War. Think of it. This man lived before our country was born.

A visitor stares incredulously. He parts the prairie grass to read the tombstone's inscription – and is struck by the irony.

Suddenly, two centuries become a mere eye-blink. The bluestem and Indian grass and asters and goldenrod have survived for eons.

The surrounding hills have been plowed up, fenced in and built on, but the prairie in which Daniel Dow was buried endures, more than 130 years later.

It's a natural island in an altered landscape, like a pencil dot on a sheet of paper, said Jerry Abma, director of the Page County Conservation Board.

In Page County – as in the rest of Iowa – less than one-tenth of 1 percent of the native prairie has survived. Abma treasures the county's few remaining prairie tracts: the cemetery, a handful of roadsides and railroad rights-of-way, an abandoned schoolyard, a forgotten hay field.

Grove Cemetery is a kind of museum, Abma said. It's a storehouse of cultural and natural history.

The conservation board helps manage the area, occasionally burning the prairie vegetation to invigorate it and keep out encroaching trees.

Abma also has begun the slow process of trying to restore prairie-like plant communities on county land.

That's why office manager Charly Stevens often leaves this sign on her desk: "Out seeding – back later."

Stevens regularly visits prairie remnants to harvest seed to plant elsewhere. She's come to love the prairie.

"I don't like to use the word 'therapy,'" Stevens said, "but it feels good to get out there. It's wide open, no phones, not too many people – and you just pick to your heart's content – or as much as your back will allow!"

Just to the north, in Montgomery County, roadside manager David Carlisle has found another benefit of prairie. Native vegetation is saving county road crews time, money and chemicals. Planting or enhancing prairie species will help stabilize road rights-of-way and crowd out weeds, he said.

Road ditches, which total more than 600,000 acres statewide, also could be the keys to preserving Iowa's vanishing fragments of prairie, Carlisle said.

A network of prairie roadsides could become genetic pathways for prairie plants, insects, birds and wildlife, he said. Isolated prairie tracts are at greater risk of being destroyed. But natural roadsides could help maintain their diverse character.

Those corridors also beautify the roads, noted Dorothy Franek of Red Oak, who sometimes helps Carlisle harvest prairie seeds. She loves the flowers, butterflies and birds of the prairie.

Iowa has become a leader in restoration of prairie roadsides, said Kirk Henderson, who coordinates the state roadside office. After a few counties pioneered the effort, the Iowa Legislature set up the Living Roadway Trust Fund, which helps pay for county roadside management. At least 26 counties now have hired roadside managers, and many others have begun using native vegetation, rather than chemicals, to control weeds along their roads.

"Rather than dumping herbicides, we're investing in something long-term," Carlisle said.

Roadside management also may help make people more aware of their prairie heritage, Carlisle said. They may begin to notice the rattlesnake master along the railroad track, the compass plant in the road ditch, the clump of Indian grass in the fence row or the butterflies swarming around the goldenrod.

And that awareness may make people want to save a part of their heritage, Carlisle said.

"If you don't, who will?" he reflected.

"Once it's gone, it's gone forever."

September 5, 1993

Heritage flourishes on peaceful field

HASTINGS, IA – It's the envy of many an Iowa black-dirt farmer: 60 acres of some of the richest riverbottom land on Earth. The soil could be growing 150-bushel corn, like millions of acres in other Iowa fields.

Instead, it supports nothing but an assortment of odd-looking flowers and grasses. There aren't even any cattle grazing on the plot.

A waste? Not to Otha Wearin. That little scrap of native prairie perched on the banks of the West Fork of the Nishnabotna River, near Hastings, is part of his heritage. He'd no sooner plant it to corn than he would use a family history book for kindling.

When Wearin's grandfather came to Mills County in 1854, he settled near that prairie – and the Wearins have preserved it ever since.

Not Always Unusual

In the 1850s the prairie was not particularly unusual. Iowa was blanketed with similar prairies that almost begged to be put to the plow. A century and a quarter later, however, the conversion to farmland is virtually complete – and the little preserve along the Nishnabotna is a unique remnant of a vanishing ecosystem.

State ecologist Dean Roosa said Wearin's tract may be the only flood plain prairie left in the state. Every other river bottom prairie has been turned into $3,000-an-acre crop land.

Why has Wearin elected to preserve a natural area that could add to his farm production and income?

"That's a good question!" laughed the 77-year-old former Iowa legislator and three-term congressman.

"I've always been very interested in the original condition of this country. And I kept thinking 'There's some virgin land that's never been plowed.'

"We ought to save some of it so our children can see what this country looked like when the pioneers came."

Indeed, it's like a leap back in time to stroll across the valley, with feathery goldenrods, dainty prairie clovers, purple gayfeathers, and knobby rattlesnake masters waving in your path. Shoulder-high compass plants grow in profusion, and stalks of bluestem bend in the breeze.

A Rare Sight

Few modern Iowans have seen such a sight – although the Hawkeye State's whole economy is deeply rooted in the same rich prairie soil that sprouts those "weeds."

But the visions of the land as the first settlers found it are very real to Wearin. From his youth, he recalls huge flocks of prairie chickens on the prairie, and great squadrons of migrant pelicans in the springtime.

Wearin and his wife, Lola, and two married daughters treasure the prairie for its history – and to be able to "mosey around and look at the flowers." Despite his failing eyesight, Wearin can recognize many of the plants from their shape, texture, or smell.

The Wearins have no thought of ever plowing or developing the land – and they have discussed permanent preservation with the Iowa Natural Heritage Foundation.

"I've been in the conservation business a long time," Wearin said. Lola Wearin, who manages her own farm, shares this conservation ethic, he said.

Wearin has written a number of books on Iowa history, family history and his experiences in politics. He hopes to preserve Iowa's heritage on paper – as well as on the land.

Wearin on the Green

In "A Century on an Iowa Farm," Wearin observed that: "There is too much of a tendency on the part of most Iowans to think that no wild things have a right to live lest they consume a small portion of the product of the land. There are those who think that every penny the soil produces should go to enrich their fortunes."

Thus, the Wearins have tried to maintain wildlife habitat, as well as the prairie. Wearin orders his farm workers to protect the deer – even though the plentiful white-tails often eat some corn.

When a neighbor complained that beavers were eating his corn and flooding his crops with their dams, Wearin said he told the man that "you kind of owe it to them. They're trying to save some water for you!"

We need to conserve our water, land and wildlife, Otha Wearin believes. Those natural resources hold the keys to our future — but they also tell the story of our past.

September 17, 1980

Stepping back in time with new prairie fires

Enthusiasts take a page from history

WATERLOO, IA – When Russ Prichard lit a match to burn a strip of prairie grass along a Black Hawk County roadside last week, he kindled more than just a few clumps of bluestem.

The flickering flames and the billowing smoke also became a history lesson. As he set the fire, Prichard, who is roadside biologist for the county, briefly turned back the clock to pioneer days.

Before European settlers came to Iowa, fire was a natural part of the state's environment. Lightning strikes probably ignited grass or forest fires. American Indians may have set fires to drive game or invigorate wildlife habitat.

Evolution

Iowa's famous tallgrass prairie evolved in part because of those fires. Without periodic burning to kill encroaching saplings, the prairie might have become a savanna or woodland.

Twentieth century prairie enthusiasts quickly learned that it was not enough to just save a tract of virgin sod from the plow. The native vegetation also needed a regular tonic of fire, lest it be swallowed by woody invaders.

Prichard is one of dozens of Iowa resource managers who have learned to use fire to invigorate prairie remnants or speed prairie restoration.

"Most of what we're trying to do is speed up the succession," Prichard said.

Benefits

Pauline Drobney, wildlife biologist at the new Walnut Creek National Wildlife Refuge near Prairie City, said fire benefits prairie species in several ways.

Burning the dead vegetation releases nutrients, which may go back into the soil to be recycled. And, since most prairie plants have vast root systems that escape fire, they respond quickly by sending up vigorous new growth.

The soot and ash also darken the soil, which warms more quickly in the spring sun and stimulates earlier plant growth.

Timing

Timing is critical, Prichard and Drobney agreed. It usually is best to burn in the spring before the warm-season prairie species have begun to grow. But burning too early can stimulate cool-season weeds instead of the prairie plants. Burning too late may jeopardize nesting birds.

It's possible to burn too much, Drobney added. Natural prairie fires probably were patchworks, leaving refuges for insects, wildlife and less fire-tolerant plants.

Fire has become such a common tool in prairie management that many county conservation boards sponsor public programs where people can watch controlled prairie burns.

But the pioneers may have been a little more apprehensive about prairie fires. An early history of Pocahontas County told of a fire that swept Lizard Township.

"To the observer in the Lizard settlement no flame was at first visible, but as the moments passed the horizon gradually grew brighter and about 8 o'clock the flames of the 'head-fire' could be distinctly seen. A little later several fine, luminous lines, like threads of tiny, sparkling beads,

47

became visible . . . the observers well knew that in those faint, glimmering lines of beauty there dwelt, in an ungovernable form, the most fiendish of devouring elements, fed by an abundance of dry prairie grass and driven by a powerful wind."

Perhaps today's Iowans no longer need fear a prairie fire – but they still can be awed by it.

April 5, 1992

New breed of pioneer aids prairie

ST. ANTHONY, IA – Neat rows of corn march gracefully around the gentle hillside. Other typical Iowa farm fields stretch to the horizon.

But Carl Kurtz hardly glances at his corn crop. Instead, he plunges into a tangle of vegetation that most people would call "weeds."

The St. Anthony farmer and freelance photographer is swallowed up by a sea of sunflowers, milkweed, goldenrod, big bluestem, Indian grass and a dozen other species.

He smiles as he wanders through the flowers and grasses, dreaming of the not-so-distant past when three-fourths of Iowa was covered with tallgrass prairie. The state had 30 million acres of a now-vanishing 140-million acre ecosystem that stretched across the Midwest.

Kurtz is bringing back a fragment of that prairie. Since 1975, he's seeded about 50 acres of his 172-acre farm with native grasses and forbs.

He began with the goal of restoring an old pasture that had been over-grazed by a tenant's cattle. He said he thought prairie grasses and flowers would hold the tired soil and provide wildlife habitat.

In addition, Kurtz hoped to create his own scenic vistas for photographs.

"I wanted to take pictures of prairies, but I didn't know where there were any," he said.

Eventually, he said he realized there was a potential to make money by selling seed from his reconstructed prairies.

Kurtz has fought drought, downpours and weeds. He's picked prairie seed by hand, dug up plants ahead of bulldozers and paid for the privilege of using his old combine to harvest seeds from private prairie preserves.

His prairie project is taking shape, with more than 24 species now established. Given a few more centuries – and a couple hundred more plant species – his farm may once again look like it did before the first settlers came, Kurtz says, jokingly.

Even that time frame might be optimistic, assuming the prairie has been evolving ever since the glaciers retreated more than 10,000 years ago.

Ever-so-slowly, those prairies built their rich soil – the fertile ground that fuels Iowa's farm economy.

And as the prairie soils are depleted, and the last remnants are plowed, more Iowans – like Kurtz – are trying to save some of that heritage.

"We're destroying our options," said Linda Kurtz, Carl's wife, who noted the potential value of native plants for medicines or alternative crops.

Prairie vegetation also is good for roadsides, where a mix of native species can create a stable, almost maintenance-free community, Kurtz said. Restored prairies also could be used for grazing, wildlife habitat, erosion control or open space.

Kurtz said he hopes his pioneering efforts to save some prairie also could prove profitable, if there is demand for seed from his plots to plant elsewhere.

But for the time being, it's reward enough to watch the sun rise over the compass plants, photograph a blazing star or host a wintering flock of pheasants.

September 8, 1991

49

Iowan patches state's prairie heritage –
one seed at a time

NEW SHARON, IA – Walking-stick in hand, Rayford Ratcliff waded into the shoulder-high tangle that sprawls across his back yard.

He admired the clusters of compass plant blossoms, then pointed out purple coneflowers, butterfly milkweed, rattlesnake master and a half-dozen other species.

"I love that prairie," he declared. "It grows on me."

Ratcliff, 77, is one of a rising number of Iowans who have discovered the state's prairie heritage.

The patch of prairie he planted in his yard eight years ago launched him into a hobby that has become a passion.

Ratcliff and his wife, Eleanora, learned about prairie from a relative who worked for a county conservation board. Intrigued, they began visiting a few native prairie preserves, such as Hayden Prairie near Lime Springs.

They liked what they saw: tall grasses rippling in the breeze, a kaleidoscope of flowers, a fragment of pioneer Iowa.

Prairie also looked like a good alternative to the big lawn Ratcliff had tired of mowing. He decided to seed prairie species – some purchased and some gathered from roadside relicts – in a 50 by 100-foot tract.

The first couple of years were discouraging, Ratcliff said. He still had to mow to control weeds.

"It's slow, and it's not going to be like a beautiful flower garden," he said.

By the third season, however, the native plants had crowded out most of the aliens. With an OK from the fire department, he burned the tract to further stimulate the vegetation.

Ratcliff now has counted 34 species in his prairie. He ticked off a few: Indian grass, rough blazing star, gayfeather, white larkspur, little bluestem, leadplant.

He delights in the first spring blooms, the ever-changing patterns of flowers and grasses, the miraculous revival after a long winter or a spring burn.

Ratcliff's fascination with prairie has made him an ideal volunteer to help with prairie reconstruction now under way at Walnut Creek National Wildlife Refuge near Prairie City, refuge biologist Pauline Drobney said.

Ratcliff regularly gathers seed for the massive project of replanting prairie and savanna on the 8,654-acre site.

"I have a great deal of respect for that man," Drobney said. "He's such a sharp observer of characteristics of plant communities. He's really an ecologist."

Ratcliff, a retired woodworker, also used his creative talents to build a "little piece of prairie" display for the Mahaska County Conservation Board. The glass case contains dozens of dried prairie plants, along with life-like artificial flowers that Ratcliff made.

These attempts to simulate some of Iowa's lost landscape are vital to teach people about the importance of prairie to the state, University of Northern Iowa biology professor Daryl Smith said.

"I could persuade almost all Iowans of the value of prairie preserves if I could just walk with them on a prairie remnant," Smith said.

But if everyone hiked those fragile areas, they would be destroyed.

Prairie reconstructions – from plots the size of Ratcliff's back yard to the 13 square miles at Walnut Creek National Wildlife Refuge – may be the answer, Smith said.

Laura Jackson, a prairie researcher at the University of Northern Iowa, hopes prairie plantings also may catch on in farming operations.

Most prairies now are "tiny fragments isolated by oceans of hostile corn and soybean habitat," she said.

But Jackson is studying ways to use intensive, rotational grazing of native species to make it profitable to preserve prairies on farms.

The approaches may be different, but the goal is the same, according to participants in the recent Iowa Prairie Conference at Cedar Falls.

Perhaps Rayford Ratcliff said it best: "My grandkids are going to get to see some things I never got to see!"

July 30, 1995

Guthrie County
© The Des Moines Register

CHAPTER 4

FORESTS

They're not just trees.

To loggers, they're a crop, to be harvested, cut into boards and sold for profit.

To squirrels and owls and chickadees, they're homes, complete with food and shelter.

To some farmers, they're barriers to growing corn.

To naturalists, they're an ever-changing ecosystem, subject to the whims of weather, time, insects, disease and man's manipulations.

To park managers, they may be tourist attractions or campground hazards.

We have not yet learned to look objectively at trees. When we do, we may begin to see the forest.

Benign neglect: Is it right way?

Planning future of Iowa's forests

Picture a dense canopy of trees, rolling across pre-settlement eastern Iowa's pristine hills and valleys . . . But it's only a fantasy.

"What we had here was something very different from the primeval forest we grew up believing was here," said Donald Farrar, botany professor at Iowa State University.

Fires – whether natural or set by Native Americans – left a mosaic of forests, prairies and savanna, Farrar said. There was almost no such thing as a mature, undisturbed woodland.

Thus, the State Preserves Advisory Board and other conservation groups face a dilemma when they try to "preserve" forests, researchers agreed at a symposium in Des Moines last week.

Preservationists once thought "benign neglect" – letting nature take its course – would assure the future of a preserve, said John Pearson, an ecologist for the Department of Natural Resources. But scientists realize that plant communities change, even without direct human management.

With no fire or mowing, many prairies would become overgrown with trees. Forest communities may evolve, as plant succession replaces oaks with maples or basswoods.

With some trees living 150 years or more, people may not perceive that a woodland is changing, Pearson said. They may see only the big oaks, and fail to understand that seedling maples eventually will take over – unless humans interfere.

"It really comes down to a philosophy of what do you want to happen in a preserve," Pearson said.

At White Pine Hollow near Luxemburg, for example, the huge conifers that gave the preserve its name are slowly dying. Browsing by deer and shading by other trees is suppressing seedlings.

Should the state intervene to fence out or remove deer, or to kill competing trees, Pearson wondered.

"What is White Pine Hollow without white pines?" he mused.

Jerry Kemperman, forestry management supervisor for the Department of Natural Resources, said esthetics aren't the only consideration. The Iowa white pines may be unique – different from trees farther north.

"Should there be extra concern at the genetic level, as well as the community level?" he asked.

Farrar said he could agree with managing the forest to stimulate white pines at White Pine Hollow. But just how much should humans tinker in other places?

Old growth forests, which are rare in Iowa and elsewhere, should be kept for research, Farrar said. Woodland preserves can provide a standard by which to measure other forests. The plots are essential for ecological and genetic studies. And the trees' age, form and growth rates may hold clues to historical changes in the environment.

Other woodlands may be manipulated for wildlife, park use or wood production, Farrar said. But some preserves should be allowed to "do their own thing," to become a haven for rare, fragile or unusual organisms.

"What is it that we don't have *without* preserves?" Farrar said.

Terry Little, wildlife research supervisor for the Department of Natural Resources, said the

53

loss of forests leaves scattered bits of woodlands that may not support some species of wildlife. But he questioned whether Iowa ever had deep woods.

"Were Iowa's forests ever anything *but* fragmented?" Little asked.

And despite foresters' complaints that deer eat oaks and other tree seedlings, Little questioned whether that phenomenon is unusual. Perhaps the oak forests that developed when early settlers wiped out the deer should be termed an oddity, he said.

"If we want to manage for the forest that was here in 1830, maybe the presence of deer isn't as unnatural as we think," Little said.

Others' suggestions for preserve management covered a wide spectrum: "hands off," periodic burning, clear-cuts, deer control.

Farris said foresters are planning a series of experimental fires at Shimek State Forest near Farmington to study burning as a management tool.

But in some cases, there's not even consensus on what a preserve should protect – much less how to do it.

The top priority may be to agree on preserve management goals, Farris said.

"Unless you know where you're going, it's hard to get there."

December 22, 1996

Early bloomers

*Spring wildflowers are beginning to appear,
and some of the best places to find them are in the parks around Iowa.*

Put on your old shoes. Walk slowly. Speak softly. Breathe deeply. And look around.

Nature is putting on her spring finery: The season's first wildflowers are blooming.

Subtly at first, the miniature blossoms poke through the dull, brown leaves. Tinges of pink or white brighten the winter-weary woodlands.

With each spring day, more clumps of flowers burst into bloom. They steal the glory of still-dormant trees like mischievous children snatching candy from their sleeping parents.

Woodland flowers *must* bloom and produce seeds early in the year. If they wait too long, tree leaves will block the life-giving sun.

Thus, as early as March, the white, three-petaled flowers of snow trilliums may cling to the ground like lingering patches of snow.

Hepatica flowers pop up quickly, not waiting for the slower emergence of the three-lobed leaves that earn the common name "liver leaf."

Bright-white bloodroots, with golden-yellow stamens, almost shine in the sun.

Indeed, their dish shape can turn some flowers into tiny solar collectors. Insects seek out the blossoms, where they bask in temperatures several degrees warmer than the surrounding air.

The arrangement benefits the bees, which conserve their own energy, and it helps the flowers, which get pollinated as early as possible.

Of course, flowers can be good for people, too. They're a spring tonic that's free and close to home.

But – just like people – they need peace and quiet and solitude. Wildflowers don't like herds of cattle or bulldozers or hordes of picnickers or blossom-pickers or plant-diggers.

Many state, county and city parks contain wildflower preserves.

Then again, almost any undisturbed remnant of woods might hide a wildflower haven. Some of the best may be little-known sites that hardly anyone ever visits.

For example, look under the old oak in a corner of the yard that escaped the lawn mower and weed sprayer.

Watch the sides of the bike trail where it curves along the edge of a secluded woodland.

Get away from the cow path to the neighbor's hillside grove where his livestock seldom go.

In the early spring, look first on south-facing slopes, which warm up the quickest. Later, try cool, damp sites at the base of north-facing bluffs.

Of course, southern Iowa flowers probably will bloom first, while the season in northern Iowa will last later.

Don't expect to find the spring flora in shopping malls or TV rooms or mini-vans.

Do savor the spell that flowers seem to cast over all who see them.

Hikers tread more softly, lest they trample a delicate violet.

Children gasp in delight at the upside-down trousers of the Dutchman's breeches.

Curiosity-seekers probe among mats of fuzzy, heart-shaped leaves to find ground-hugging flowers of wild ginger.

Photographers flop on their stomachs in search of perfect close-ups.

Botanists peer through hand lenses, studying pistils and anthers and other flower parts in search of an iron-clad identification.

Even bird-watchers may temporarily lower their binoculars. Flowers can be relished. They don't fly away.

Wildflowers aren't loud or brassy or strident or demanding – yet they still captivate us.

April 20, 1995

'Morel' of story: Mushrooms hard to find

Dear Boss:

You remember that mushroom hunting story I was going to write? Well, I'm afraid I can't do it.

Oh, I tried – really I did. But did you ever take pictures of a mushroom hunter? Such a fuss! They're more elusive than gulley cats – and twice as ornery. One lady even offered to feed me my camera if I so much as clicked near "her" mushroom timber.

It may not be a very good year for mushrooms, anyway, Boss. One fellow blamed it on a shortage of box-elder bugs. You see, the best mushrooms grow in places that have been fertilized by box-elder bug wings. (Gee, it was kind of that guy to tell me his secret! At least I learned something on this assignment.)

But, good year or not, I tried to sniff out a story. In fact, I was sure I was on the right track when I heard of an old Norwegian who hunts mushrooms by smell. He even agreed to let me join him!

We'd just started huntin' when that darned volcano erupted. Well, my source's volcanic ash allergy flared up, and, wouldn't you know, he sneezed so hard he blew every last morel back in the ground before we could get close enough to pick 'em. (He even showed me the spots where they would have been, if he hadn't sneezed so!)

But you've always told me to have another idea to fall back on – right, Boss?

How about the theory that morels come out when oak leaves are as big as a squirrel's ear? I had it figured that you'd love to see some close-up pictures of leaves and ears . . . .

I'll try to "fall back" from a little lower limb, next time, I promise. (Our company insurance does cover X-rays, doesn't it?)

Maybe I wasn't working hard enough on this story at first. (Don Muhm says you've got to sweat to find mushrooms.) But I persisted. I even did a lot more research.

It didn't bother me a bit (well, maybe a little) to learn that folks have died from eating mushrooms. Most aren't poisonous, but some of those little fungi can really zap you. They're full of monomethylhydrazine – stuff they put in rocket fuel, for crying out loud! (I resolved to be very careful!)

I kept at it, checking all over town for fresh asparagus shoots and May-apple blossoms and lilac blooms. (Sure signs of mushroom time, they tell me.)

I even wished for thunderstorms. All that lightning really makes 'em pop. (But you KNEW that – didn't you, Boss?)

I really got inspired by all this information I turned up, too. I even found out that the old-timers used mushrooms for a love potion. (Don't let the word get out!)

There's even a potential story in hunting techniques, I discovered. One ol' boy showed me how he carries a three-foot stick and always keeps his eyes glued right to the end of it. (I tried it Boss, and it seemed to work OK. But I was so busy watching that stick it took me half a day to get out of the timber. Never did figure out where that man went after he gave me the stick!)

But the best system sounded almost too good to be true. All you've got to do is find one mushroom and lay your hat down by it. Then you just keep crawling in circles around the hat until you fill your bag with morels.

I'll have to admit, it took me a while to find the first one – but I suppose you expected that! (Please, no more jokes about the Stone Jinx.)

But I found a morel, Boss! It was a fresh, light brown, spongy-looking morel mushroom – poking right up through the dead leaves beneath those sweet Williams growing under a two-year-dead elm tree. Just like it says in the book!

And I did just like I was supposed to – I laid my hat down beside it and I crawled around and around, looking under every leaf and wildflower.

But it didn't work, Boss . . . .

I couldn't even find my hat.

May 25, 1980

Naturalist teaches kids about new tricks for old logs

MANCHESTER, IA – When Betsy Paragamian leads nature hikes, her students sometimes are surprised to find they're studying death, as well as life.

Who cares about a dead elm snag, or a barkless oak or a rotting log, the kids may wonder.

"Most people see a dead tree and think it's useless," said Paragamian.

But when she lifts a mossy log to reveal a salamander, or points out the intricate bark beetle tunnels on a dead elm, or spots a downy woodpecker in a basswood snag, or finds mouse tracks entering a hollow stump, the kids see the light: a tree dies so other creatures may live.

"Actually, a dead tree has more life inside of it than a living tree would," said Paragamian, who is a naturalist for the Delaware County Conservation Board.

Cycle of Life

Think, for example, of the insects and larvae that begin burrowing into the wood almost as soon as it dies. Next come woodpeckers and other birds, probing and pecking for a meal. In winter, the wood-chip crumbs from their dinner tables may litter the snow around a snag.

Often, the woodpeckers may chop out a hole big enough to nest in. Other cavity-nesters – chickadees, bluebirds, screech owls – also move in.

Squirrels love the holes for winter shelter or to escape marauding owls and foxes. Flying squirrels find secluded hide-aways in rotting trees. Raccoons raise their young in the hollow trunks.

Paragamian regularly gets springtime calls from firewood cutters who find baby raccoons or owls in dead trees they've cut to burn. Often, the wood cutters are surprised to learn that their harvest of apparently worthless trees is so destructive to wildlife.

Far-reaching Damage

But the damage extends to more than just the obvious game or non-wildlife that uses tree cavities, said Doug Reeves, nongame wildlife biologist for the Iowa Department of Natural Resources.

"If that was the most important thing," he said, "we could just stick up nest boxes and not worry about dead trees."

Reeves said endangered Indiana bats need loose bark – not just tree cavities. The bats may crawl up under the protective bark to raise their young.

Hawks and owls seek out limbs on dead trees as hunting perches, Reeves added. Meanwhile, the raptors' prey – such as white-footed mice – may be hiding in the dead-wood holes and crevasses.

Dead wood also contributes to a complex food chain, which nourishes fungi, insects, mosses, earthworms, snakes and a host of other often-overlooked organisms. The rotting wood eventually turns to humus, enriches the soil – and nurtures the forest community of the future. Even when it falls to the ground, the tree is alive.

Yet casual observers too often view the dead trees as unsightly or wasteful, contributing nothing to a growing woodland, said Mike Brandrup, head of forestry services for the Iowa Department of Natural Resources.

A dead tree doesn't hurt other trees, however, Brandrup said.

Once dead, the tree no longer competes for sunlight or moisture, he said. Instead of growing wood, the tree's role becomes one of recycling nutrients to the ecosystem, and of wildlife production.

Biologists often recommend leaving two to five dead trees per acre of forest, just to provide wildlife habitat.

"What you have [with a dead tree] is an apartment house," Brandrup said, "and the more it decays, the more valuable it is to wildlife."

Despite the variety of insects, fungi and other organisms that live in decaying wood, dead trees do not pose a disease threat to the living forest, added forestry supervisor Jerry Kemperman. Most harmful insects or diseases exist only on live wood, and the organisms have moved elsewhere by the time the tree is dead.

In fact, dead trees could attract birds that may eat harmful insects and therefore protect live trees.

"It doesn't help your woods to take out the dead trees," Kemperman said.

Cutting dead trees for firewood or to clean up the forest may even damage the woodland – and endanger the sawyer, he added.

To a human, a dead tree may be just another chunk of firewood. But to woodland wildlife, it's home sweet home.

January 17, 1988

Iowan pays $286,000 for unique timber stand

GARNAVILLO, IA – Bob Livingston stretched his forester's calipers to nearly their full 30 inches, stuck them against the massive red oak, and leaned back to stare in awe at the slate gray trunk that rose 35 feet to the first limb.

"Just look at that," he said softly.

"Ain't that one – – – of a piece of wood?"

Livingston had a right to be proud of that magnificent "piece of wood." He'd just paid more than $286,000 for a 40-acre patch of woods where that oak, and scores more like it, had lived undisturbed for nearly 150 years.

Now, he stood among the giant oaks and ashes and the healthy young maples, satisfied – after 40 years of prowling northeast Iowa forests – that he owned the ultimate.

"There ain't another timber in the country that's worth half this much," he said. "It's the best one I know of."

Possible Record Price

That's why, Livingston said, that he was willing to pay more than $7,000 per acre for the land and the right to log it. That price, more than double the runner-up offer in a sealed bid auction, probably is a record for Iowa timberland, said state forester Bill Farris.

But the site just can't be compared with more typical Iowa woodlands, which may sell for $200-$400 per acre – sometimes less, Livingston said.

"This is one of a kind," he said. "It's as near virgin as we've got."

The timber's value was enhanced even more by the rich, rock-free soil, the long-time protection from grazing and the high proportion of top quality red oak.

There may not be another plot of private timber in Iowa worth $7,000 per acre – and few are worth even a fraction of that – agreed Farris. But the unique value of the site illustrates the potential worth of Iowa forest-land.

"If you don't graze it and take care of it, timber can develop into something quite valuable," he said.

Owned by Muellers

The property had been in the Valmah Mueller family since 1874, and never had been commercially harvested. A nearby 40-acre parcel, which Livingston bought for $116,000, had belonged to the Mueller clan since 1865.

Mueller cherished the unspoiled timber, where he gathered mushrooms, hickory nuts and fern bouquets, said his nephew, Lloyd Biederman of Elkader. When Mueller died last April, however, the land had to be sold.

Bob Livingston, the tree-lover, almost reverently acknowledged the century-and-a-half of history in those oaks. But Bob Livingston, the logger, had envisioned the trees' fate ever since he first saw the tract 35 years ago.

Eventually, most of the trees will be cut and sold through Livingston Lumber Co., the Guttenberg sawmill Livingston began in 1946 and now operates with his son, Ralph. The best logs will be cut into veneer and paneling, either domestically or in Japan. Lower quality trees will make oak furniture or lumber, while the poorest wood goes into pallets, railroad ties or firewood.

Cruel End?

Is it a cruel end for such stately old trees? State ecologist Dean Roosa thinks so.

"I think these ancient trees, the truly mature woodlands, have so many secrets we haven't yet extracted," Roosa said. Because virgin timbers are so rare in Iowa, there have been almost no studies of their ecosystems.

"They have so much to offer as laboratories," Roosa said. "It bothers me that we're going to lose those centuries of accumulated wisdom."

Even Livingston admitted to having mixed emotions about cutting the oak monarchs.

"I've got a lot of real deep feelings about that," Livingston said. "It's about like burying that old friend of mine; it's gotta be done. I don't enjoy going to his funeral, but we must do it."

Many of the old oaks are near the end of their life span, Livingston rationalized. Some of their tops had broken out, some had been toppled by the wind, disease threatened others.

"They're gonna go," Livingston shrugged, "one way or the other. What we'll be harvesting is something on the way out."

"I guess we have to go back and look at Genesis," he said. "The Lord put all that here for man to use."

Harvesting trees is *wise* use, Livingston insisted. His conviction that Iowa forests should be saved for their long-term timber crop is another reason he bid high enough to be sure he bought the Mueller woods, he said.

"At least half this is an investment in the future," he said.

It irks him to see timberland grazed or cleared and converted to farmland, as happened so often under the farm policies of the past 30 years.

"We encouraged farmers to clear it and then paid [cost-sharing subsidies] for them to terrace it and then paid them [through government programs] not to farm the – – – stuff," Livingston bristled.

His timbers won't ever see a plow – not while he's alive, Livingston vowed. And he'll keep planting up to 10,000 trees annually, as he has for years.

He pointed at the woods.

"One thing I know about that S.O.B.," he declared, "it isn't going to be a – – – cornfield!"

It *will* see a chainsaw—but even that may wait awhile. On a recent hike through the timber, Livingston spray-painted orange rings around only a few oaks with damaged tops, resisting the urge to mark more for the sawyers.

Mostly, he buried the berries of ripening ginseng, gathered acorns to plant elsewhere – and just admired his trees.

"I'll get in here after the leaves are down, and maybe hunt a few squirrels," Livingston said, "and I'll have a paint can in my hand" to mark trees to cut.

"But would I rather have [the money] in the bank or out here on the land?" he mused. "Where . . . else can I go and lean up against a tree like that and look up and say 'it's mine'?"

September 6, 1987

Turning a field into a future forest

Like a ragged but comfortable pair of jeans, our old farm needed a little mending.

That's why several delightful May days found my family and me on our knees in the misused dirt, planting trees.

We were trying, in our own imperfect way, to put back what nature had intended our hills to grow.

Sadly, some ambitious or ignorant farmer, decades ago, had chopped the oaks and basswoods and maples off the steep slopes and planted them to "worthwhile" crops: corn, oats, hay.

A pitiful field of corn clung to the incline when Margaret and I bought the land in 1979. To halt the erosion, we seeded the first thing that came to our Iowa farm-bred minds: alfalfa and brome.

The sod held the soil, and even attracted a few turkeys and deer. We hunted and skied and picnicked and bird-watched in the field.

But the clearing also was a magnet for cowbirds and raccoons and coyotes and other invaders that thrive when man cuts holes in the landscape. "Fragmentation," ecologists call it.

Eventually, we decided to try to undo the damage, and to turn our old field back into forest.

- •

Five hundred red oak seedlings didn't *seem* like many when we placed our order with the State Forest Nursery. Of course, the forester *would* have lent us his mechanical tree planter, but the machine seemed so, well, mechanical . . .

How much more personal to hand dig each hole, to select the right seedling for the site, to gently fit it into the depression, carefully cover its roots with loam, and step beside it to scrunch out the air pockets.

Besides, the process gave us time to reflect on the young oaks. Like children, each had its own identity.

Some – straight, tall and robust – sat in the root-soaking bucket, begging for attention.

"Plant me first!" they almost shouted.

A few hung back, like shy grade-schoolers. With crooked stems and tiny roots, they hardly looked worth planting.

But we tried to do our best with each. After all, how could we know which seedling might get gnawed by a mouse, choked by a drought or browsed by a deer? If a sickly oak endured the hazards and found a fertile site, it might – like a late-blooming child – outpace its more conspicuous cousin.

We tried not to begrudge the long-ago farmer who'd first cleared the plot. His was the "conquer-the-wilderness era," when a "good" farmer grubbed out all the trees he could.

He didn't foresee how the topsoil would ooze down the slope, leaving little but yellow clay on the ridges.

He'd have learned a lot, had he helped with our digging.

We learned, too – about more than just dirt and trees.

Our son, Andy, 19, shovel in hand, laughed as he recalled his sandbox days as "Samuel P. Gopher, excavation expert," star of a favorite "Winnie the Pooh" tale.

Home from college for a few days, he could polish those digging skills before beginning a "real" job on a road-construction crew.

Silently, Margaret and I wondered which task Andy will remember longer – building culverts or replanting a forest.

Daughter Emily, 15, joined the party after school. She brought cookies, cold drinks and an inborn love for running her fingers through the dirt.

Together, we pondered whether these oaks would be a timber crop that could pay college tuition for our children's children.

We wagered how long it would be before the squirrels could jump between the treetops, and when the first acorns would fall to feed our turkeys.

We studied our barren field, with the emerging goldenrod, mustard, box elder, ragweed and other "weeds," hoping the green fuzz would become a jungle, guarded by raspberries and tree seedlings. Such a thicket might lure the ruffed grouse back to our farm, after a long absence.

And if we are successful in restoring trees to our hill, we mused, which of our kin might begin to call it a "forest"?

We talked of transplanting wildflowers from our nearby woods, or of scattering their seeds. Would these tiny oaks some day shed enough leaves, build enough duff and cast enough shade to support Jack-in-the-pulpits, spring beauties, bloodroots or showy orchis?

When our backs cried out for rest, we stopped for a drink and to listen to the bird chorus. Indigo buntings and field sparrows sang from the field edges.

Would we live long enough to one day hear deep woods songsters, like the scarlet tanager and ovenbird, call from the same spot?

Later, as we surveyed our work, a palm warbler hopped among our dirt piles. Migrating Swainson's thrushes scoured the field.

And then, to our amusement and delight, a tiny flycatcher perched on a freshly planted, foot-tall oak seedling, where it launched repeated forays in pursuit of an insect breakfast.

Our faith was rewarded.

If the birds were happy, so were we.

June 6, 1997

Eagle Lake

CHAPTER 5

© The Des Moines Register

WETLANDS

Like the prairies, wetlands once covered so much of the state that no one thought of needing to save any. Hurrying the water off the land made room for farm fields and highways and cities.

But drying up the puddles and ponds and sloughs, those natural sponges, destroyed trumpeter swans and ducks and muskrats. Speeding the runoff brought more floods and longer droughts. We sacrificed an array of water-loving plants.

To grasp the extraordinary wealth of a wetland, you must literally and figuratively immerse yourself in it. Then, after you've smelled the muck, felt the mosquitoes, heard the cacophony of bird songs, seen the cattails bending in the breeze and tasted a roast duck, you may sense both our ancestors' urge to drain the swamps and our own determination to re-flood some of them.

Tranquility runs amok in muck

BRITT, IA – They're despised as stinking wastelands by sophisticates; they're coveted as potential cornfields by farmers; they're shunned as weed-filled jungles by pleasure boaters.

But Iowa's few-thousand acres of marshes and wetlands – all that remain undrained from the millions of acres the first pioneers saw – contain some of the richest ecosystems on Earth. Our marshes produce more plant and animal life than any other land type.

Terns wheel overhead. Coots and grebes and sora rails chuckle and grunt and hoot from hiding. Yellow-headed blackbirds buzz and rasp from swaying perches. Muskrats scurry to build food caches against the winter. A maze of cattails and bulrushes and water weeds stretches out under the June sky.

Just an instant ago, in geologic time, this watery wilderness covered much of northwest and north-central Iowa. Potholes and shallow lakes, the 10,000-year-old footprints of the retreating glacier, shimmered all across the prairies.

Early settlers avoided these soggy lowlands, but industrious farmers soon found ways to drain the marshes. Cornfields now grow where once there was more water than dry land.

Only a handful of private wetlands and a few scattered state-owned marshes are left for the modern naturalist in search of a piece of this vanishing part of Iowa's natural history.

That call of history lured Ken Formanek and me to Eagle Lake, near Britt. The 900-acre "lake" in reality is a shallow marsh, managed by the Iowa Conservation Commission for wildlife – an ideal place for photographing abundant marsh wildlife.

Ken grew up on a farm on the shores of Eagle Lake, so he's felt the call of the marsh for years. His love of the outdoors and his present job as a photographer for the Conservation Commission no doubt have their roots in the mucky bottom of Eagle Lake.

As we poled a borrowed duck boat out through the cattails, the hub-bub of deadlines and telephones and work-a-day cares melted under the hot sun. We paused to look and listen, to smell the marsh smells and to feel the marsh serenity settling over us.

"This is what I call getting in tune with the marsh," Ken sighed. Each of us hated to move, for fear of breaking the other's tranquility.

The black terns broke our idyll with a series of screaming dives over the boat. We must have floated too near their nesting colony, for they swooped and hovered and scolded until we moved on.

Chattering calls from the dense cattails caught our attention. We watched with amusement as young yellow-headed blackbirds fluttered, crash-landed, then struggled up the stems to launch on another practice flight.

Fragrance of the marsh

As we slid through a corridor in the rushes, Ken spotted a watery heap of vegetation. Perched on the mound were two freshly-hatched coot chicks, along with several unhatched eggs. What a sorry sight those chicks made, with their red bills, orange-tinged down and greenish, match-stick legs!

We slipped into the water for closer pictures, and sank calf-deep in the rotting marsh bottom.

"Ah, the fragrance of the marsh," Ken grinned, as the aroma of methane gas and decaying plants oozed into our nostrils.

Each step in the muck was a struggle, as the clinging mixture of silt and organic matter closed in around our feet. It was easy to imagine why the gunk in marsh bottoms has earned the irreverent nickname "loon puke."

As we coursed through the cattails, our boat occasionally flushed nesting ducks. Several pairs of redheads circled around us, protesting our intrusion with their purring calls.

Last home of whoopers

We heard – but did not see – several American bitterns, with their unusual "slough-pump" calls. The "glug-glug" sounds came from the depth of a cattail meadow – but it's doubtful we'd have spied the bittern even if he'd been alongside our boat. The bird's brown stripes and habit of freezing in a vertical pose give it almost perfect camouflage.

A century ago, an Eagle Lake visitor might have been lucky enough to see the magnificent whooping crane. Whoopers nested in Iowa before the marshes were destroyed – and the last known whooper nest in the United States was found near the lake in 1894.

Today, however, we have to be content with the wonders of more common marsh wildlife – and with the satisfaction of knowing that this one tiny remnant of our wetlands is being preserved.

We didn't try to put dollar signs on our experience – but some economists have valued marshes as high as $60,000 per acre. Biologists say the marsh ecosystem is worth that much because of its sponge-like ability to hold water and release it gradually during dry seasons, and because of its great capacity to absorb pollutants in runoff. A marsh is really a flood control device, water storage reservoir and pollution control plant.

Come to think of it, that day on Eagle Lake – with nobody around but the birds – may be as close as Ken or I will ever come to being millionaires!

June 24, 1979

Listening to an Iowa frog opera

TODDVILLE, IA – You'd think it'd be easy to ignore a frog.

At least you *might* think that, if you haven't spent a spring evening in frog country.

But when a pond full of spring peepers or chorus frogs or tree frogs begins a concert, the music can be almost deafening. You may not see the inch-long vocalists, but there's no mistaking their presence.

It's mating time, you see, and that's when male frogs demand attention. They get that attention by singing – loudly.

You can't blame the frogs for the racket; after all, that's the only way they know to attract females.

The frogs are singing for each other – but humans, too, can enjoy the music.

Neil Bernstein and K.E. Goellner of Cedar Rapids recently attended a frog opera in an open air theater near Toddville. The performance was at Behrens Ponds and Woodland, a Nature Conservancy preserve, where several shallow ponds and surrounding woodlands make ideal frog and toad habitat.

The natural area is one of Bernstein's favorite retreats. As a biology professor at Mount Mercy College, he often takes his classes there. Goellner, a retired Coe College biology professor, was instrumental in the Conservancy's preservation of the site.

Hip Boots

Hip-booted, the pair eased into the vegetation-choked ponds as darkness fell.

Spring peepers serenaded them with clear, bell-like notes. To Goellner, the peepers' songs sounded like "little blacksmiths pinging on tiny anvils."

Two kinds of tree frogs called urgently with bird-like warbles. Bernstein distinguished between the similar species by their calls: one rapid and high-pitched; the other slower and lower.

A chorus frog croaked slowly, sounding vaguely like a thumbnail scraping the teeth of a pocket comb.

In the distance, an American toad tuned up with a pleasant trill that floated above the near din of a hundred other competing frog vocalists.

Bernstein said frogs and toads begin singing in the spring as the weather warms. Each species is most active at a different temperature, so the voices in the frog chorus can change with the season.

After mating in shallow ponds, adult frogs and toads may head for woodlands or meadows, leaving their eggs to hatch. The tadpoles stay in the water until they mature and develop lungs.

"Why?" a passer-by might have asked, had he seen the men exploring the darkness of the dank, musty marsh.

Explaining Why

Bernstein could have explained his scientific interest by stating the importance of frogs and tadpoles in the food chain. They eat insects, larvae and other small animals – and in turn are eaten by fish, birds and larger predators.

Or Bernstein might have lectured on frogs and toads as indicators of the health of the environment. Any complete checkup of Mother Earth would include a survey of her frog and toad populations.

68

But if, after hearing the wondrous frog chorus, the visitor still had to ask the question, he probably wouldn't have understood the answer.

Bernstein or Goellner might as well have responded by pointing to Venus, hanging like a jewel just above the western horizon. Or they could have shushed the onlooker so he could hear the distant chatter of the whip-poor-will. Or perhaps they could have nodded in the direction of the barred owls trading hoots in the timber down by the river.

Frogs, after all, are just another part of the great ecological web, Bernstein noted.

For his classes, the frogging trip to the ponds is a highlight of the year, Bernstein said. Even the reluctant students often get caught up in the marvels of a marsh at night, he said.

"To stand in the dark in a wet place and hear all these things, and then be able to find them, seems to open up a whole new world."

May 11, 1986

Fen Pal: Nekola delights in Iowa's floral treasures

LAWLER, IA – With water squishing underfoot, the ground bouncing like a trampoline and rare plants spread out before him, Jeff Nekola was in paradise.

"What a place!" he beamed. "What a *place!*"

Nekola was exploring his favorite haunt: a seepy Chickasaw County hill that is home to some of the state's most rare plants.

The site is a fen – formed when ground water oozes up through peaty soil, providing habitat for plants found virtually nowhere else.

Once common in northeast Iowa, fens now are among the state's least-known communities, said Nekola, whose fen research recently earned him a PhD in ecology from the University of North Carolina.

Nekola, 29, began his studies about 10 years ago as a Coe College student, when he was intrigued by the water, hummocks and strange plants in northwest Iowa fens. He soon located similar sites in northeastern Iowa.

After a tedious hunt through soil surveys and other maps, Nekola identified more than 2,300 potential fen sites in 30 counties. But a 10-year field search turned up only 160 remaining fens. The other 93 percent had been destroyed.

"It's just a small piece of the story of the destruction of Iowa's natural history," Nekola said.

The loss of fens is especially tragic because of the variety of ferns, sedges, mosses and other plant life they support, he said. He found about 320 plant species – 18 percent of the entire state flora – in the fens he studied.

Unfortunately, about half those species are rare in northeastern Iowa and the rest of the state, Nekola said.

Fens are more than just collections of peculiar plants, however. Nekola said fens can help scientists learn how to preserve other environments.

The idea struck him as he compared fens with another unusual environment, the cold air slopes. Both are isolated habitats in northeast Iowa, but they have markedly different histories.

Cold air slopes and their plant communities are survivors of the Ice Age that ended more than 10,000 years ago. Most fens were formed and colonized by plants less than 6,000 years ago, long after the glaciers had retreated.

Nekola found that fens are dynamic, containing many species that disperse their seeds by the wind. Cold air slopes are more stable, dominated by plants that grow from fruits or berries dropped at the site.

"These two habitats make a really neat system of comparison of how different habitats form," Nekola said.

"I think it's better than any computer model because it's telling you for a fact what did fragmentation do in the natural world."

The comparison also should make conservationists re-think strategies to preserve natural areas, he said.

Saving a cold air slope might be as easy as protecting it from physical damage, Nekola said. But fen preservation may require attention to several areas among which different species can move.

"You have to look at a bigger landscape perspective," Nekola said. "Not every habitat is the same and you can't save one habitat by using methods you used on another."

At North Carolina, where Nekola studied for seven years, and at the University of Wisconsin at Green Bay, where he has accepted a job teaching conservation biology, friends have teased him about working in Iowa, where so much of the land has been altered. But Nekola defends his home state.

"These are globally important ecological questions you can ask here – in the cornfield," he said.

Nekola intends to keep asking, and to keep searching for new habitats and rare species.

His quest started in earnest in junior high school, when he learned his house had been built on the site of a rare orchid. He began walking or biking to other areas, teaching himself about botany. The pace has accelerated through high school, college and graduate school.

"I have a real sense we're rushing against the clock. If we don't find it in the next 25 years, there won't be anything left to find."

May 29, 1994

The goal is to flood cornfields

ESTHERVILLE, IA – Ron Howing pointed across the rolling corn and soybean fields, but in his mind, he saw water.

"I've dreamed for years of plugging tiles and putting water back on land where there used to be a marsh," said Howing, who is a wildlife biologist for the Iowa Department of Natural Resources.

And now, with tile valves in place, the stage is set to flood a 50-acre basin, a 24-acre pool and six other, smaller potholes at 288-acre Four Mile Lake Waterfowl Production Area near Estherville.

When the rains come, cattails and bulrushes will grow where corn has been king for decades.

"It's really satisfying to flood a cornfield," Howing said with a smile.

More than 30,000 acres of Iowa cornfields and other crop land will revert to prairie or marsh in the next decade, said Richard Bishop, wildlife bureau chief for the Iowa Department of Natural Resources.

The effort is part of the Prairie Pothole Joint Venture, a plan to protect 1.1 million acres of land in five states by the year 2000.

Under the North American Waterfowl Management Plan, similar wetland protection efforts are under way in other parts of the country. The $1.5 billion, 15-year plan, which began in 1986, is aimed at reversing habitat losses that have devastated waterfowl populations. Biologists hope to see a fall flight of 100 million ducks by the year 2000, up from a low of just over 60 million birds in 1985.

Iowa's goal of restoring 30,000 acres of wetlands in 35 north-central counties pales beside those of North Dakota, South Dakota and Minnesota, each of which will protect more than 200,000 acres. But given Iowa's almost total loss of the state's original 7.6 million acres of mixed prairie and wetland, the 30,000-acre target is an ambitious one, Bishop said.

"And we're going to make it – no question about," he said.

From 1987 through 1989, $3.8 million is to be spent to protect nearly 5,000 acres in the state, Bishop said. The money includes more than $1.6 million from the U.S. Fish and Wildlife Service, plus funds from state waterfowl and habitat stamps, the Iowa Lottery, county conservation boards and private groups.

A recent 305-acre project, Meredith Marsh near Forest City, used money from the Department of Natural Resources, the U.S. Fish and Wildlife Service, Ducks Unlimited, Pheasants Forever, Wetlands for Iowa, the Hancock County Conservation Board, Winnebago Industries, the Iowa Trappers Association, students at Forest City Middle School and other private donors.

Scores of farmers also have allowed Department of Natural Resources biologists to restore marsh basins on land idled by the Conservation Reserve Program, Bishop said. Those projects could total 1,800 acres by the end of this year.

Wetlands shelter not only waterfowl, but also yellow-headed blackbirds, great blue herons, painted turtles and muskrats. The marshes slow runoff, reducing floods and recharging groundwater. Wetlands also filter out pollutants and slow erosion.

The best wetland complexes include one to three acres of nesting cover for every one acre of water, Bishop said. Those uplands are habitat for deer, pheasants, rabbits, upland sandpipers and dozens of other wildlife species. Often, the sites may protect rare remnants of native prairie vegetation, as well.

For some people, the idea of flooding a crop field may take some getting used to, Howing said.

"For the old-timers who fought the water all their lives, it's tough to talk of plugging up a tile," he said.

But attitudes are changing, Howing said.

Iowans have learned to see a marsh not as a potential cornfield but as a source of clean water, a home for wildlife, a place of beauty – and an asset to the state's quality of life.

August 6, 1989

Reviving the wetlands

Projects bring wildlife back along the Missouri

ONAWA, IA – Clouds of ducks and geese swarmed over backwaters and wetlands.

Sandbars lured basking turtles, loafing water birds and nesting terns and plovers.

Pools and cutbanks sheltered sturgeon, catfish, paddlefish, northern pike and a myriad of small fish.

That was the Missouri River a half-century ago. A maze of channels, forests, sloughs and shallows, the untamed river roamed a broad floodplain.

The rowdy stream was treacherous to navigate and often flooded cities and farms—but the "Big Muddy" was a paradise for fish and wildlife.

Then came "progress." In 1944, Congress authorized five dams on the upper Missouri. That work, plus channelization in the 1950s and 1960s, harnessed the river for navigation and flood control. The once ever-changing river became a straight, rock-lined canal.

With their homes destroyed, fish and wildlife populations plummeted. Some species became rare or endangered.

Now, some are reviving. State and federal agencies have begun to repair a bit of the damage, with "mitigation" for past sins against the natural river.

It's been a slow process, said Allen Farris, fish and wildlife administrator for the Iowa Department of Natural Resources. He's worked on Missouri River mitigation since 1976.

In 1981, the U.S. Army Corps of Engineers agreed to restore, preserve, acquire or develop 48,100 acres of habitat along the river in four states, including 9,600 acres in Iowa.

The cost, based on 1994 estimates, could be more than $69 million, and is to be paid by the Corps, Farris said.

Last month, the Department of Natural Resources and the Corps of Engineers dedicated the first of several projects to compensate for some of the habitat losses.

At Louisville Bend, southwest of Onawa, the Corps is restoring 225 acres of wetlands. Pumps will control the water level. Where old pilings once squeezed the river into an artificial course, a new levee now backs water over shallow wetlands.

Ed Weiner, a wildlife biologist for the resources department, said the lower end will be open to the river in the spring to allow fish to move into shallows to spawn. The upper area will be managed as a wetland for wildlife.

But Weiner is even more enthused about the proposed Blackbird-Tieville-Decatur Bends project a few miles upstream.

"It's the jewel" of the planned restoration efforts, he said.

The work will cover about 3,500 acres, involving three wetlands along about 11 miles of river.

The heart of the plan is to divert or pump water from the Missouri River into an old channel, creating a meandering "mini-river" through the site, Weiner said. Rock jetties or other structures may be used to cause the stream to form sandbars and pools like those once found on the main river.

Culverts and weirs will allow fish to move up into the wetland from the present Missouri River channel.

The wildlife area, at a site once proposed for a national wildlife refuge, is a joint effort of Iowa and Nebraska state agencies, the corps and two Indian tribes, Weiner said. He expects construction to start in 1997.

At least two other mitigation projects are being planned. Wetlands will be restored at Winnebago Bend, west of Salix. That will complement the nearby Snyder Lake project, where the Department of Natural Resources used cooling water from a coal-fired power plant to re-fill a 400-acre oxbow lake.

Engineers also are designing a flow-through diversion to improve fish habitat at California Bend, west of Missouri Valley.

Other projects await political approval, engineering studies and money.

"It's sometimes maddeningly slow and maddeningly bureaucratic," Farris said. But patience pays off.

"You're darned right, it's worth it."

He cited Snyder Lake, where fishing, camping, hunting and wildlife habitat all have greatly improved with the water from the power plant.

Results are almost immediate, Farris said. With high river levels this fall, waterfowl poured into the few natural or restored wetlands along the river.

"I think it's only going to get better in the future," Farris said.

December 3, 1995

Gladys Black and kestrel

CHAPTER 6

© The Des Moines Register

BIRDS

Maybe it hit me first on a high school trip to see the spring snow goose migration at Forney Lake, in southwest Iowa. "Awesome" says it well.

But that should be no surprise. People no doubt have been in awe of flight, and of birds, since the first human saw his first bird.

Perhaps it was inevitable that, for some, the fascination evolved into life lists and Christmas counts and computerized field guides. But, the shut-in who feeds sparrows outside her window can enjoy birds as much as the "lister" who will travel hundreds of miles for a brief glimpse of a rare species.

Gladys gives personal zing to 'Iowa Birdlife'

Friendly. Feisty. Folksy. Colorful. Opinionated. Packed with information.

That's Gladys Black of Pleasantville, Iowa's best-known "bird lady."

And Black's new book, "Iowa Birdlife," is just like her.

The book, like a conversation with Gladys (does anybody call her Mrs. Black?), leads the reader on field trips around Lake Red Rock, explores the intriguing world of bird behavior, introduces bird-watching friends and shares her wealth of knowledge on natural history.

The volume reprints more than 100 essays, which first appeared in The Des Moines Register and Pleasantville's Marion County News. It is an expanded version of a popular 1979 compilation, *Birds of Iowa.*

Black, who'll be 84 in January, has been fascinated with birds since childhood. After a career in nursing, she became an accomplished amateur scientist, conducting hundreds of bird nesting, banding and migration studies.

The work led to frequent columns in The Register, beginning in 1969. The articles continued in the Pleasantville paper, after disagreements with editors led Black to end her submissions to The Register.

Black's down-to-earth style, which made her one of The Register's most popular writers, and the independence that ended the relationship, permeate her writing.

Tireless Conservationist

What begins as a report on a recent field trip may turn out to be a detailed natural history lesson on several species of birds seen on the outing. Likely as not, there also will be comments on environmental problems, such as pesticides, and a jab at bureaucrats who aren't addressing those concerns.

Black is a tireless conservationist – and not bashful about it. A casual pre-election conversation quickly turned to politics.

"If we have the Republicans in for another 12 years, we won't have a damn thing left of the environment," she bristled.

Black seldom misses a chance to blast agricultural chemicals, which she calls "poisons." Several of her columns describe pesticide poisoning of birds and other wildlife.

Despite her successful crusade against an Iowa dove-hunting season and her continued criticism of some hunting regulations, Black resents the anti-hunter label given her by some hunters.

"It makes me so mad I could just fight," she said. "I was hunting before they were born."

Black grew up on a farm near Pleasantville, where she often hunted rabbits. She still likes to eat wild game.

But Black also was an astute observer of wildlife. Her mother taught her 25 species of birds before she was age seven. She recalls seeing flocks of turkey vultures that still frequent the Red Rock area, along with prairie chickens that are long-gone.

She Made Her Own Guide

Gladys Black didn't have a bird guide, so she made her own. She bought a series of bird cards offered by Arm & Hammer baking soda, then pasted the pictures and information into a book.

As a high school senior, Black "raised Holy Hell" to get permissions to take a newly-offered biology class.

She attended the Mercy Hospital School of Nursing in Des Moines, graduating in 1930. She also received a degree in public health nursing from the University of Minnesota. Black worked as a public health nurse in Clarke County and later in Warner Robins, Ga., where she moved with her husband, Wayne.

After her spouse's death in 1956, Black came back to Pleasantville to care for her mother. Her free time was devoted to birds, including up to 300 nesting studies per season.

When Lake Red Rock filled in 1969, Black dropped her plans to return to Georgia.

"I think Red Rock is the top spot in the state for real good birding," she said. The Des Moines River reservoir, ringed with thousands of acres of state-managed wildlife areas, is a magnet for waterfowl, songbirds, raptors and other species.

"When the white pelicans come in, I think they're my favorites," Black said. "Then I think the eagles are my favorite . . . and then I go nuts about the ducks and geese. . . ."

Black sprinkles her conversations, and writing, with dry wit. She laughs at a turkey vulture's uncanny ability to find a rotting animal carcass.

"What to us is a stench is to them an alluring Chanel No. 5," she writes.

An Untidy Yard

Black makes no excuses for the wildlife habitat in her untidy yard, with trees, bushes, assorted bird feeders and several cages where she once kept sick or injured birds.

She still nurses an occasional unfortunate critter, such as "Killy," a broken-winged kestrel, or "Strixie," a barred owl with eye trouble. Her patients sometimes are kept indoors, necessitating plastic bags over the furniture and newspapers on the floors.

A mild heart attack last June slowed Black only a trifle. She recently spent a day gathering wildflower seeds for the Walnut Creek National Wildlife Refuge prairie restoration project.

At least once a week, often more, friends come for bird-watching trips to Lake Red Rock. Between outings, she's reading, writing or answering phone calls about birds.

Black also has given hundreds of talks to groups ranging from pre-schoolers to college classes to nursing home residents.

"You'd be surprised how much those dear little old ladies talk about that," she said.

She also annually visits several schools, and has participated for about 20 years in an outdoor day for sixth-grade students at Lake Red Rock.

Making the Connection

No matter what the group, Black always links birds to environmental issues.

"Birds are indicators of the quality of our environment," she says.

Protecting birds – and the Earth – "is a matter of eternal vigilance."

"Iowa Birdlife" wasn't intended to be a comprehensive work on Iowa birds. But it is vintage Gladys, with interesting observations on many of Iowa's more common species and unusual visitors.

"Gladys knows an awfully lot about birds," said James Dinsmore, who teaches ornithology at Iowa State University. "She's a very keen observer."

Black has received awards from the Iowa Women's Hall of Fame, the Iowa Academy of Science, the Iowa Ornithologists' Union, Simpson College, the Iowa Governor's office, The Nature Conservancy and the U.S. Army Corps of Engineers.

While the book is mainly a tribute to Gladys Black, it is set off by 32 striking color photos taken by Carl and Linda Kurtz of St. Anthony. The couple also took many of the book's black-and-white photos. (Editor's note: Some of the reviewer's black-and-white photos also are included.)

The book also includes a useful chapter on Iowa's natural communities and wildlife habitats by Wayne R. Ostlie, director of science and stewardship for the Iowa Chapter of The Nature Conservancy. The 5,000-member land-conservation group sponsored the book and will receive the proceeds from its sale.

November 15, 1992

We know where birds go, but how and why?

Primitive people reasoned that nothing less than a miracle could explain the sudden rush of birds that appeared every spring. To account for the mysteries of what we now know as migrations, the ancients devised stories of birds spending the winter on a journey to the moon, burrowing in the mud, or riding to a distant hide-away on the back of a larger bird.

Twentieth century scientists scoff at those beliefs, since ornithologists have used banding, radios, satellite tracking and other sophisticated means to pinpoint birds' movements.

But even though we know "where," we still have big gaps in our knowledge of "why" or "how."

Researchers are finding that birds' navigation systems are incredibly complex. There are studies to show that migrating birds can find their way by the sun, stars and light polarization. Other research indicates birds can detect small changes in Earth's magnetic field and in barometric pressure.

Some scientists are even working on the theory that a bird's sense of smell is somehow connected to its navigational ability.

These senses may be used together to help birds decide not only where to go, but when. Birds might use changing air pressure to guide them to favorable migrating conditions, for example. Having a tail wind instead of a head wind could be of life-and-death importance to a tiny bird with meager fat reserves traveling thousands of miles to a breeding ground.

But how do birds know which migration routes to take – or whether to migrate at all? What prompts a young bird to leave the nesting area and travel across continents to a wintering site it has never seen? Or to race back north – often before winter has eased?

Perhaps these mysteries are what make bird watching such a fascinating hobby.

"To me, it's spring when the first Canada geese show up," said Pleasantville ornithologist Gladys Black.

The migrating honkers usually come in February, ahead of blue and snow geese, she said.

Common mergansers, goldeneyes and scaup also are among the earliest migrants, Black noted. These "cold water ducks" push into Iowa as soon as there's the tiniest bit of open water for them.

The first spring robin – usually "sort of a forerunner" of the rest of his clan – also makes an appearance in February, she added. And some bluebirds begin arriving in March.

But smaller birds use more caution than waterfowl, she noted.

Ducks and geese often take the option of temporarily retreating southward in the face of foul weather, but bluebirds or other songbirds sometimes perish in spring storms if they move north too early.

Killdeers are the earliest shorebirds, arriving in early March. Most shorebirds wait until warm weather has thawed their favored mud flats and marshes.

But ornithologists believe most birds instinctively migrate according to the changing amount of sunlight and only temper their urges by the weather conditions. The seasonal and sexual responses triggered by the day's length are too strong to be curbed by weather for very long, however.

Thus, red-winged blackbirds usually show about March 1, as familiar "harbingers" of spring, Black said.

Marsh hawks are much earlier, and many already have passed through Iowa on their northward journey, she said. Song sparrows also come very early, and many even winter in southern Iowa.

Warblers, on the other hand, are much less tolerant of cold, so they restrain their travels until spring has fully committed itself.

Birders may watch and study and identify and tally each spring migrant, but we may never fully understand the birds' unerring flights or unquenchable instincts for semi-annual travel.

In fact, I hope we never do. As Aldo Leopold said, "What a dull world if we knew all about geese."

March 23, 1977

Eruption of geese at Forney:
Awesome, indescribable sight

THURMAN, IA – Ever see a bedlam of geese, or a horizon of geese, or 400 acres of geese?

I've yet to come up with a word that adequately describes the sight when a whole river valley seems to take wing.

Such was the scene at Forney Lake near Thurman last week, at the height of the spring migration of snow and blue geese. Perhaps a half-million birds moved into Fremont County.

Forney Lake erupted before sunrise – and hundreds of thousands of goose wings beat skyward. The roar of the combined voices of 200,000 geese was the only sound to be heard.

Not Frightened

The geese swept like a cloud over the lake, then smaller swarms of the birds peeled off and spread out over the Missouri River Valley.

From horizon to horizon, the sky was filled with geese, as flock after flock moved out to feed in grain fields on the river bottom.

Near a roadside cornfield where the geese were breakfasting, the birds chuckled, grunted and chattered like a litter of baby pigs fighting for their mother's milk.

The birds waddled suspiciously away from the road – but most did not fly. How different from the fall migration, when geese flare at a strange shape a half-mile away.

The birds must know that springtime gawkers are only to be tolerated – not feared, as are the fall hunters.

The geese sometimes jumped and circled nervously, however—perhaps because they're anxious to get on with their trip to arctic breeding grounds.

The late spring delayed the birds' flight, since ice-bound lakes and snow-covered fields offer little food or protection for traveling birds. Even after the snow melted, the geese found slim pickings in the parched southwest Iowa grain fields.

The birds adapted – as they always seem to – by spreading out in their search for meals. What are a few more miles of flying to a bird that twice annually spans the North American continent under its own power?

Perhaps this ability of the geese to be their own masters, and to remain unfettered by the complications of civilization, explains the attraction of the birds to sight-seers.

Awesome

The migration of bird-watchers to southwest Iowa for the annual goose spring spectacular is as much a sign of spring as the first tulip or a returning robin.

It's a natural wonder and the person doesn't live who can fail to be humbled by the spectacle of a world of geese blocking out the horizon with their wing beats.

As we sat by Forney Lake before dawn, a solitary figure in an old car shared our parking spot. He slouched in the seat, listening to country and western music on the radio, seemingly unaware of the mass of birds sitting on the lake.

Suddenly the birds swarmed skyward, and the man turned off his radio, crawled from the car and stood staring in wonder.

He finally raised his sagging jaw, and spoke: "You sure don't see that every day."

March 24, 1975

Bald eagles on rise

Make dramatic comeback in Iowa

Over the hill behind the barn, along the secluded creek valley, well up in a towering cotton-wood, sits a wildlife success story.

Two half-grown bald eagle chicks are peering from their massive, stick nest. They stretch, scratch, yawn and blink, waiting for the next feeding time. Their parents circle protectively, just over the treetops.

The Clayton County eagle nest is part of an encouraging trend, said Bruce Ehresman, a nongame wildlife technician for the Iowa Department of Natural Resources.

Bald eagles are making a dramatic comeback in Iowa. The number of nesting eagles has grown steadily since 1977, when the birds finally returned after an absence of about 70 years.

There were at least 23 active eagle nests in Iowa this spring – up from a record 19 nests last year – Ehresman said. At least 24 young birds fledged from those 1992 nests, and Ehresman hopes the total will be even higher this season.

Allamakee County has the most birds, with at least eight nests, Ehresman said. Most are along the Mississippi River. Four nests are in Clayton County, with two in Jackson County. Benton, Black Hawk, Fremont, Howard, Iowa, Jefferson, Mahaska, Marion and Winneshiek counties each have at least one eagle nest.

In fact, there could be even more, Ehresman said. Despite their large size – adult birds have a wing span of 6 feet or more – nesting eagles can be quite secretive.

Good habitat, successful nests in other parts of the Midwest, public education and bans on some pesticides have combined to aid the eagles, Ehresman suggested.

The birds probably vanished from Iowa almost 90 years ago because of human disturbances, including the clear-cutting of bottomland forests and shooting, he said. Later, pesticide poisoning nearly wiped out the birds in other parts of the country.

With bans on DDT and some other persistent chemicals, the birds began recovering in many areas, Ehresman said. At the same time, Iowa's forests were recovering and people became more sensitive to protecting the birds.

Declining human populations in some rural areas also may have given the birds more of the seclusion they seem to seek, Ehresman said.

Food usually isn't a problem. Eagles' preferred diet is fish but they also will eat ducks or even carrion.

Ehresman predicted a continued growth of eagle numbers, barring an increase in habitat loss.

"Probably the biggest limiting factor is nest site availability," Ehresman said.

The birds need large trees, such as cottonwoods or silver maples. In the northern United States and Canada, eagles often nest in white pines.

Jody Millar, bald eagle recovery coordinator for the U.S. Fish and Wildlife Service, said eagles have fared well throughout the United States.

In the early 1960s, there were fewer than 460 pairs of eagles in the lower 48 states, she said. By 1992, that number had jumped to more than 3,700. In the upper Midwest – Iowa, Illinois, Minnesota, Missouri, Wisconsin and Michigan – the total climbed from 989 in 1990 to 1,141 in 1991 to 1,205 last year.

The cool, wet spring could limit population increases this year, however, Millar said. Floodwaters may have made hunting difficult for the birds, while the poor food supplies and cool weather may have reduced egg laying.

Biologists from state and federal resource agencies hope to complete a survey of nesting success later this summer.

Some officials still worry about sporadic reports of nesting failure due to chemical contamination, Millar said. Others cite the need for better wintering sites, such as protected valleys near a plentiful supply of fish or waterfowl.

"There are still problem areas," Millar said, "but we've solved enough problems that the birds are coming back."

June 20, 1993

Wanted: Falcons

Odd 'welcome mat' prepared as lure

Along the Mississippi – Rattlesnakes. Sheer cliffs. Loose rock. Bird excrement. Bloody feathers. *Perfect!*

"The welcome mat is out," declared Pat Schlarbaum, as he pondered the rugged bluffs along the Mississippi River in northeast Iowa.

That kind of hospitality might not appeal to humans, admitted Schlarbaum, who is a wildlife diversity biologist for the Iowa Department of Natural Resources. But the conditions could be just the ticket for peregrine falcons.

Schlarbaum and several other falcon experts have been studying the towering cliffs along the Mississippi as nesting sites for peregrine falcons.

Up to 50 pairs of peregrines once may have nested along the river and its tributaries and at other sites in the upper Midwest, Schlarbaum said. But the birds were wiped out in the 1960s – victims of poisoning by DDT and other chemicals.

Falcons have made a comeback, however, thanks to the release of captive-hatched birds in cities in about 10 states. In Iowa, 50 birds were released in Cedar Rapids, Des Moines and Muscatine between 1989 and 1992.

That paved the way for falcons to breed successfully for the past two seasons in Cedar Rapids and Des Moines.

Iowa biologists would like to see at least five nests in the state, Schlarbaum said. Ideally, they hope falcons eventually will return to historic eyries on bluffs along the Mississippi and a few other rivers.

Several falconers, peregrine breeders, biologists for government agencies and other naturalists from Iowa, Minnesota and Wisconsin met last week to discuss the potential of peregrines returning to the cliffs.

The group debated the need to protect the bluffs from human encroachment or development. They outlined strategies for managing peregrine habitat. Schlarbaum talked of the spiritual, as well as scientific importance of the project.

Bruce Ehresman and Sara Thompson, of the Iowa Department of Natural Resources, scaled a bluff to examine a former eyrie and to "prime" the rocks with falcon excrement. The white liquid, carefully collected from captive birds, could help attract passing peregrines.

Ehresman and Thompson also left a few bird wings on a ledge, as if a falcon had been feeding there.

Barb Schoenherr of Wauwatosa, Wis., led a hike to the ridge above the cliff, where she and her companions left offerings of sweet grass and tobacco, in a ritual borrowed from Native Americans.

Many of the river bluffs have spiritual significance to Native Americans, said Schoenherr. Respect for that culture should be an integral part of efforts to return falcons to the cliffs, she said.

The Native American belief is that a hawk is a messenger, Schoenherr said.

"Maybe by investing in the peregrine we're sending a message of faith to our future," she said.

After Schoenherr's group had descended, 14 bald eagles circled the site.

"That was a really nice uplifting experience, almost like a high sign of approval," she said.

Mark Washburn of Wilton, former president and director of the Iowa Falconers' Association, said getting peregrines back to traditional nest sites may not be easy.

The birds that historically nested there have died out, he noted, and the re-introduced peregrines have slightly different genetics. They might not be as adapted to the predators or habitat of the bluffs.

Or it may just take time for birds from an urban environment to learn to use the cliffs. In Germany, biologists have tried using nest boxes to lure birds back to cliff eyries, Washburn said.

Scientists may need to study nuances of the birds' behavior, habitat and genetics for keys to help them adapt, he said.

"We can't do it all," Washburn said. "The bird has to do it – but there may be little things we can do to help."

"Ultimately, I'm confident they're going to be back there. Maybe our involvement may allow us to see it in our lifetime."

February 26, 1995

Spring on the Prairie

Prairie chickens rebound after decades-long absence

KELLERTON, IA – The moon begins to wane. A March sunrise flecks the dead grass with pink and gold. A restless farm dog yaps in the distance.

Then, as if on cue, an eerie, musical "oo-ooo-ooo" floats over the low ridge.

Strutting, stomping, fluttering, running, sparring – male prairie chickens begin their age-old territorial dance. In their frenzy, the performers puff out orange sacs on the sides of their necks, cock their long neck feathers (pinnae) and sometimes jump more than a foot in the air.

The knoll rings with their clucking, cackling, booming calls.

Spring has come to the prairie.

After an absence of several decades, prairie chickens once again are the stars of a spring spectacle in several southern Iowa counties.

Driven from the state by intensive agriculture that destroyed their grassland habitat, the birds are staging a comeback. More than 500 birds were transplanted from Kansas between 1987 and 1993. Their offspring have gained a foothold in counties on either side of the Iowa-Missouri border.

There have been prairie chicken reports in Adams, Adair, Clarke, Dallas, Decatur and Ringgold counties.

Some of the birds have traveled more than 50 miles from their release site.

"Habitat is the key," said Melvin Moe, a wildlife management biologist for the Iowa Department of Natural Resources.

The federal government's Conservation Reserve Program, which has replaced many crop fields with grassy cover, is restoring the prairie conditions the birds need.

Moe said prairie chickens were common before Iowa was settled. Populations even increased around early farms, because the crops boosted the birds' food supply.

"A lot of grass and a little agriculture was ideal for them," Moe said.

Farm families and pioneers shot prairie chickens to eat. Market hunters killed thousands of birds in the mid-1800s. Sport hunters also took hundreds per day.

Populations declined sharply after the 1880s, as more of the native prairie was plowed.

Most prairie chickens were gone by the early 1900s. The last known nest was in 1962, in Appanoose County.

In 1980 and 1982, the Iowa Conservation Commission released 101 Kansas prairie chickens in the Loess Hills in Monona County, but the birds apparently did not survive.

The southern Iowa stockings have fared better.

Friends credit Moe, a lanky, blond, soft-spoken man who fondly recalls his father's tales of hearing prairie chickens on their North Dakota farm.

Moe prefers to praise ranchers in Kansas, where the birds were trapped, and the farmers at release sites in Iowa and Missouri for the birds' survival. The landowners have cooperated with grazing and burning plans that tailor cover to the birds' needs. Prairie chickens need short grass on open "leks," or booming grounds, while they nest and roost in denser vegetation.

The prairie tracts also must contain several hundred acres, with few trees to attract winged predators like red-tailed hawks and great-horned owls.

The future of the birds depends upon preservation of grasslands and prairies, either public or private, Moe said.

"If a lot of this land goes out of (the Conservation Reserve Program), it could have a detrimental effect," Moe said, adding that more public prairie land could help.

The chickens probably don't know that their fate hangs by a political thread, or that the price of corn could lead to their demise.

All they care about is that sunny spring mornings are made for dancing.

March 17, 1996

This bird-count stuff is for the people!

Larry Stone spent a day with several Iowans
on a Christmas Bird Count near Readlyn and Tripoli recently.
Here is one observer's impression of the outing.

By Strix Varia
(alias Barred Owl)

"Whoo-hoo-hoo-hooo . . . Who-ha-ha-who-ah."

Oh, whiskers; here they come again. Can't a self-respecting bird have some privacy?

That barred owl imitation wouldn't fool anybody – except Uncle Howland – and he's half deaf!

Why do those humans torment us every December? It's bad enough with hunters banging through the woods. And now come these characters waving binoculars and trying to sound like birds!

Before daylight, even! Their friends must think they're nuts, tromping around in the dark listening for owls. Heck, I'd hoot in the daytime if they'd just ask!

We owls aren't the only ones they harass, either. Why, they chase anything with feathers! They carry clipboards and pencils and write like fury if they see so much as a sparrow.

Celebrities on the Wing

They call it a "Christmas Bird Count." Aunt Owlice said they do it all over. They mark off big circles on a map and write down every bird they see there – even starlings.

Rumor is, they've done it since 1900. I suppose they've even got it computerized!

Gosh, does that mean we're celebrities?

'Course, some are more celebrated than others. Those humans sure made a fuss about that pileated woodpecker. But they hardly noticed Charlie Chickadee. Poor little guy never did get much respect.

And they drove miles looking for Rupert Rough-leg. They wanted that ol' hawk on their silly list so bad . . . .

The rascal decided to have some fun with 'em. He stayed just below the tree line, and it took them all day to find him. (He flew right overhead at noon, but those people were too busy eating to notice!)

Just wait! Tomorrow, when they don't have that list along, Rupert will sail right above 'em and just grin.

Nervy Bird

He'd better be careful! Randy Red-tail flew across the road and almost caused an accident. Those humans gawked out the window of their car and nearly ran off the highway.

Chester Cardinal made it easier for them. He perched in the sun, bold and brassy as anything, just daring them to count him. (Boy, what an ego!) Even called the Missus to pose. And they both flew down the road and sat in a plum thicket in front of that bird-watcher-mobile, just to show off.

Barney Brown Creeper had the right attitude. The little tyke just ignored the peeping people; he kept on poking in the tree bark like they weren't even there. Funny thing, he was right in front of their noses and they almost missed him!

I felt sorry for Cousin Stanley's screech-owl family, though. They're so shy. They hunkered down in a wood duck box for hours to keep those folks from seeing them. Can't really blame Stanley for hiding – but I guess those people don't hurt too much. Maybe we should let them stare, if it keeps 'em happy!

Picky, Picky, Picky

Our other cousin, Shirley Short-ear, is kind of fickle, too. She jumped out of the pines, then darted right back in after they'd passed. That photographer guy should have gotten a picture. But, no, he was daydreaming. He wasn't even sure if it was her or me.

Geez, we birds can tell a barred owl from a short-eared owl. Who needs fancy picture books, like those people carry?

But, oh, they're serious; got to make dead sure of what they write on their lists.

The sassy little Cooper's hawk over at the marsh teased 'em about that. He could have hidden from them, but he had to be a daredevil. He zipped out, then dived back into the woods quicker than anything, to see if he could catch 'em napping.

A sharp-eyed kid spotted him – or he might have pulled it off.

The whole group got pretty excited about that. Those Cooper's hawks don't stop for autographs!

The pheasants thought it was kind of a dull day, though. Usually, the roosters are out waving their tail feathers at hunters with guns. (They generally make monkeys of those humans, too!)

But bird-watchers spoil the ringnecks' fun. It's no challenge if people only want to look at you.

The roosters are too cocky for their own good. Word is, a couple of them got invited to Christmas dinner – as the main course!

Well, gotta fly. Think I'll see if they fall for my sandhill crane routine . . . .

See ya next year!

December 25, 1988

Winging their way into our imaginations

Soaring and circling, feathers spread like outstretched fingers, the season's first turkey vultures drift north on March thermals.

Honking urgently, Canada geese slice their tight V through the gray sky, cutting winter's shackles.

Scolding, a defensive robin swoops and dives at a wandering cat.

The miracle of flight: It has awed humans for eons.

Marvel at Birds

Even in this age of jet airplanes, scientists still marvel at birds, said James Dinsmore, professor of animal ecology at Iowa State University.

But bird or airplane, the "why" of flight is the same, Dinsmore said.

Swiss mathematician Daniel Bernoulli proved in 1738 that air moving past an object exerts less pressure as it goes faster. An airplane or bird wing, flat on the bottom and curved on top, forces air to move faster over the top. With less pressure on the upper surface, the effect is upward lift on the wing – and flight.

But, unlike an airplane, which has an engine, a bird must get its forward thrust from the wings. Part of that thrust comes from the backward push of the wings, like oars against water.

Different Species

The bird's primary feathers also act like miniature wings, Dinsmore said, with air flowing faster past the curved, upper surface than the flat, lower surface. The front edges of the feathers turn downward as the wings flap, translating the lift into forward motion, rather than an upward push.

Each bird species has refined those principles, Dinsmore said. Birds with short, rounded wings – like pheasants or Cooper's hawks – are built for bursts of power to flush from danger or dart after prey.

Long, pointed wings are best for speed – as proved by falcons and swallows.

Sea birds' long, thin wings – similar to a glider plane – are ideal for long-distance gliding on the winds.

Broad, slotted wings help turkey vultures and hawks soar for hours on rising thermals.

Many Variations

The variations are almost endless, Dinsmore said. A heron, for example, flaps and sails on wings that are a compromise between power and soaring.

Soft-edged feathers on owl wings silence the flight of the night hunters.

The hummingbird has perfected hovering. Its downward wing beat is like that of other birds, giving lift and forward motion. But the hummingbird negates those effects by turning its loosely jointed wing to produce downward force and backward motion on the up stroke. As a result, the bird seems to hang in the air.

Easy? Hardly.

A hummingbird may beat its wings 60 to 70 strokes per second, using 10 times the energy per body weight as a running man, according to John K. Terres, in the book *"How Birds Fly."* He estimated a hummer must eat half its weight in sugar daily to produce that energy. By comparison, Terres said, a human working as hard would need to eat 285 pounds of meat or 370 pounds of potatoes.

Strong Heart

Birds in flight also require huge amounts of oxygen, Dinsmore said.

Pumping the blood to carry that oxygen requires special adaptations. A hummingbird's heart, in proportion to its body, weighs five to six times that of a human's. And it beats more than 600 times a minute – nine times the rate of a human heart.

A bird also needs strong breast muscles – making up 15 percent to 25 percent of its body weight – to power the wings. The well-developed muscles of ducks, pheasants and other game birds make tasty eating.

But after he's measured air flow, counted heart beats, photographed wing-flaps or eaten roast grouse, a human still can't appreciate the wonder of birds. The best way to do that is to lie back, look up at a wheeling red-tailed hawk – and dream.

April 1, 1990

White-tailed deer

© Larry Stone

CHAPTER 7

CRITTERS

From deer to dragonflies, from snakes to skunks, many kinds of wildlife have adapted to habitat that is shaped as much by man as by Nature. Still, some people are surprised to learn of the diverse fauna that live in our fields, roadsides or even back yards.

Have the critters adapted TOO well? Deer have become pests in some cities, and vermin in the eyes of many farmers. Raccoons and opossums fare as well in city storm sewers as they do in hollow trees.

When our tinkering favors a population explosion of one species, what are the effects on the land, or on other wildlife? We've learned to manipulate the numbers of some creatures. Maybe someday we'll grasp the implications of our experiments.

94

Shoot them or live with them?

Deer have become unwelcome guests in Iowa cities

CEDAR FALLS, IA – Remember when deer were reclusive creatures found only in the wildest areas?

Back then, most Iowans would have been thrilled at even a glimpse of the graceful animals.

Some of today's white-tails are city slickers. They have become jaywalking, traffic-stopping, tulip-munching, backyard-dwelling suburbanites.

And many Iowans now see more deer than they would like.

Nixon Wilson, a University of Northern Iowa biology professor who lives near the Hartman Reserve Nature Center in Cedar Falls, must fence his evergreen trees to protect them from hungry deer.

Angela Tenborg of West Des Moines has hit two deer with her car in that suburb since November.

Three men in Council Bluffs last week had a narrow escape when their twin-engine plane collided with a deer on takeoff from a private air field.

And some Cedar Rapids gardeners have given up their hobby because they are unable to protect their vegetables and flowers from marauding deer.

At George Wyth State Park in Waterloo and nearby Hartman Reserve Nature Center, researchers are studying the citified deer and seeking ways to minimize conflicts between deer and people.

Steve Finegan, director of the Black Hawk County Conservation Board, said a deer task force was formed in 1991 in response to complaints about deer damage to shrubbery and ornamental plants near the nature center and the state park.

The situation was complicated by Highway 218 construction and related fencing that disrupted the animals.

But the deer also have plenty of defenders.

George Kunz of Cedar Falls enjoys the deer's visits to his bird feeder, where the animals eat corn and sunflower seeds.

Kunz occasionally has damage to his shrubs, but most are protected with deer repellent and fences.

"I don't consider them a problem," he said. "I think they're beautiful animals."

At George Wyth State Park, deer are a major attraction, assistant ranger Tim Gedler said.

"On weekends, it's bumper to bumper at times," he said.

But the deer that lure the people are damaging the park, Gedler said. He pointed out trees and shrubs that had been nibbled off by the animals.

Willie Suchy, deer management biologist for the Iowa Department of Natural Resources, said the less obvious impacts may be even more important. Deer can change an entire plant community by eating new seedlings, he said.

To learn how deer affect the vegetation, researchers have built fences to exclude deer from small plots in the park, the nature center and a greenbelt south of Waterloo.

The biologists also have been capturing and tagging deer. About 20 will be fitted with radio collars to allow tracking of their movements.

The Nature Center has begun an "Adopt-a-Deer" program to raise money for the collars. People in the Waterloo-Cedar Falls area also are asked to call a deer hotline to report sightings of tagged deer.

The study could answer some questions, Suchy said.

How many deer winter in the Waterloo-Cedar Falls area? Do they leave in other seasons? and fall? Do the animals go outside the city, and are they hunted?

The answers may help show whether there are too many deer, or if the population is compatible with the habitat.

Officials in other cities – Cedar Rapids, Davenport, Des Moines, Iowa City, Sioux City – also are concerned about growing deer herds, Suchy said, and there's hope the study may apply in other urban areas. Differences in topography, human populations, highway corridors and other factors could make each site unique, however.

Suchy cited the growth of Des Moines' western suburbs into nearby fields, streams and woodlands that are ideal deer habitat.

"We're going to see Des Moines probably be the worst place in the state in a few years," he said.

In Cedar Rapids, herds of 30 or more deer already have caused problems, said Dave Kramer, commissioner of parks. He is working with city police to do a helicopter count of the deer.

Rich Patterson, director of the Indian Creek Nature Center in Cedar Rapids, said he often gets calls about deer in the city. Some people want to feed and protect the animals, Patterson said. Others wonder how to keep the pests away from gardens and shrubs.

There is a deer problem, Patterson said, and it must be addressed. People will not tolerate increasing property damage, car-deer collisions or the fear that Lyme disease may be spread by ticks on the deer.

In an extreme case, the deer might even destroy their own habitat, bringing a natural decline from disease or starvation.

"Deer are going to have to die," Patterson said. He said trained gunners eventually may have to cull urban deer herds.

Efforts to teach people to use fences or repellents to foil the deer are only short-term solutions, Patterson said.

"Education is fine, but the problem won't go away," he said. "It'll get worse."

February 7, 1993

Coping with winter, critter style

How Iowa's smaller wildlife survives harsh weather

Tiny pock marks in the snow, with a faint line between, told of the mouse's winter ramblings.

Dragging his tail, the little creature had hopped between tufts of grass, burrowing here and there in search of seeds. Occasionally, he'd dive beneath the surface, tunnel along for a few feet, then pop back on top.

But the tracks ended abruptly beside a steel fencepost. Where had that mouse gone? Could it have known that a bluebird house sat atop the post?

Gingerly, the lid of the house was opened – revealing the inquisitive stare of a pair of shiny-black eyes peering over a whiskered nose from under two round, gray ears.

Then, the box came alive as several brown, furry bodies scrambled down under a fluffy pile of grass and debris. The small, wooden house, which had served a bluebird family last June, now sheltered a dozen white-footed mice.

Each critter has its own way of coping with winter.

We shouldn't be surprised to find mice in a birdhouse, said William Clark, associate professor of animal ecology at Iowa State University. White-footed mice are inveterate climbers. Their explorations easily could lead them to the cozy winter quarters.

The mice also may remodel old bird nests for shelter, Clark added.

By contrast, meadow voles (often called "field mice") stay on the ground, Clark said. They burrow through networks of tunnels in the grass or under the snow.

But this year, with very little snow cover, could be a tough season for mice and other small mammals, Clark said. Without the protective blanket of snow, they're more vulnerable to hawks, owls, foxes, weasels and other predators.

Chipmunks and ground squirrels, on the other hand, probably don't know what the weather is – and they couldn't care less. They're almost dormant in underground burrows, with lowered body temperature, heart rate and breathing rate. True hibernators, chipmunks and ground squirrels won't surface again until spring.

Raccoons, squirrels, skunks and opossums like to sleep, Clark said, but they don't actually hibernate. Even on the coldest day, a dozing 'coon or squirrels may rouse for a quick snack at a nearby corncrib.

In balmy weather, squirrels prowl for hickory nuts on sunny hillsides, and raccoons may roam the creek banks at dusk.

The creek runs crystal-clear now, fed only by springs, seeping tiles and drips from sun-warmed snow patches. You can see three feet to the rocky bottom, where a school of suckers dance and chubs fin lethargically in the chill water.

Unseen crawdads, caddis fly larvae and other stream organisms nestle under rocks, waiting for spring in a sort of suspended animation.

But not all streamside life is dormant. The sunlight seems to flicker as the rays catch the wings of tiny grey insects – gnats or midges, perhaps – drifting on the breeze. Upstream, a dimple breaks the glassy surface. Did a trout inhale a buggy snack?

Insects normally winter in sheltered crevasses or cracks, protected from the cold by antifreeze-like chemicals in their blood, said Donald Lewis, extension entomologist at Iowa State University. But insects may venture out on mild days when their surroundings are sufficiently warmed to break their dormancy.

Wingless soil insects, called spring-tails, have earned the nickname "snow fleas," for their habit of hopping on patches of snow when the sun warms their usual earth homes.

Along the field edge, bulging galls on dead goldenrod stems mark the winter home of another insect. A tiny white grub nestles in the center of each gall, waiting until spring to emerge as an adult fly.

But the downy woodpecker also knows what's hiding in the gall. With its needle-like bill, the downy can drill in for a tasty meal.

Wild turkeys won't have to work that hard for their lunch this winter. They can easily scratch through the thin layer of snow to feast on waste corn.

Deer, too, wax fat and healthy on leftovers in Iowa farm fields. Most white-tails probably need to travel only a few hundred yards from daytime beds on a sheltered hillside to evening banquets in the cornfield.

As the deer steal through the dusk for supper, great horned owls shake themselves awake for a night's hunting. Although the calendar still says winter, the owls soon will be laying eggs to start this spring's family.

An owl swoops over the snow in the twilight, glimpsing a faint movement near the fencerow. He dives on muffled wings, razor-like talons flashing in the moonlight.

And back in the bluebird house, the "White-foot Hilton," there'll be an empty bed.

January 18, 1987

Dragonflies make a feast of mosquitoes

GARNAVILLO, IA – Hate mosquitoes?

Then you should love dragonflies.

They're the hawks of the insect world – aerial predators that feast on mosquitoes.

"They'll sort of grab one and eat it in passing, like a dollop of ice cream," said University of Iowa biology professor Bob Cruden. And a dragonfly nymph – the immature form that lives under water – devours countless mosquito larvae.

But hungry dragonflies aren't finicky, said Cruden, who has studied the insects for several decades.

"They'll eat anything that's smaller than them."

Worms? Insects? Small fish? Tiny frogs? Other dragonflies? *Chomp.*

Diet is just one of the intriguing things about dragonflies, Cruden said.

Take their history: some ancient species had wing spreads of more than 30 inches.

Many species of dragonflies are best identified by the appendage the male uses to hold the female during mating. The genitalia also may be diagnostic.

"Once you've got those patterns in mind, you just take a look at them and say 'aha!' and let them go," Cruden said.

"Aha!" has been an important part of Cruden's vocabulary the past three summers.

He, field assistant Bud Gode of Iowa City and several Iowa Lakeside Laboratory students have searched for dragonflies, and closely related damselflies, in at least 70 Iowa counties. They plan to update an inventory from the early 1900s. The Iowa Science Foundation has helped pay for the study.

Cruden said biologists wonder which dragonflies and damselflies have survived, whether new species have moved in and what the changes mean for the ecosystem.

"We can begin to use our knowledge of these critters to answer ecological questions and biogeographical questions," Cruden said.

For example, the researchers have found nearly 70 species of dragonflies and damselflies in northwest Iowa, where only 45 kinds were reported at the turn of the century. Nine of the original species are gone, while more than two dozen others have moved in.

Cruden cited habitat changes: the loss of shallow wetlands and the proliferation of deep gravel pits.

"It's surprising so many of the things that were here back then are still here . . . given the incredible changes in the area," he said.

Cruden also expressed surprise at how fast the creatures will colonize in a new area.

"The neat thing is, these animals have just responded incredibly quickly to changes we've rended in the landscape," Cruden said. "And probably that adaptation and movement of these species is still going on today."

Gode shares Cruden's fascination for "odonating," the men's name for their study of the scientific order "odonata," to which dragonflies and damselflies belong.

So far, Gode has recorded more than 4,400 odonate observations from the study.

Sometimes, the work includes wading into streams, like Buck Creek near Garnavillo, insect net in hand, to capture flitting dragonflies or damselflies.

Often, the men can identify passing odonates in flight by wing patterns or flight characteristics. "The same way you know it's a turkey vulture," said Gode, who also is an avid bird watcher.

Gode said a few people even have started observing dragonflies as a sport, just as others watch birds.

But dragonfly-watchers have an advantage, Gode joked, because they don't have to get up early or go out in bad weather, as birders sometimes do.

Dragonflies and damselflies are most active on warm, sunny days, he said. That's when they spend most of their time basking on rocks or sticks, patrolling stream banks or skimming over the water.

And eating mosquitoes?

August 13, 1995

Butterflies give insight into nature

CENTER POINT, IA – Mention butterflies, and most people probably think monarchs, the common black-and-orange insect of summer roadsides. Talk of butterfly collectors, and we envision the stereotype of a pith-helmeted, net-waving scientist dashing through the grass.

But to Dennis Schlicht of Center Point, the most exciting butterflies are tiny, inconspicuous creatures most people never see. And butterfly collecting is just one phase of a survey to pinpoint some of Iowa's most unspoiled natural areas.

"I chased birds and everything else as a kid" growing up on a farm between Hudson and Cedar Falls, Schlicht said. But his interest in butterflies really took wing in the early 1970s, when Schlicht was a student under University of Northern Iowa entomologist John Downey, a butterfly authority.

Since then, Schlicht has combed much of Iowa in search of the state's 100 species of butterflies, sometimes doing studies for the Iowa Conservation Commission.

Some of his favorite butterflies are "skippers," which include more than 30 species in Iowa. Most are only three-fourths to one inch across and are rather dull brown. They're easily mistaken for small moths.

Skippers apparently were named for their characteristic hopping flight. When disturbed, they seem to bounce or "skip" into the air, dart around, then drop back to a perch. They fly fast enough to create a faint buzz with their wings.

"If skippers were birds, we'd be in trouble," Schlicht said. "They're ferocious." He's even seen the little butterflies dart at birds in a territorial defense.

But there's little danger of butterflies taking over the world. Many types of skippers live in grasslands and prairies, so they're becoming as rare as those vanishing habitats. In a sea of corn and soybean fields, where is a skipper to live?

Skippers are even more threatened because they're so specialized, Schlicht said. Some species may feed on only one type of plant, and they may defend a tiny bit of habitat only a few yards across. If that site is plowed, burned, grazed or otherwise disturbed, the butterfly may be eliminated.

Schlicht, a science teacher at Central City High School, is fascinated by the butterflies and their habits. For those who don't share that enthusiasm for little "bugs," however, he offers the argument that the presence of the rare insects may be an important indicator of the quality of a natural area. If the site's vegetation has been undisturbed enough to support unusual butterflies, it may be a botanical refuge, as well.

"When you find the butterfly, you find this kind of extended community," Schlicht said.

Schlicht and other biologists also have begun to question the management of some natural areas that supposedly have been protected by public or private conservation groups. For example, the common practice of burning prairie preserves to keep out invading trees and shrubs could wipe out butterflies and other insects if the fire is too widespread, Schlicht fears.

He also thinks state and county conservation officials should put more emphasis on preserving the natural prairies that remain, rather than trying to create prairie-like sites by seeding native grasses. This planted grassland may be good for large species of wildlife, Schlicht said, but it never can be as diverse – or attractive to rare species – as native vegetation.

As an example, Schlicht cited a Buchanan County site where he has found the olive hairstreak and other unusual butterflies. Although not a spectacular tract to look at, the site has prairie plants, sand dunes and marshy vegetation.

The Buchanan County Conservation Board and the Iowa Natural Heritage Foundation have leased the area for a year to study its future protection potential.

Another wet prairie near Rowley is slated for development as a county lake, Schlicht said. But he advocates maintaining the natural area for its plant and insect life.

Iowa's butterflies, obscure though they may be, really are "beautiful little bugs," Schlicht said.

"These are as much of the prairie as the buffalo was. These are pure prairie critters," he said. "Here's some of real Iowa."

July 28, 1985

Reptilian discovery

Naturalist introduces children to snakes

STOCKPORT, IA – Even snakes have personalities, Verne Downard has discovered.

In that regard, they're kind of like the school children to whom the 76- year-old Keosauqua naturalist annually introduces his reptilian friends.

"A king is one of the more gentle snakes," Downard said. "I like them for a class because they don't get excited."

Black snakes, on the other hand, are "iffy," he said. It's hard to predict how they will react to people.

Blue racers live up to their names.

"They can move," Downard said.

A hognose snake won't bite, Downard said.

"But water snakes always bite," he said. "Always."

He doesn't worry about an occasional bite, however, since Downard handles only non-poisonous snakes. He's just careful to "unhook" the teeth, rather than pull the snake loose and risk tearing his skin.

Iowa has four species of poisonous snakes, but they're all relatively rare, Downard said.

Massasaugas inhabit a few marshes in southern and eastern Iowa. Timber rattlers like secluded, rocky woodlands in the south and east. Prairie rattlers live only in a few sites in the Loess Hills. And copperheads exist only in far southeast Iowa.

The 23 other kinds of Iowa snakes are harmless.

And they're fun, said first graders in Roberta Stephenson's Van Buren Community School class at Stockport.

Some students bubbled with excitement at the prospect of even seeing a snake. Some grabbed at the slithering visitors.

Others tried oh-so-hard to be gentle. A few children waited for their friends to be first. Several wrapped snakes around their necks or tucked them into their shirts.

Although Downard let a half-dozen snakes loose in the room, no one felt threatened by the sometimes-maligned creatures. The students sat on the floor, with the snakes crawling on a huge sheet of plastic. Anyone who didn't want to get close merely had to lift the edge of the tarp, and the snakes would slide away.

The problem is protecting the snakes from the children, Downard said.

"If you're going to handle them, take your thumb off and put it in your pocket," Downard said.

Downard's daughter, Judith Andrews, of Des Moines, helped demonstrate proper etiquette with snakes, encouraging the children with hands-on learning.

It's a show her pupils always look forward to, Stephenson said.

She's even come to enjoy it, too, confessed the teacher, who admits to a long-standing fear of snakes. After 15 years of Downard's classroom programs, Stephenson is still not a snake lover.

"But I don't run over them with the lawn mower any more," she said.

Students' attitudes about snakes also improve when they meet Downard and his legless companions.

103

We need snakes to "keep the mice away," to "eat insects" and to "save our environment," said the budding herpetologists.

Downard listened patiently to their stories, and shared a few of his own.

He recalled the "privilege" of spending two and one-half hours watching a king snake swallow a black snake.

Downard described how a black snake climbed a tree for a meal of wren nestlings.

The students squealed as he told how the bulge of a snake's meal — often a mouse — can be seen in its stomach.

But Downard said a snake's prey probably dies quickly. Most snakes squeeze the animal until it suffocates, then swallow it whole.

In contrast, he noted, a hungry hawk may tear apart live prey.

"A snake doesn't make the animal suffer," he said.

He joked with students about snake traits — such as their darting tongues.

"They're not threatening you, they're sensing their environment," he said.

A snake's sense of smell is in its tongue and roof of its mouth, he explained.

Snakes "hear" with their bodies, Downard added. They don't have true ears, but they're very sensitive to vibrations.

The children were intrigued by the thought of how a snake molts.

"Their skin gets the shivers," one youngster said.

Iowa's snakes are important parts of our environment, Downard emphasized.

And he's convinced that helping children discover these reptiles is all it takes to recruit a new generation of snake conservationists.

May 14, 1995

Iowa's lakes and ponds
full of more than just cold water

CEDAR FALLS, IA – Has the heat wave gotten the best of you? If so, why not go jump in a creek?

If it's too muggy to go camping, too sunny for fishing and too hot for boating, don't just loaf in front of an air conditioner. You still can find outdoor entertainment by wading in a cool, refreshing, shady creek or pond. And you might be surprised at how much company (human or otherwise) you'll have.

Several curious aquatic explorers joined Black Hawk County Conservation Board naturalist interns Jim Debner and Laura Frisch for a hike in Snag Creek, near Cedar Falls, on a recent steamy Sunday. The group found not only cool feet but a new appreciation for the wonders of water.

Conservation Board naturalist Mary Duritsa said the aquatic hike in the county's Black Hawk Park was one of a series of programs designed to get campers to "leave their campsites and come *do* something with us."

The adventurers found themselves "doing something" up to their waists in the cooling creek water. With a minnow seine, they captured small fish, tadpoles and crayfish. And they found a whole host of lesser critters living under submerged rocks and stream-bottom debris.

"They learned that something really lives in there besides fish," Duritsa said.

That's an important concept for anyone with even the mildest interest in ponds, streams, lakes or other aquatic habitats, Duritsa said. Water areas are intricate ecosystems, with hundreds of different interdependent members of the natural community.

"There's a whole city of things under the surface of the water," Duritsa said.

"Most people are amazed when they turn over (submerged) rocks and find all kinds of little creatures," she continued. They just don't expect that much life under water.

"The diversity is the thing that's most exciting to me," Duritsa said. For example, the water may be home for several different kinds of algae, from free-floating plankton to filamentous "moss" clinging to streambed rocks. Dozens of almost invisible animals zip around in the water, feeding on algae and in turn being eaten by larger creatures.

Insect larvae – juvenile forms of mosquitoes, mayflies and dragonflies – often live in the water or on the stream bottom. They feed on plankton, dead or dying plant and animal matter – or each other.

Crayfish scavenge the stream bottom, eating whatever plant or animal goodies they can find. The crayfish may themselves become supper for raccoons, catfish or bass. And the fish? Well, man sometimes works them into his food chain.

It's a web of life that's quite complex, Duritsa said. She said one of the best ways to study that web is to get wet. While wading, use a large tea strainer to dip up stream bottom critters for closer examination under a magnifying glass in a white-bottomed pan. You may find wriggling fly larvae, mean-mouthed dragonfly nymphs or camouflaged caddisfly larval cases.

Don't worry if you can't identify the creatures you find, Duritsa said. That knowledge can grow with your excitement about "magical" water ecosystems.

For starters, try comparing the life you find in a flowing stream with that in a pond or lake. Sleek minnows are more at home in moving water, for example, while flat-bodied sunfish may prefer

105

quiet ponds. Many smaller life forms also are restricted to only one type of aquatic habitat.

"The discovery of it is really the neat part," Duritsa continued. When people realize how much life there is in water, "they're just fascinated by it," she said.

"Look at all that stuff that lives in here," marveled one wet-footed hiker.

"We never knew that!"

August 7, 1983

Clint Fraley

CHAPTER 8

© The Des Moines Register

FISHING

Fishing is FUN! That's been my bias ever since Grandpa took me to the creek and taught me to watch the bobber.

Is it any wonder, then, that my favorite Iowa fishermen (and women!) take a laid-back, enjoy-life approach to their sport? And maybe that explains why most of my fishing trips always have involved more "fishing" than "catching."

Whether they're lounging on the bank, not caring if there's a fish within 100 miles, or diligently probing the depths in search of a lunker, it's the SMILE that makes the fisherman.

300,000 bluegills – and counting

Clint Fraley, a 51-year-old kid,
hasn't outgrown a love for battling the feisty fish.

SIOUX RAPIDS, IA – Maybe Clint Fraley never grew up.

No kid could have more fun than Fraley, 51, when he finds a farm pond full of bluegills.

He grins, he laughs, he whoops, his eyes sparkle. You almost expect him to dance a jig.

"Bluegill fishing is just fun!" he said with a chuckle.

And the merriment is contagious, Fraley's fishing partners soon discover.

He recently shared the revelry with a reporter, who just happened to bring a flyrod, along with a notebook and camera.

The frolic started early.

The men hiked in at first light to the mist-shrouded hideaway. Robins sang "cheerio" from the wooded shores. The pool shown like a mirror.

Fraley broke the spell with a wave of his rod. The line straightened, settled, then dropped a brown nymph onto the silvery water.

The fly sank – deeper, deeper – until the leader twitched and Fraley cocked his wrist.

The 7 1/2-foot rod bowed and bounced. The line cut corkscrews in the water.

"How about that 'gill?" Fraley beamed, as he landed the plump, orange-bellied fish. He guessed the weight at close to a pound – then gently slipped the prize back into the water.

Soon two rods were waving, as the men fought bluegills, compared lunkers and feigned fatigue from battling the monsters of the deep.

Fraley spoke almost reverently of the scrappy fish.

"*All* bluegills are nice," he said. "Some are just bigger than others."

Before the sun peeked over the horizon, the two men had caught a dozen hefty bluegills.

Stopping only for occasional pictures and bragging, Fraley and friend plied the pond waters for more than an hour. The big bluegills, apparently still on their spawning beds near the face of the dam, obliged by sucking in the artificial flies.

The fishermen returned the favor by releasing each fish to fight again.

Although Fraley likes to eat fish, this trip was just for fun. Really big bluegills are hard to find, he said. He didn't want to fish out this hole.

Besides, Fraley respected the bluegills' spunk almost too much to want to keep them.

"If they averaged five pounds apiece, we'd declare largemouth bass a noxious fish," he joked.

"And if (bluegills) took steroids, fishermen would be an endangered species."

Fraley admits he's biased. His love affair with bluegills is long-standing.

He was seven years old when his father showed him how to use an old bamboo flyrod, then pointed young Clint at the nearest pond.

"I caught two five-gallon buckets full," said Fraley, with characteristic fisherman's modesty.

For the next 20 years, Fraley was obsessed with bluegill fishing.

Flyrod in hand, he'd walk or ride his bike to ponds around his hometown of Milo.

He carried a small notebook, in which he kept track of every fish he caught. The tally, over two decades, topped 300,000 fish.

"A lot of days I caught 1,000 bluegills," Fraley said. "That was work!"

He'd occasionally save a few to eat, but Fraley threw back most of the fish. After all, what's a kid to do with 300,000 bluegills?

Fraley never tired of catching bluegills, though that meant he also had to learn to tie flies to replace those he lost or wore out.

"Tying can be as much fun as fishing," he said. He still teaches a winter fly-tying class through the Clay County Conservation Board, where he is director.

Fraley's friends occasionally tease him about bluegills, but it doesn't faze him. On the contrary, he's founded "Bluegills Forever," a whimsical group with the credo "No dues, no banquets, just fun."

It's for kids, and for fishermen who haven't forgotten the fun of their first bluegill.

"Bluegills Forever," Fraley declared. "It's a state of mind."

June 12, 1994

Dad's gone fishin' – for patience

Avid sportsman changes pace during outing with kids

WAHPETON, IA – Patience.

Now *there's* a Father's Day gift a dad really needs – especially if he's a fishing dad!

Jeff Lenz of Wahpeton can thank sons Reid, 5, and Chase, 7, for his patience.

As an avid sport fisherman and part-time fishing guide, Lenz is on the water – and working hard to fool fish – several times a week.

But he also reserves time for another kind of fishing. When Reid and Chase go along, the pace changes.

Instead of hunting muskies or stalking walleyes on West Okoboji, Lenz may take the boys on a bluegill safari in the lake's network of canals.

Staying Simple

"Don't get too sophisticated," Lenz advised.

A simple spin-cast outfit, with an ice-fishing jig, a pinch of worm and small bobber, is fine for bluegills.

Lenz eased his bass boat into a canal, then instructed the boys to cast toward shore, where several bluegills lurked on their spawning beds in submerged vegetation.

The hours of backyard practice paid off as both deftly dropped their bobbers near the fish.

"Now tighten your line . . . move the bobber . . . just a little bit," Jeff coached.

"There he goes! Now set the hook!"

Reid jerked – and something jerked back.

"I've got him," cried the exuberant 5-year-old.

"He's a big one."

Big? Depends on your point of view.

Any Size

Several of the bluegills were chunky fish that could make respectable fillets for anyone's table. Others were, shall we say, "dinky?"

Didn't matter.

When their bobbers moved, Chase and Reid yanked and cranked with gusto – whatever the size of the catch.

The boys gamely – if not always gently – unhooked their fish, dropping the bluegills over the side or into the live well, depending on size.

Diversions

But even a successful fisherman needs a change of scenery.

(Translation? "Time for a boat ride.") .

"I want to go as fast as this boat can go!" Chase said with a wide grin.

Lenz eased out onto the lake, then opened the throttle for a brief run to a new spot. His laughing sons relished the bouncing ride over the waves.

The family stopped in the middle of a bay, and Lenz tied on jigs for his sons.

A jig needs a minnow: good excuse to play in the minnow bucket! (Wiggly critters, aren't they!)

110

A few splashes and giggles later, the boys were ready for more action.

Chase cast his lure into the waves, then glared intently at his rod tip, waiting . . . .

"Got one!" Suddenly Chase was reeling frantically as his rod bowed against the weight of a fish.

He beamed as his dad netted a small northern pike.

Reid, without a bite, looked glum.

"I'm bored," he announced.

Sandwich and pop time.

And how about another boat ride?

Dad and kids headed for another canal – and more sure-fire bluegill action.

(The action also included tangled lines, a broken bobber, sunburn, spilled pop and escaped worms. That's where the patience part comes in!)

Too soon, it was time to go.

"Can we come back here sometime?" Reid pleaded.

'Nuf said.

A few tips for fishing with kids:

• Keep it simple. An inexpensive spin-cast outfit, rigged with 6-pound line, will do for most fishing. For bluegills, use the smallest bobber possible, along with an ice fishing jig and bit of worm or a waxworm. For walleyes or bass, try a jig and minnow.

• Keep it short. If the child tires of fishing and wants to stop, don't fight it. A short, fun trip will leave the youngster eager for more; if kids are forced to fish too long, they may not want to go again.

• Bring food! Kids always are hungry. Snacks are a must, even if the fish *are* biting.

• Be safe. Get a properly-fitting, comfortable life jacket and have the child wear it whenever he or she is in a boat or near water.

• Plan diversions. A coloring book or favorite toy may help entertain a child who temporarily loses interest.

June 2, 1992

Porky lands bass amid lots of laughs

LANSING, IA — KABLOOEY! KARASH! WHOOOEEE!

With a whoop and a holler and a splash and a belly laugh, Orville "Porky" Meyers landed yet another Mississippi River bass.

"This is what you call livin'," he chortled as he swung the largemouth into the boat. "We have more fun than ordinary people!"

Porky's far from "ordinary," that's for sure.

At 73, the jovial, silvery-haired river rat lives fishing. If there's a fish to be caught, Porky can catch it.

But as a long-time fishing guide and former host of Quad Cities-area radio and TV outdoors programs, Porky enjoys seeing others catch fish even more than catching them himself. That's why he invited me to join the "party" upriver from his Lansing home.

Two frequent angling companions accompanied Porky. Dick Pierce of Waterloo bought a summer cottage next door to Porky several years ago – and soon caught an incurable case of fishing mania. Gary Schreiner of Sterling, Ill., is an avid tournament angler who shares Porky's love for the Mississippi.

Out on the river Porky hardly had time to jockey his 20-foot johnboat into a tangle of flooded willows when the bass started flying.

Porky, Schreiner and Pierce all tied into largemouths within minutes. Fishing in currents and eddies in flooded timber, they dangled pork rind tipped jigs along the brush.

"Make it look alive," Porky coached, as the anglers used the bait that earned him the title of "Porky the Chunker."

"I was dunkin' them suckers when they first made 'em – 50 years ago," he said with a chuckle.

The men used stiff rods or "flippin' sticks" rigged with 17-pound line to gently plop the "jig-and-pig" baits into saucer-sized holes in log jams right alongside the boat.

"Sometimes [bass] back right in" to their hideouts, and may take a lure only if it's dropped right in front of their noses, Schreiner said. And when fish hit in the brush, it takes a sturdy rig to horse them out.

As the water cools in the fall, a jig-and-pig in the brush will continue to be a prime bait for lunker largemouths, Schreiner said.

"The colder it gets, the bigger they get."

Heavy cover often is a good bet for big bass, Porky agreed.

"They're not where people are running around."

Thus, he headed into the "wilderness," using a trolling motor to slip the boat around willow cuts, over sunken beaver dams and through weedy tangles.

Porky hit some favorite spots, but he tried new holes, as well. "Research," it's called.

"I like to keep checking. That's how you learn," Porky said.

Where to check? Try thinking like a bass.

He slid the boat just a few yards toward a sheltering line of trees – and KA-CHUNK! A four-pound largemouth slammed my spinner bait.

"Wild!" Porky laughed with delight, scrambling for his camera to record the flopping fish and grinning journalist.

As they cast in the lee of the timber, the men practiced Porky's theory of versatility. They dangled jigs-and-pigs in the brush, clattered buzz baits across open water, twitched spinner baits through lily pads and slithered "Moss Bosses" across tangles of duck-weed.

What's the secret of using the different lures?

"Stick it on and throw it in front of a fish," Schreiner said, only half facetiously. He traded grins with Porky and Pierce.

Anglers fret over lure color or scent, line size, speed of retrieve, weather reports and a dozen other variables – but they still may not catch fish.

"Ah, the missing link," Porky said. "How to put it in front of one's mouth. They're easy to catch if they grab it.

"Finding 'em – that's my hobby," he declared.

The ability to find fish sets Porky apart. On this trip with high, murky water flooding usual fishing holes, many an angler would have given up.

But not Porky. Confidence was on his side, along with a major solunar period and overcast skies. He'd find 'em.

The fish were moving into the shallows with the rising water, Porky figured. He fished chutes through flooded islands or shorelines, submerged weeds and other spots that could attract a migrating bass.

Where Porky predicted bass, there were bass. Without depth finder or pH meter or thermometer or even a map, Porky beat the fish at their own game.

But Porky had two advantages: "65 years of experience" and a living computer under his cap.

"The first thing you take bass fishing is your head," he said. And you never allow yourself to stop learning, he might have added.

Schreiner and Pierce marveled at Porky's fishing knowledge and perception.

"He never catches a fish but what he's thinking about why was it there and how did it hit," Schreiner said.

Porky laughed – again.

"Neither you nor I nor anyone else will ever know everything there is to know about bass fishing," he said. "That's what makes it such a sport."

September 23, 1985

Granddad's painless pill: More fishing

And if the luck goes bad, blame the lightning bugs

LENOX, IA – Cecil Cordell stretched out on the grassy pond bank, leaned on his elbow, lit up a Pall Mall and tucked a thumb in the suspenders of his bib overalls. As an afterthought, he glanced at his fishing rod propped up at the water's edge.

"I used to think a guy who'd lay around fishin' on a day like this was a lazy S.O.B.," he said.

But five years ago, Cec ("everybody calls me 'Cec'") was ordered to reduce his work as a custom butcher.

"I paid the doctor $1,700 to tell me to work less and fish more," Cec said – as if the prescription pained him.

He's adjusted quite well, however, with the net result that he has more time to spend fishing with his 14 grandkids – especially David Haidsiak, 10, of Gravity.

"Since he was 3, he has follered me," Cec said.

"And, by God, that boy can FISH!"

When David was still a toddler, Cec tied himself and the boy together with a 20-foot sash cord, then let David walk ahead as the pair fished around farm ponds.

Since then, a friendly grandfather-grandson rivalry has developed – and the two constantly trade barbs about each other's fishing prowess – or lack of it.

Most trips start out with nickel bets on who'll catch the first fish, the biggest fish and the most fish.

"The last guy to catch a fish is supposed to dress 'em," Cec added.

Cec has no shortage of fishing holes, since he knows all the farmers in the area from his nearly 30 years of butchering. Most farms have a few ponds – and many are stocked with fish.

He used to be a "river rat," Cec admitted, but now he prefers the easier fishing in ponds.

"I don't know if I'm getting old or if the dogs they've got now are getting tougher," he pondered.

"When I was 20 years old, there wasn't any dog I couldn't wear out – but now a dog 20 years old can wear ME out!"

Bank fishing in a farm pond really is no handicap, Cec said, since the fish usually are close to shore anyway.

"I like to come out here in the morning or evening -- daylight to sunup and sundown to dark-- and not fish over 10 feet from the bank, or maybe five."

He chuckled at the quirks of human nature that tempt most bank fishermen to cast as far as possible – while boat fishermen cast as close to the shore as they can.

Of course, it makes a difference what you cast, as well as where, Cec said.

David likes to fish for bass, so his favorite lure is a "rooster tail" spinner – perhaps a yellow one. Cec is more of a catfish man, so he sticks with bait.

What kind of bait?

"I try about everything," he shrugged.

In the spring, cut shad is good – the more rotten the better.

In the summer, mudpuppies are good catfish getters, as are crawdads, he said. Nightcrawlers and chicken guts also are worth a try.

"That ole beef spleen is a pretty good bait, too," he added. "It's got a tough skin on each side –

114

and it's bloody as hell."

Cec's favorite bait he makes himself, simply by leaving scraps of raw beef in a jar of prepared "stinkbait."

But nothing worked on a recent, sunny afternoon.

Was the excuse the time of day – too early or late? Perhaps heavy rains.

Or, more than likely, it was the fault of the lightning bugs.

"I really don't catch many catfish until after the lightning bugs begin to come out," Cec explained. Naturally, he'd yet to see lightning bug No. 1 this season.

David almost saved the day when he hooked a huge bass. But his recycled fishing rod snapped, the bass shook free – and immediately grew by several pounds.

Cec's chance came when an equally large bass made a mighty swirl and splash at his rooster tail. Bass and rooster tail escaped unharmed. Cec's feelings got bruised.

Both incidents were duly noted, however, for they were the stuff of which fish tales are made.

On another lazy day, or winter evening, or whenever fishermen assemble, they'll be retold – not necessarily with any respect for accuracy.

But Cec confided that he'd just as soon catch small fish, anyway, since they're better eating. "A lot of guys use bigger fish for bait than I take home," he said.

Cec's eyes twinkled.

"Now, the *STORIES* get kinda big . . . ."

June 18, 1978

Little luck, but lots of laughs

Watkins derby isn't just about fishing for carp

WATKINS, IA – "How many carp did you catch?"

Dan "Squeak" Stramer pushed back his cap, scratched his head and digested the question.

Stramer and his partner, Mark "The Shark" Frese, both of Fairfax, stared at each other, obviously deep in thought.

"All together?" Stramer finally said, frowning. "Both of us?"

He hooked his thumbs in the bib of his overalls, shrugging at Frese.

"Counting the first one and the last one? And the ones we kept and the ones we threw back?" Stramer's eyes brightened, and his mental computer clicked.

"One!" he said, beaming.

Of course, as tournament director for the fourth annual greater Watkins invitational carp derby, Stramer had an excuse. He had to worry about more important things.

You know – details like potato salad and brats and sauerkraut and beer and barbequed deer ribs.

The food – prepared by Stramer's parents, Ray and Lois – was the focal point of the contest. Who wants to think about carp all day?

Blames Weather

Wally Dusil and Orville Butz, both of Watkins, gave it their best shot, though. They found a shade tree beside a canal by the Amana Woolen Mill, and spent a relaxed day drowning worms, dunking corn and soaking dough balls.

They almost caught four carp, too – except Stramer called their bluff and ruled that a buffalo (even the kind with fins and scales) isn't "almost" a carp.

Dusil blamed the weather, which he said has been too cool and wet for his secret weapon: dough balls.

He usually tempts carp with a mixture of oatmeal, corn meal, flour, vanilla, sugar, water and Jell-O – either strawberry or raspberry.

Oh, there's one other "secret ingredient," Dusil admitted. But he refused to divulge the complete recipe. "I might go to jail," he said with a grin.

But nobody else's secrets worked any better. Carp experts figured Iowa River floods had given the carp too much room to roam and too much food to eat. The 40 die-hard contestants mustered only 27 carp.

Stramer's brother, Bill, came all the way from Lexington, Ky., to help catch one carp.

Loren Meredith and Pat Bombei of Fairfax met with jeers when they proudly hefted their catch: four chunky channel catfish.

"No rough fish!" scoffed Stramer, always a stickler for rules.

It's a tall order to keep carp fishermen honest, Stramer teased. One year pranksters Dick Wessling and Dan "Coon Dog" Nolte of Watkins, when asked about their bait, pulled fake sticks of dynamite from their pants pockets.

Rookies Win

Much to the chagrin of the old pros, a rookie team caught the most fish this year. Cousins Andrew and Scott Schulte of Norway caught five carp.

Appropriately, the lunker award went to a not-so-tiny fisherman, Richard "Bull" Boddicker of Norway, who landed a 6 1/4-pound carp.

"The one I lost was bigger than that," he dead-panned.

Boddicker figures his carp trophy will be the envy of his younger brother, Mike, whose only taste of such glory has been occasional pitching duties for East Coast baseball teams.

Stramer concedes the carp derby isn't quite as big a deal as the World Series – but so what?

"We drink some beer, eat some brats and have some fun," he said.

"And we might even try to catch a few carp if we have time!"

July 22, 1990

'You've gotta be at the river to catch fish'

FREDERIKA, IA – A raw northeast wind skipped across skies that alternately promised a glimpse of sun and yet another dose of showers. It was a blustery morning on the banks of the Wapsi.

But were Fred and Ole Buss discouraged?

Ha! Here are two fishermen who laugh at the weather and grin in the face of adversity.

"If the weather is so we can get out there, we're fishin'," Fred said.

But some folks say the water is too high, protested the stranger. And it's too late for the walleye run and too cold for catfish and too early for bass and . . .

"There's fish there to be caught – fish of some kind – if guys want to try for 'em," Fred countered.

Probably should be some northerns moving up the Wapsi, he decided. And a fella just might catch one if he dunked a chub long enough.

"You just wait 'em out," Ole mused. "Just spend your time and all at once one can grab it."

The two brothers relaxed on the river bank, content to let time slip by.

"But the odds are against you," Fred finally acknowledged, as he stuffed in another chew of tobacco.

Then he waited, watching the stranger for the question he knew was coming: If the chances of catching anything are slim, is it worth going fishing?

"Absolutely," he grinned. "We might come up with a 15-pounder. You never know when he's gonna come up and grab it.

"You've gotta be at the river if you're gonna catch fish," he said. "You can't catch 'em at home watching television."

The stranger didn't say it, but he wondered how many folks might think riverbank-lounging a waste of time.

It was Ole's turn for mind reading.

"Time don't mean anything to us," he shrugged.

The bachelor brothers have been retired from farming for 12 years, Fred explained. And what better to do with your time than go fishin'?

"The old walls get kind of close," Fred mused.

But even in the days when the brothers were farming, they did their share of fishing, Fred conceded. If the fish were biting when the farm work needed doing, the fish often got priority.

"We always was outdoor guys," Fred reflected. He recalled the brothers' 1947 purchase of their farm near Tripoli. The 240-acre tract of sloughs, timber and pasture sprawls along the wandering Wapsipinicon River.

"Everybody said we was crazy to buy a damned old farm like that."

But the deer and ducks and coons and wild turkeys and squirrels and pheasants don't think the brothers are at all crazy. The wildlife thrives on habitat so rich that the farm has been included in the Iowa Nature Conservancy's Registry of Natural Areas.

Fred's mood turned somber when he thought of other landowners draining sloughs and bulldozing trees and otherwise destroying wildlife habitat to clear a few more acres for crops – all for a few more bucks.

"That's all it is — they've gotta make money," Fred lamented.

Then he brightened. "But they're not near as happy as Ole and me!"

Indeed, to Fred and Ole, happiness is fishing. Even in the 1930s, when they worked as farm hands for a dollar a day, the brothers would take a week off and go to Minnesota fishing, Fred said. They'd fish from dawn to dark, all day, every day "to get our money's worth," Fred said.

In 50 years, that fever obviously hasn't subsided.

The brothers fish all year — through the ice for bluegills, in the river for northerns or walleyes or even suckers. And if the fish don't bite?

"We're gonna have enough fish for supper anyway, because we're gonna go down to Plum Creek and catch a mess of bullheads," Fred said confidently.

"That's our diet," he said. "Every night for supper we eat fish."

Fred has even kept on fishing despite a mysterious ailment that felled him earlier this spring.

"On the last day of February, the boys picked me up off the riverbank and took me to the hospital," he said. After a brief hospital stint, Fred went back to fishing — but he concedes he's wading less now.

Fishing, the Buss brothers agree, is good therapy. People would be happier and healthier if they took more time to hunt and fish and enjoy the outdoors.

Then Fred Buss wrinkled his weathered face, twinkled his light blue eyes, grabbed the stranger's shoulder and gave some gentle — but firm — advice.

"Do it before you retire!"

May 8, 1983

Fly fishing isn't just for trout –
in fact, it's a philosophy of life

"Fly fishing."

If those words evoke only a vision of a splashing trout on its way to the frying pan, then you haven't met Dave Halblom.

The Des Moines man is absorbed in a sport that's also art, history, science, recreation, a test of skill, an occasional source of food, and a vocation.

"It easily becomes all-encompassing," said Halblom, who is a representative for several tackle companies.

"I look at fly fishing not so much as a way of catching fish as a way of thinking."

He has fly-fished for bluegills in Iowa farm ponds, northern pike in North Dakota reservoirs, striped bass in the Ozarks, trout in Rocky Mountain streams and steelheads in the Great Lakes.

As an adult education instructor, he's taught hundreds of people to tie their own flies.

"If you can tie a shoelace, you can tie a fly," he said.

His first creation, tied at age eight or nine, was "a bunch of buck-tail lashed (with white sewing thread) to a long-shanked hook." But it worked! He caught a smallmouth bass from the Iowa River near Marshalltown.

"I can't think of anything that's meant more to more people than catching their first fish on their own fly," Halblom said. "That's putting it all together."

But the fish is just a small part of a fly fisherman's realm, Halblom said.

A dedicated fly fisher may observe weather patterns, chart stream conditions, study aquatic insects, try to "match the hatch" and strive for pinpoint casts.

"The pursuit becomes more important than the act of catching," he said.

That attitude may develop gradually, he said.

Beginners just want to catch a fish. Later, they hope to catch the biggest or the most fish. As their skills improve, the fisherman or woman may want to use ultra-light tackle or other special equipment.

"And if you continue on with it, you'll probably end up fly fishing," Halblom said.

Fly fishing equipment can get complicated, Halblom admitted, but it need not be more confusing than other fishing gear. Just as people use an ultra-light spinning rod for panfish and a heavier casting rod for muskies, there are fly rods and line for special situations, he said.

A main difference between fly fishing and other fishing is in the relative weights of the line and lure. In spinning or casting, a heavy lure pulls out light line. In fly fishing, the heavy line carries the light fly.

"I use the longest rod possible for the conditions," Halblom recommended. He prefers a nine- or even 10-foot rod, unless close quarters force him to use shorter gear.

A beginning fly fisher should choose a rod at least eight or nine feet long, Halblom suggested. Modern graphite rods are light and easy to handle, even at that length, he said.

Be sure to use line of the weight specified on the rod, Halblom added.

And don't forget the sunglasses!

Polarized sunglasses are a must to help see into the water to locate structure or see rising fish, Halblom said.

120

Once you're hooked on fly fishing, don't be surprised if you get the urge to tie flies, Halblom said.

Fly tying can be a satisfying hobby, as well as a winter pastime, a creative outlet, a study of fishing history and a way to beat the expense of costly, faddish lures.

To learn to tie flies, seek help from a good book or a good friend, buy a high-quality vise and other tools – and practice, Halblom said. And don't be afraid to ask for advice.

Despite their stereotype as solitary souls, most people who fly fish are eager to help novices, Halblom said.

"On the stream, we avoid each other," he said, "but there's nothing that turns into a coffee klatch faster than a couple of fly fishermen OFF the stream!"

That gregarious nature led Halblom to the presidency of the Great Lakes Council of the Federation of Fly Fishers, which is an international fly fishing organization.

Fly fishing, he noted, is more than just fishing.

"It's a philosophy of how you approach the world," Halblom said.

April 18, 1993

Forget those ugly fish –
try butterflies, or berries, or rocks

It's too hot or too cold or too windy or too calm or too dry or too wet or too early or too late, and the fish won't bite. So what do you do?

Fear not, fellow anglers, I'm the state's undisputed authority on the subject of "What to do when the fish aren't biting."

It has taken years of unproductive fishing trips, jinxed outings and muffed chances to acquire this knowledge. But I feel obligated to share these gems of information with fellow bumblers who "can't catch a cold."

• Ever try butterflies?

Forget about the stupid fish! They're ugly, anyway. Look around next time you're near water with a funny pole in your hand. Butterflies are fun to watch and photograph, and it's even legal to catch them with a net.

• With a little luck, a flitting butterfly might lead you to a wild strawberry patch. Strawberries won't swim away or swallow the hook or turn up their nose at your new $2.95 super-whiz spinner. Strawberries just sit there and wait for you to eat them. And I'd rather eat strawberries than fish any day!

If you miss the strawberry season, try wild grapes, or plums or raspberries.

• Or go rock hunting – there's no season on that.

We kids seldom had much luck fishing in a creek in a pasture, but we never failed to bring home a pocket full of interesting rocks.

Some purists might not settle for just "interesting rocks," but they would abandon their tackle in an instant at the prospect of finding an Indian arrowhead. Streamside ledges often are productive sites for such artifact hunters.

• Wildflowers are more photogenic than arrowheads, however, so I often spend more time flower-snooping than fishing or artifact hunting.

• Or try bird watching.

Birds frequent brush and trees along most rivers, lakes and streams – and they're often tame enough to let a slow-moving angler get a close look.

If I can see a flame-orange oriole in an overhanging tree, or hear a yellowthroat singing its "witchity-witchity" song, I don't worry about the fish.

• And if I tire of looking up, I sometimes stretch out and peer into the watery depths.

A school of minnows darting about in search of plankton meals, or a crawdad groping in the gravel on the creek bottom can keep you entertained between bites.

When I took on the chore of teaching my younger brothers all I knew about fishing, I used to chastise them for their lack of interest in the finer points of the sophisticated sport.

But my instruction did little good – the restless tads soon would be dangling their lures in front of bullfrogs.

Needless to say, Mom usually ended up cooking frogs' legs instead of fish – much to my chagrin.

In recent years, I've simply given up trying to conquer the fish world. I still cast a line into a lake or river on occasion, but I'm not really "fishing," if the word means "catching fish."

What I'm really doing is paddling around or exploring the river or engaging in a little photography or bird watching or practicing my casting or testing equipment or looking for turtles or watching the sunset or counting mosquitoes – and I'm usually successful.

June 16, 1976

Ron Kaiser and friend

© The Des Moines Register

CHAPTER 9

HUNTING

Why do we hunt? Sure, we speak wistfully of communing with Nature or our pioneer heritage or of the fulfilling experience. But, truth is, most hunters simply can't explain it.

Oh, I've tried, countless times over 25 years. Occasionally, I've even struck a responsive chord with fellow hunters, who share the lure of the hunt.

But the urge to hunt, the satisfaction of the hunting experience and the connection to the natural world, are too personal to communicate in words that a nonhunter can comprehend. So, I write of my feelings, and of the feelings I see in others – and hope *someone* will understand.

Hunting – It's a tribute to Iowa, he says

I like to hunt.

There. I've said it and I'm glad. I'm not ashamed of being a hunter – although it's chic these days to abhor hunting and view all hunters with contempt and ridicule.

True, some incompetent or inconsiderate hunters deserve this scorn – and I'll criticize them as I defend the legitimate sportsmen, and champion their rights.

Why do I hunt?

Certainly not just for food – though I love to eat roast duck and creamed pheasant and rabbit simmered with mushrooms. I could go to the supermarket and buy a plucked chicken easier and cheaper than I could chase and kill and clean a quail – but the meat would be a lot less satisfying.

I don't hunt for a test of shooting skill, either. A visit to a trap or skeet range would assure lots more targets – and you don't have to clean clay pigeons.

Do I hunt for trophies? Not really. I've saved the skinny rack from my first deer, and there's a mounted grouse poised above my desk – but I treasure the memories more.

Some claim to hunt for the benefit of the animals – to kill them before they die of hunger or old age or overrun their habitat – but I don't buy that. Nature usually does a fair job of controlling her numbers, despite man's meddlings.

Nor do I hunt to out-do other hunters, to bring home a limit or to fill the freezer with game. Such competition would tarnish the joy of the outing.

Hunting isn't necessarily a social experience for me. I enjoy a quiet bird hunt with a buddy and his dog – but I shy away from opening day at the duck marsh and 20-member deer drives.

I don't even hunt for excitement – though my heart jumps when mallards turn to the decoys or a grouse explodes from an oak top.

I DO hunt to enjoy the outdoors. I also hike, watch birds, smell flowers, photograph wildlife, camp and canoe to enjoy the outdoors – but hunting spawns a kinship with Nature that no other pastime can.

Perhaps it's the feeling of actually participating in a natural system, instead of being just an observer, as a photographer must.

It could be a desperate attempt to stem the march of civilization, to resist the pressures that have converted this country from a wilderness of woods and prairies and rivers to a maze of roads and farm fields and cities and power lines.

When a hunter finds and kills game amidst the scars of "progress," he's whisked back to the era of pioneers and uncharted frontiers that every youth reads and dreams of.

Maybe hunting is a family tradition. My grandfathers told of epic duck hunts on the Missouri River bottoms, of clouds of pheasants in South Dakota, of blackberry brambles hopping with rabbits.

The stories awed me as a kid – so it was a red-letter day when Dad and I went out with the .22 to shoot my first cottontail.

Perhaps hunting and its rituals link me spiritually to unknown ancestors, who crouched around campfires planning treks to kill the winter's supply of game.

Whatever my motivation, and whether or not I understand it, I've learned alot about hunting in two short decades. In retrospect, I NEEDED to learn a lot.

Hunting "way back then" was simple – you took the gun and shells and went. The neighbors didn't mind if you used their land, and nobody thought of asking "How can you stand to KILL that poor bird?"

But suddenly there are people who don't like hunting – who see a difference, somehow, between butchering a hog and shooting a rabbit; who prefer not to think about animals dying.

Thus, a hunter today must – above all else – be an ethical and responsible individual. He must have the courtesy to seek the farmer's permission; the training to safely handle a gun; the compassion to honor the rights of those who choose not to be exposed to hunting.

These are solemn obligations, since the hunter has only his conscience to enforce his unwritten code. No umpire looks over his shoulder; no referee calls fair or foul.

His reward for sportsmanlike conduct is mostly satisfaction – and the continuation of his hunting privileges. The consequences of misbehavior are more direct, for a host of eager jurors wait to render an instant "guilty" verdict if a hunter trespasses or drops trash or frightens livestock. And each hunter suffers for the transgressions of others, simply by association.

Let's face it – hunters are a small but visible minority. Only 20 percent of Iowans hunt – and the proportion nationwide is even smaller.

But hunters shoot loud and potentially dangerous guns and wear orange hats and go out in droves on opening day, so they have the ability to touch the lives of many other people. Hunters must realize this, and strive to make their contacts with non-hunters as untraumatic as possible.

By the same token, anti-hunters who are opposed to killing should remember that animals also must die if we are to eat meat or wear leather clothing. They also should understand that an animal killed by a gun can be replaced with next year's breeding season – while wildlife lost to habitat destruction from farming, chemical pollution, mining or urban sprawl is gone forever.

It's a tribute to Iowa and her people that hunting still is possible here. If the quality of our environment or the mood of our society ever precludes hunting, the state will be immeasurably poorer.

October 29, 1978

The first hunt is the best hunt

For Iowa pheasant hunting, the early 1960s were the best of times.

The "soil bank" program had turned half a million acres of Iowa into undisturbed hay field nesting havens for pheasants. And the ravages of intensive farming hadn't yet grubbed out the abandoned farmsteads and plum thickets that sheltered the birds in the winter.

As an eager, southern Iowa farm kid, I grew up in that era, dreaming of hunting in the fabled pheasant Mecca of the wilds "up north." My first hunting trip to "pheasant country" is etched in my mind more vividly than any of last year's remembrances.

I'd gotten my first gun – a little Ithaca 20-gauge pump that I still cherish – but had shot only a few cottontails. The only live pheasant I recall seeing was a stray hen my grandpa kicked up while we were rabbit hunting.

My big break came when a neighbor and fishing buddy, John, conned his dad and uncle into taking us two novices on an opening day pheasant hunt all the way up to Wright County. The BIG TIME!

I reread advice in old "Outdoor Life" magazines, trying to decide whether sixes or fives or fours were the best loads for pheasants. Indecisive, I settled on a combination, tucking in a few magnum fours for long shots.

How many sweatshirts should I wear under my new hunting coat – the one from last Christmas? Would my manure-stained work shoes serve as hunting boots? Should I clean my gun . . . again?

Dad counseled me to be careful, recalling with trepidation a party hunt he'd been on when an army of hunters, tempted with swarms of flying pheasants, shot dangerously close to their companions.

Mom baked a batch of her world-famous cinnamon rolls for the occasion, knowing that John and I could devour the sticky treats by the dozen.

Naturally, John's mom came through with a pan of her widely acclaimed brownies. And we packed enough sandwiches (roast beef and ketchup, probably) to feed an infantry on maneuvers.

I must have slept some on opening day eve – although I can't imagine how. Excited? Who, me?

Before dawn, we were headed north in Uncle George's big Oldsmobile. Up front, George and John's dad, Pete, tried to outdo each other with tales of pheasant hordes in the good old days. In the back seat, John and I sat staring out the window, expecting to see ring-necks dancing in the headlights.

When dawn broke and we complained that we still hadn't seen a pheasant, Pete and George solemnly reminded us that it was bad luck to see a rooster before shooting time.

Our hopes sank for an instant when George gleefully heralded "birds" as we neared our destination. But George guffawed as we sprained our necks turning to see a pen of domestic turkeys.

Trip over, we greeted the farmer, invited him along and checked the time. At 9 a.m. (the starting hour in those days), we marched down a railroad right-of-way bordering an immense picked cornfield. Almost immediately, hens began flushing near us. In the distance, other hunters' guns boomed steadily.

In the November sunlight, a gaudy rooster burst from the grass under Pete's feet. Cackling vociferously, the giant bird zoomed toward the cornfields. I froze, too awed to do anything but gawk. Boom! Pete folded the noisy cock with one shot.

"I like it when they cuss at me," Pete grinned, retrieving the bird.

That was the first of many birds we shot – and even more that we missed – as we tromped fencerows, draws and those long, long corn rows.

Several other roosters stick out in my mind – like the one that sailed in front of our line of five hunters, escaping the hail of pellets until Pete, on the end, rolled the cock with his old 12-gauge pump gun.

"I had a long time to aim," Pete laughed, when teased about the feat.

Another special bird was the one John shot and galloped to retrieve as he, George and I made a final pass along the railroad tracks to end the day.

But the most vivid memory is of a rooster that flushed at the end of that mile-long cornfield. As before, I automatically brought my gun up and shot, expecting to see the cock fly away or fall near someone else. But the pheasant crumpled, and my heart lept as I realized I alone had killed it. My first pheasant!

The trip home was satisfying, as we rehashed game in the bag and fun in the field. We laughed at our misses, ribbed Pete about his deadly aim and moaned at the length of those corn rows.

And George entertained us with a yarn about the pheasants he rescued from an ice storm, only to have the birds flying around his basement after their feathers thawed out.

John and I have hunted together most years since then but we still share that memorable adventure, and measure all other pheasant trips against it.

Pete and George recall it fondly, too.

"I haven't seen that many birds in a long time," George reminisced.

"I've been hunting a lot, but I don't think I ever had a better time," Pete added. "Just to see a couple of young guys really enjoy it made it even more fun."

For this "young guy," that day will last a lifetime.

November 4, 1984

Hunting with Dad: Son's dream finally comes true

"Dad, when does the squirrel hunting season open?"

"Yesterday."

A light flashed in those 10-year-old eyes.

Uncharacteristically speechless, he just grinned, and looked at his father with those wistful, puppy-dog eyes.

The question was clear: Is it finally time for the first hunt?

After all, he'd paid his dues.

For three seasons, he trudged along with Dad, just learning.

The first year – draped in his too-big orange vest – he'd walked and watched his father try to set a good example.

Always – always – keep that gun pointed in a safe direction. Be sure of your target – and of what's beyond. Know where your partner is. Check – then check again – to be sure that gun is unloaded before you put it down.

Later, he earned the right to carry a wooden gun. Dad and son had sawed it out, using a pattern copied from a dog-eared gun catalog.

But wooden or not, the safety rules were the same. He pointed the pine muzzle carefully, unloaded the make-believe shell when crossing a fence, pretended to check the chamber before hanging it on the rack above his bed.

Then he graduated to the real thing: a BB gun. Not a toy, a BB gun can kill a sparrow or starling – or put out an eye.

Shooting at a cardboard box against a ditch bank, he practiced. And he eventually won permission to plink that first sparrow off the shed roof.

The came another year of target shooting with the .22, breaking clay pigeons with the .410 and more sparrow control with the BB gun. And now, maybe it was time . . .

•

A hint of fall hung in the air. Yellow tinged the elm leaves. Dew-spangled spider webs shimmered in morning sun.

"Turkeys!" blurted Dad, as the car clunked down the farm lane. Four jakes raced along the alfalfa field fence, then melted through the raspberry thicket into the woods.

The father was still savoring the moment when his son hopped from the car. Patience is not a virtue of 10-year-olds.

Reason prevailed, however, as he uncased and checked the guns. No hasty mistakes.

But before they'd walked a dozen steps toward the timber, the hunters froze. High-stepping across the alfalfa came two fawns, then the doe.

Stopping to nibble-sniff-munch, the deer ignored the two humans downwind behind the sumac thicket.

The white-tails eased down the bank, glided onto the road and floated over the fence.

Dad and son exhaled in unison. Then they crept along behind the fencerow, until the browsing deer snapped their heads up and bounded away, white flags waving.

A trail wound down a sunny, wooded hillside, beckoning the hunters.

Through the trees, a pileated woodpecker scolded: kuk-kuk-kuk-kuk. Amber walnut leaves glowed against the September-blue sky.

The boy saw it first: a flash of rusty-gray at the base of an oak. The intruders had interrupted a squirrel at breakfast.

After a glance back for reassurance, the young hunter tip-toed ahead. Step – wait – step – wait . . . The .410 eased to his shoulder.

It was a clean head shot. The young gray squirrel thumped to the ground.

The boy stroked the soft tail, felt the sharp toes, admired the tiny ears. His first squirrel.

Beaming, son and Dad exchanged "high fives."

Then, once more, they stalked the trail.

"Squirrel!" whispered the boy, as the leaves rustled ahead.

But the gun stayed down. A chipmunk scolded, then darted into a hollow log.

Be sure of your target. Yes, he'd learned well.

More flickers of movement ahead. No doubt this time. A bushy tail waved in the oak top.

Strategy: son on the left, Dad on the right. Spread out and scan the canopy. Slowly. Quietly. "Bang!"

The little .410 barked again.

Another head shot.

Nice job.

Enough for supper. Time to go home.

But first, another lesson: squirrel skinning. The tough part is getting started. Then, pull – hard!

A turkey vulture wheeled low over the treetops. Good. He could feast on squirrel innards. Nature is not wasteful.

The midday breeze had begun to rustle the cottonwoods. Two red-tails soared in the distance, specks against the blue.

"Nice day!" the boy said, sighing.

•

"Guess what's for supper, Mom!"

Without waiting for an answer, he held up the freshly cleaned carcasses.

And she gave him a hug. (Now *that's* a special kind of mother.)

The glow lasted through the squirrel and gravy.

The warm feeling returned as son and Dad pinned the tails out to dry, once again admiring the soft, gray hair. They'd hang in a place of honor, next to the Hawkeye clippings and autographed Twins baseball.

But the hunt was not over. As they cleaned their guns, Dad and son shared the moments again.

Turkeys, hawks, deer, leaves turning, pileated, chipmunk, squirrels, autumn air, companions.

Some day.

Some memories.

September 25, 1988

Sometimes a hunt just means a watch

RANDOLPH, IA – Chris Slutz curled a massive hand around the duck call, huffed deeply from his barrel chest – and played a love song to the shy hen mallard.

"Talk to me, sweetie," he whispered.

The "Suzie" swung over Slutz's decoys, then set her wings above a flock of real ducks feeding in the flooded smartweeds 50 yards away.

"Quack-quack-quack-quack." Slutz huffed harder, pleading in duck talk, "Please don't go!"

The bird flared, flapped faster and flew over the decoys for one last look.

Mesmerized

Slutz laughed. Enough playing. He let the bird sail on by to join the other flock.

Call it "duck hunting" if you must – but the term doesn't adequately describe Slutz's fall passion.

"There's a lot more to the sport than just killing," he said.

"When the mallards are in, I can sit and watch ducks all day and be totally mesmerized by the way birds fly."

Slutz, 45, has hunted since his boyhood in the waterfowl meccas of south-central Nebraska. And the Council Bluffs man has killed his share of ducks.

Slingshot Hunt

But lately he's lamented the decline of duck populations pushed to the brink by drought, wetland loss and illegal hunting. And he's decided to give the birds a break.

"I *can* make a difference in my world," he declared.

For the last couple of years, he's decided to hunt in different ways.

In 1988, he hunted all season with only a slingshot. His take? One green-winged teal.

"I picked that bird and baked it in a mushroom sauce and it was the best duck I've eaten in a long time," he said.

The memory was interrupted by a high-pitched chorus of honks trickling down from the hazy-gray November morning. Goose music!

Enjoys Surroundings

Slutz froze, then peeked skyward at the black-and-white flicker of wings from a flock of southbound snows.

He beamed at the passing geese, then began a tour of the 137-acre private marsh that's his second home.

Slutz grinned at a huge deer track in the dirt. He picked up and studied a snail shell. He chuckled as a swooping red-tail flushed a panic-stricken flock of mallards from the shallows.

He admired a cardinal flitting through the willows. He smiled at the busy-body chickadees playing hide-and-seek in the willows.

He stood savoring the shimmering water and bobbing decoys and nodding marsh grass and the streaks of sunlight filtering through the clouds.

"This is more than a duck pond."

Still, the scene wouldn't be the same without ducks.

"I've never seen anything else like a special sunrise or a special sunset, with a flock of ducks that shift on the wind and drift back in over the marsh."

And hunting those ducks is a paradox, Slutz conceded.

"How can I kill something with so much beauty . . . something that gives me so much joy?" he wondered.

As a hunter, Slutz figures he's motivated 45 percent by a love of watching wildlife, 45 percent by camaraderie – and 10 percent by ego.

"When you're young and full of . . . vinegar, you get into that ego thing," he said. "You're out there to prove something to the whole world.

"But as I get older, I realize what's important is the necessity of balance."

Value Isn't Financial

The hunt becomes a social event.

"It's kind of a ritual thing. Every year we go through getting the blind ready – and it's never quite right."

"The best part of duck hunting is a hot cup of coffee, maybe a bowl of soup and some B.S."

Although he and several partners own the marsh, they don't view their land as property with a dollar value, Slutz said.

"A person who sees everything in monetary terms scares me," he said.

"To me, this [marsh] is a priceless resource I'm privileged to utilize for a while.

"This is my Sistine Chapel."

Slutz the hunter has yielded to Slutz the philosopher.

"Perhaps the time has come in my life to see the other side of a limit," he wrote in an introspective essay about bagging a quota of game.

"Somehow in keeping score we've missed some of the joy at being there," he said. "We've missed the full satisfaction of what we have [by] wishing for what we don't have.

"Perhaps more days should be spent in not taking any," Slutz continued.

"Then on the day I take one, I'll appreciate it, rather than [complain about] being one duck short."

Personal Standards

Each hunter must set his or her own standards, Slutz said.

"Killing a duck is a personal, moral question," he said. He'd no more tell someone to hunt or not to hunt than he would tell them what religion to follow.

But protecting the environment so there can be ducks is a moral obligation, Slutz believes.

"I've got a 15-year-old daughter, Katherine, and I want her to have the choice to shoot a duck or to just look at it."

Nothing in nature quite compares to the sight of a flock of mallards against a blustery sky, Slutz said.

"When they break out and come down like this [wings set], something happens inside of me, he said. "That's what gets me cranked.

"If they closed the season for a year, I'd still be here," Slutz said. "I'd still camouflage my blind, I'd still have my decoys out and I'd be calling like a son-of-a-gun."

November 12, 1989

132

Coon hounds can make beautiful music together

ESTHERVILLE, IA – There was an unusual concert near here recently. Four major performers sang choruses in an open air theater along the wooded hills of the Des Moines River valley.

Reviewers probably would have panned the production, however, since the supporting characters failed to appear. And without them, the stars of the show couldn't display their full musical talents.

But despite the disappointing performance, the attentive, two-man audience promised to give the choristers another chance. Music lovers Herb Aldridge and Gary Grange, of Spirit Lake, even invited the vocalists home for a meal and overnight lodging after the final curtain.

Aldridge and Grange always take the singers home from their recitals, however. After all, a good coon hound is hard to find!

Call it a coon hunt if you like, but a night-time romp through the timber with their hounds is a musical experience for Aldridge and Grange. No opera fan is more enthusiastic.

"I like to listen to the hounds," Aldridge confided. "I just like hound music."

Music? From a coon hound?

Of course. It's just that you've got to know how to appreciate it. (Just like opera, some would say!)

Having owned "three or four hundred" coon hounds since acquiring his first dog at age eight, Aldridge should have an ear for hound vocalizations.

An uncultured listener might just hear a pack of dogs howling – but Aldridge can name each animal by its voice. Not only that, but he can almost tell what the unseen hound is doing and thinking as well.

The hounds' trailing bawls tell him how fresh the coon's trail is, whether all the dogs are following it and how close they are to the coon. When the dogs switch to their treeing "chop," Aldridge can judge whether the coon is cornered or if it may have jumped to another tree or otherwise eluded the dogs.

For Grange and Aldridge, the success of a coon hunt depends on how their musical dogs perform – not on whether they shoot any raccoons.

"The race is half the fun – listening to them trail and listening to them tree," Grange said.

Thus, Grange and Aldridge are satisfied to kill only a fraction of the raccoons their dogs tree. When they find a family of several raccoons, they usually shoot only one.

And they run their dogs all summer for training, without shooting any raccoons.

With raccoon pelts selling at $20 or more, how do they overcome the temptation to harvest as many animals as they can?

"If you (hunted) just for the money, you'd be out of it before long," Grange laughed.

"We won't even make our dog food (expenses) back," Aldridge concurred.

It costs several hundred dollars annually to train, feed, house and transport each dog – but few serious coon hunters have only one hound. Aldridge has seven, while Grange has four.

The initial cost of a hound can be staggering, as well, judging from the stories hound men tell about animals selling for several thousand dollars.

Are those tales of gold-plated dogs, really true?

"You betcha!" Aldridge grinned.

"I offered a guy a $4,200 van for a dog once," he admitted, "but he wouldn't trade."

Grange acknowledged paying as much as $1,500 for a coon hound.

"I'm always looking for a little better dog," Grange smiled. "It's a never-ending habit."

"You go through them like hotcakes until you find the one that does the job," Aldridge said.

"The main thing I like about one is when you get ready to go home, you can catch him," he added, only half joking. "He's gotta mind."

When you hunt five or six nights a week, as Aldridge and Grange do, you don't need a rebellious dog wandering off at quitting time. There are enough late nights as it is, Grange said.

"By the end of two or three weeks, you're ready for a weekend in bed," he chuckled.

Despite lost sleep, long hikes through the dark timber and occasional "no-show" nights by coons, Grange and Aldridge keep hunting until winter sets in.

"It's just something about the dogs," Aldridge mused.

November 28, 1982

Hoots, caws, squawks . . . and finally, a few gobbles

The pre-dawn bird chorus singing reveille. A spine-tingling gobble of a lovesick tom turkey. The soft greens and pinks and whites of the April woods in bloom.

If you think turkey hunting is just about meat or trophies or game in the bag, think again.

•

It's still dark outside, but you wake up before the alarm goes off. Can anyone but another hunter understand the anticipation?

What a morning! Stars still dot the inky sky, and Jupiter hangs like a glowing lantern in the southwest. But the eastern horizon already is turning gray, silhouetting the trees on the ridge.

Across the river, the whip-poor-wills try frantically to squeeze in a few more verses before daylight ends their songfest.

The field sparrow eagerly is warming up for its musical day shift, trilling a challenge to other birds to join the celebration.

Soon the cardinal chimes in . . . and the titmouse . . . and the song sparrow . . . and the phoebe . . . and the robin.

Off in the distance, two barred owls, in a vocal duel, interrupt the melodies with their hoots, caws and squawks.

The big tom can't stand it any longer. From his roost in the hillside oak, his gobbling rattles the creek valley.

Soon, you're engulfed in a sensory avalanche of sights and sounds.

Two pairs of wood ducks flash past in tight formation.

A great blue heron flaps methodically up over the trees.

A pileated woodpecker pounds on a hollow tree like a child beating on a toy drum.

You laugh at the contrast with a little downy woodpecker's tick-tick-ticking on the bark of the dead elm.

A mourning dove coos from a nearby tree, while a sassy crow caws defiantly to his brethren on the next hill.

A ruby-crowned kinglet searches the cedar branches just an arm's-length away.

A rooster pheasant crows from the neighbor's hayfield, arrogantly staking his claim to all hens within earshot.

His timber-dwelling cousin, the ruffed grouse, is more subtle. The grouse's rapid-fire wingbeats drum his quiet courtship invitation.

Nothing quiet about the two playful gray squirrels, though. With great leaf-rustling and chattering, they chase each other through the forest.

Suddenly, confronted by a strange, human shape seated against the base of their favorite walnut tree, they skid to a halt. Then, twitching their bushy tails, they scurry up separate maples to study and scold the intruder.

Gradually, the calm returns, broken only by the distant screeching of a blue jay and the clear whistle of a chickadee.

Crash! You instinctively look toward the sound, and see five deer, white tails waving, prance up the valley – perhaps spooked by another hunter.

You sit . . . and wait . . . and wait . . . and sit. An hour, almost two . . . Foot asleep, backside numb, you finally decide to move.

Too soon! Three toms, almost within range, see you first. Like shiny-black ghosts, they trot off through the tall grass.

•

You sigh . . . Nothing more to do but savor the warm, spring morning.

Much later, a friend asks: "Any luck?"

How do you answer?

Who else will measure success in stepping over a cluster of Dutchman's breeches . . . in close encounters with a skunk on a dark trail . . . in trying not to blink in a stare down with a hen at 10 paces . . . in the soft, green glow of the first light shining on the young cottonwood leaflets?

You smile.

"Oh, I'm learning!"

April 24, 1994

Few feathers or fowl but, oh, the memories

Hunting season 'successes'

Some sportsmen measure the success of the past hunting season with mallard feathers in their hatbands, pheasants in the freezer or trophy deer heads over the fireplace. My success – or lack of it – can be gauged only in the memories.

I recall the haunting calls of the barred and great horned owls in the Mississippi River timber as I camped with two friends along a bayou, waiting for duck season to open next morning. The owls and rustling of unseen critters in the dry leaves kept us awake most of the night – and perhaps gave us an excuse for the next day's poor shooting.

There was no excuse for the blunder of the previous afternoon that made us miss a chance to bag some Canada geese. The birds rested so quietly on a marsh pond near a duck blind that I was certain they were decoys. When my partners finally convinced me otherwise, the birds were alert to our presence and flapped away, chuckling at my poor eyesight.

Another dawn during the duck season found us floating through the mist on the Turkey River. No ducks fell to our guns, but we experienced a greater thrill when two dozen wild turkeys flushed from a nearby sandbar. The majestic birds clucked at our silent approach, strutted nervously, then boomed into the air and scattered into the forest while we watched spellbound.

The snipe migration was in full force during that float trip, and we chased small flocks of the shorebirds ahead of our canoe. The snipe season was open, but we were after ducks. Besides, the birds' sandbar ballet and darting flight was so amusing we forgot to shoot.

Grouse also are adept at distracting their pursuers. One bird lured us near with his drumming, then strode boldly into the open as I passed his home log. After an eyeball-to-eyeball standoff, I finally stomped my foot to put it to flight. Fly he did – directly at my companion, who was in the process of extricating himself from a puckerbrush tangle. All either of us could do was say "bang" as the bird flew safely away.

Word quickly spread that I was no threat to the grouse population, and four other birds successfully tested that theory when they sat contentedly in treetops near the road, watching me watching them. How could they have known I had been ice fishing and had left my shotgun at home?

Pheasants have the same smug disdain for my hunting prowess. One big ringneck brazenly flushed nearly at my feet, then flew directly toward a skittish herd of cattle. I couldn't even yell "bang" – much less shoot – without triggering a stampede.

When it comes to making a monkey of me, however, quail take the prize. We'd been hunting a favorite brushy draw, thick with bobwhites, but my total bag consisted of one thistle head, three blue skies and two patches of boxelder bark.

But my luck was due to change. I knew the bird was in a clump of grass in a ditch, and there were clearings on two sides where I could get off a shot. I had him!

But as I stepped over the bank, the quail rocketed out – straight up. The bird flew up, down, around and back into the brush.

I watched, since the attempt to swing my shotgun left me flat on my back, head downhill, with the gunstock planted against the ground like a flagpole.

If I had pulled the trigger, a white banner probably would have popped from the barrel: "I surrender!"

January 5, 1977

Hunt goes on through time

Ancestors may have sought more than food

Muzzleloader ready, the hunter dared not move as the three deer picked their way along the trail.

He eyed the clearing as the whitetails approached. One shot should do it.

That would mean a winter's food for his hungry pioneer family, buckskin and sinew for clothing, antlers for buttons and knife handles. His heart pounded expectantly.

Vrooom!

The spell was broken by a four-wheel-drive pickup truck bouncing along the logging road.

The deer, like obedient schoolchildren, stopped and watched calmly until the familiar vehicle rumbled out of sight. Then they turned and trotted along an alternate trail and over the ridge.

I chuckled at the thought of the motorized hunters, oblivious to the wildlife almost under their noses.

And I laughed at myself for – once again – being in the wrong place at the wrong time.

Then, stiff from the hours of sitting, I trudged to the warm house for a cup of hot chocolate and a fresh cookie.

I pondered my link to an earlier generation of hunters.

We no doubt shared the same thrill at seeing our quarry. As if by magic, dusky forms appear on the trail. Black noses, white chin patches, twitching ears and shining eyes take shape through the brush.

But the frontiersman was unencumbered by thoughts of a computer-printed license specifying when, where and what sex of deer he could shoot. He didn't worry about a thick rule book telling him how to tag the animal, whether he could get another license or how long he could keep the meat.

Hoping his powder had stayed dry and praying that his flint would ignite it, the early woodsman could not fathom printed "rules."

Blaze orange? He'd scoff! How could anyone mistake a person for a deer?

Auto-loading shotgun? With *five* shells? What a waste, he'd think. One well-placed, carefully-molded lead ball would kill a deer.

Party hunting? My gosh! All those people tromping around would scare every critter for miles.

But, despite my mythical forefather's disdain for "modern" hunters, I like to think he shared some of the joys, too.

He would've smiled at the comical gray squirrels boldly chasing each other up and down a walnut tree.

How could he help but marvel at the bald eagles that soared above the river bluff, then screeched and scolded in a squabble over a prime roost site?

Maybe he even sat under my ancient white oak, the tree too big for two men to reach around – the monarch that finally toppled in last summer's storm.

The old hunter might have sneered at my synthetic clothing – but he secretly would have envied my toasty polypropylene underwear, my Thinsulate gloves, my goose down vest and my felt-lined leather/rubber boots.

If he had tried to look through my bifocals, he'd have shook his head in disbelief. How could you see a rifle sight looking through those chunks of blurry glass?

Still, I sense a real kinship with the imaginary ancestor that may have stalked my woods 150 years ago.

To be sure, he hunted for physical needs. Success could mean the difference between eating and going hungry.

But while I can open my freezer and find a pre-cooked meal ready to heat in the microwave, I also savor the taste of game I've killed, cleaned and prepared myself.

Yet the fact that he *was* a pioneer says that spiritual fires also burned in the long-ago hunter.

Perhaps, like I do, he needed the chickadee, the eagle, the chill wind, the prick of the blackberry, the rotting oak stump, the screams of the blue jay and the breathless anticipation almost as much as he needed the deer.

December 15, 1996

Spider dew   © The Des Moines Register

CHAPTER 10

BEAUTIFUL IOWA

Want an argument? Just list the "10 best" of anything. Somebody's bound to disagree! We figured as much when we picked our favorites among Iowa's prettiest places. Iowans didn't let us down. People from all over the state wrote passionate letters explaining why THEIR choice deserved mention.

Now it can be told: The list was just our way of getting fellow Iowans to think about their good fortune; to spur them to take delight in this beautiful land.

Sure, we bestow park and preserve status on some natural treasures. We protect river vistas, geological anomalies, native vegetation, historic sites and wooded hide-aways. But the people who most appreciate Iowa's beauty are the ones who can savor the small wonders – Nature's little miracles that engulf us every day.

Beautiful Iowa

Natural beauty? In agricultural Iowa?

It may be hard for some people to accept, but Iowa really is more than corn and bean fields.

Sure, we've plowed and planted most of our state, but a surprising number of spots have escaped, or recovered from, the heavy hand of man.

Often, it's an accident of topography that protects natural areas – timbered hills too steep to clear and plow, a marsh too deep to drain or a river bluff too inaccessible to farm.

Sometimes, farsighted conservationists have fought to save disappearing natural wonders.

What's left are oases, bits of wilderness whose beauty lies not only in their natural vegetation and wildlife, but also in their contrast with the manicured, manipulated land around them.

Which are the 10 prettiest? Any list must emphasize the rare or unusual – high bluffs in the midst of plains, deep forests surrounded by open fields, wildlife havens in farm country.

And no part of Iowa or its natural heritage should be left out. Subtle or spectacular, each corner of the state is scenic in its own way.

The most beautiful sites must include rivers, forests, prairies, parks, wetlands and natural wonders that sweep the state's rich range of beauty.

An impossible task? Perhaps. But it *should* be hard to choose the prettiest of the pretty. And Iowans can be proud of these places that make our state "Iowa, the beautiful land."

June 12, 1988

Upper Iowa River, Bluffton

Snow geese, Riverton

© Larry Stone

Pike's Peak State Park, McGregor

© Larry Stone

Nine Eagles State Park, Davis City

Ruddy duck, Eagle Lake, Britt © Larry Stone

Butterfly milkweed, Kalsow Prairie, Manson © Larry Stone

Rochester Cemetery, Cedar County © The Des Moines Register

Ledges State Park, Boone © The Des Moines Register

Loess Hills, Monona County

Shimek State Forest, Farmington

White-tailed deer, Lamont

© Larry Stone

Short-eared owl, Tipton

© Larry Stone

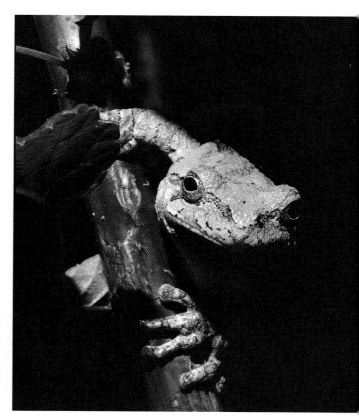

Gray tree frog, St. Olaf

© Larry Stone

Great horned owls, Ames

Red fox cub, Tama County

Deer mouse, St. Olaf

Black-eyed Susan, Elkader

© Larry Stone

Sulphur butterfly on New England aster, Elkader

© The Des Moines Register

Big bluestem and moon, Elkader

© Larry Stone

Goldfinch and compass plant, Elkader

© Larry Stone

Cedar Hills Sand Prairie, Cedar Falls

© Larry Stone

Prairie chickens, Mt. Ayr

© The Des Moines Register

Land snail, Clayton County

© Larry Stone

Dutchman's breeches, Warren County

© Larry Stone

Hug-A-Tree, Clayton County

© Larry Stone

Maple leaf and October snow, Elkader

© Larry Stone

Deep woods dawn, Garnavillo

© Larry Stone

Morel, Elkader

© Larry Stone

Pileated woodpecker, Dundee

© The Des Moines Register

Trumpeter swans, Boone County

© The Des Moines Register

Turkey River, Elkader

© Larry Stone

Blue flag, Union Slough, Titonka

© Larry Stone

Great blue heron, Roberts Creek, St. Olaf

© Larry Stone

ald eagle, Lansing

Mississippi River, near Lansing

Summer storm, Elkader

© Larry Stone

Wooden windmill, Storm Lake

© Larry Stone

Sioux quartzite and lichen, Lyon County

© Larry Stone

Loess Hills Prairie Seminar, Turin

© Larry Stone

Abandoned farm, Thornton

© Larry Stone

Moonset, St. Olaf

© Larry Stone

Ten prettiest scenes
from the Mississippi to the Missouri

Riverton goose migration

It's a world-class spectacle. Snow geese migrate twice-yearly through western Iowa, traveling between Arctic breeding grounds and Gulf Coast wintering sites.

Hundreds of thousands of birds may gather at the Riverton Wildlife Area near Riverton, Forney Lake near Thurman, or DeSoto National Wildlife Refuge near Missouri Valley. In the fall hunting season, the geese crowd into refuges.

But in the spring, the geese may scatter across the river bottoms. Huge flocks sometimes feed or rest along highways, treating travelers to a traffic-stopping wildlife show.

Shimek State Forest

Forests? In Iowa? The state may not have giant redwoods, or mountainsides covered with spruce trees – but Iowa does have real, honest-to-goodness tracts of timberland. Four major state forests are managed for their timber, wildlife and recreation.

At 8,800-acre Shimek State Forest near Farmington, in the gentle hills of southeast Iowa, native oaks and hickories blend with pine plantations up to 40 years old. Deer and wild turkeys thrive. Several ponds, campgrounds and a network of hiking and horseback trails make the forest a favorite with outdoor enthusiasts.

Eagle Lake

Before the white man and the plow and the tiling machine, much of north-central and northwest Iowa was covered with water. Shallow marshes and potholes swarmed with waterfowl, marsh birds and other wildlife.

Even whooping cranes nested in Iowa – notably at Eagle Lake, northwest of Britt.

The whoopers are gone now, but other wildlife abounds. When yellow-headed blackbirds or black terns are hatching in June, or when flocks of mallards sweep down on November snows, the marsh still sings.

Rochester Cemetery

With 150-year-old headstones framed in native prairie flowers and grasses, Rochester Cemetery, along the Cedar River near the village of Rochester, links Iowa's human history and natural heritage.

Shooting stars, columbines, prairie phlox, birdsfoot violets, little bluestem and other prairie plants thrive on the sandy hills. Huge white oaks – some three feet in diameter – also dot the pioneer graveyard. Rochester Township trustees manage the cemetery for its natural beauty in a tribute to those early settlers.

Ledges State Park

Sculptured, multicolored sandstone cliffs, rising 75 feet above Pease and Davis Creeks, distinguish Ledges State Park along the Des Moines River south of Boone. The spring-fed creeks have carved winding, tree-lined ravines through the 300 million-year-old bluffs. In the deep shaded canyons, time stands still.

In contrast, the 1,200-acre park's forested uplands are dotted with prairie remnants and rest on glacial deposits only 13,000 years old – an age that makes them mere infants in the geologic time span of the area.

Upper Iowa River

Limestone palisades climb more than 150 feet above a winding, rocky stream near Bluffton, marking one of the prettiest stretches of one of the state's prettiest rivers: the Upper Iowa.

For anyone who thinks of Iowa in terms of flat crop fields, the stream is definitely out of character. Its rapids, cliffs and wooded valleys hint of wilderness.

The Upper Iowa's rugged beauty lures thousands of canoeists, but its unusual topography also is home for a number of plants found in few other places in Iowa. For example, balsam fir trees more common in northern Minnesota and Canada have found a refuge on cool slopes above the river.

Loess Hills

They look almost like mountains. Looming above Iowa's western border, jutting up out of the Missouri River bottoms, lie the rugged, imposing Loess Hills.

Formed of windblown silt, or "loess," the unique 150-foot-high hills actually are drifts of soil piled by winds carrying sediment from retreating glaciers 20,000 years ago.

"The hills," with prairie grasses on dry southwest slopes and trees creeping up wetter valleys, stretch from north of Sioux City to the Missouri border. To best experience the hills, follow the gravel or dirt roads winding eastward up from the Missouri River floodplain.

Pike's Peak State Park

When Louis Joliet and Father James Marquette paddled down the Wisconsin River to the Mississippi, they were the first Europeans to see a towering bluff now known as Pike's Peak.

Modern Iowans atop that 500-foot summit, now a state park just south of McGregor, can gaze into history as they view bottomland marshes, wooded bluffs and the confluence of the two rivers.

It's a favorite stop in the fall, when orange and red maple, sumac and oak leaves set the northeast Iowa hills on fire.

Nine Eagles State Park

Nestled in the oak-hickory hills along the Missouri border southeast of Davis City, Nine Eagles may be Iowa's prettiest state park. I formed that opinion more than 25 years ago while camping there with a highschool friend.

It was May when Iowa is most lush. We slept in a green wall tent, listened to the buzzing cicadas – and caught a stringer full of fish in the 64-acre lake.

Those fond memories will always make Nine Eagles special.

Kalsow Prairie

Head-high grasses and panoramas of wildflowers rippled across Iowa to greet the first settlers.

But those 10,000-year-old prairies are almost gone now – buried by the plow in barely a century. The rich soil, built by prairie plants, now grows corn instead of coneflowers.

Kalsow Prairie State Preserve north of Manson is a 160-acre monument to the ecosystem that once covered 85 percent of Iowa. Butterfly milkweeds, sunflowers, prairie grasses and more than 200 other species take refuge here. But the real beauty of the preserve lies in the heritage. All Iowa has its roots in the prairie.

June 12, 1988

The best of the rest

The hardest part of listing Iowa's 10 most beautiful places is picking just 10.

As an Iowa native whose job it is to explore Iowa's outdoors, I easily thought of more than two dozen favorite spots worthy of mention as "the prettiest." I solicited votes from others, also – photographers, naturalists, resource professionals.

Here are some other top spots:

White Pine Hollow – The state's largest remaining stand of white pines grows on the rocky hills of this 712-acre state preserve near Luxemburg.

Maquoketa Caves State Park – More than a dozen caves, a natural limestone bridge and a 17-ton balanced rock highlight the geological marvels of this 272-acre park near Maquoketa. Lush ferns and wildflowers add to the natural beauty.

Yellow River State Forest – Forested bluffs, cold trout streams, scenic overlooks and abundant wildlife make this 7,000-acre state forest near Harpers Ferry a wild treasure.

Great Lakes – Spirit Lake, West Okoboji, East Okoboji and nearby lakes glisten like emeralds on the northwest Iowa prairie. The lakes, with their adjoining marshes and tree-lined shores, attract wildlife and tourists.

Dunning's Spring – Hidden in the back of a Decorah city park, this spring gurgles from the face of a limestone bluff to cascade down a 60-foot series of waterfalls.

Boone River – Out in the flattest of Iowa's flat farm country, the surprising Boone River cuts a rocky, wooded valley through Hamilton County.

Freda Haffner Kettlehole Preserve – A huge "kettlehole," left by melting glaciers, distinguishes this Nature Conservancy preserve northwest of Milford.

Big Sioux River – From a hill above the Big Sioux River, in Sioux or Lyon County, you look across the valley to where the west begins.

Mt. Hosmer – Climb or drive to Mt. Hosmer, a city park in Lansing, for a premier view of the Mississippi River.

Effigy Mounds National Monument – Indian mounds in the shape of animals, plus vistas of the Mississippi River, make Effigy Mounds near Marquette a favorite spot.

Waubonsie State Park – With forested valleys and prairie ridges, this 1,200-acre state park perches at the southern end of Iowa's Loess Hills near Hamburg.

Gitchie Manitou State Preserve – Pink Sioux quartzite, the oldest exposed rock formation in Iowa, marks this 91-acre preserve at the furthest northwest corner of Iowa.

Woodland Mounds Preserve – As a boy in Warren County, I dreamed about the wilderness along South River, east of Indianola. Now the county conservation board has a preserve there, complete with Indian mounds and wildflower woods.

North Cedar Creek – Every trout fisherman has his favorite stream. This is mine, because it's close to my home (seven miles east of St. Olaf) and requires walk-in access. No cars and no cares.

June 12, 1988

Beauty is in eye of beholder, often in small packages

Early morning dew dapples a wildflower leaf. An indigo bunting chatters from the backyard treetop. The heavy scent of wild plum blossoms sweetens the evening air.

You don't need to have your breath taken away by a magnificent vista to enjoy the Earth's beauty. The wonder of nature isn't so much the spectacular, but her subtle charms.

If you have trouble finding natural beauty, try looking inward. Stop for a moment to adjust your frame of mind. Ponder the miracle of life. Savor the small things.

Step outside at dawn. Let the dewy grass tickle your bare feet. Inhale the fresh, cool morning air. Listen to the cardinal's bright "Cheer! Cheer!"

Why long for real jewels when those pearls of raindrops hang on the spider web?

Learn to appreciate what Mother Nature gives you. Before you curse that dandelion, consider the honeybee busily probing the sun-gold flower for nectar.

It's OK for a farmer to admire his long, straight, clean rows of corn stretching to the horizon; but he shouldn't overlook the curious fox pups in the fence row, or the spunky dickcissel singing from the mulberry shrub.

My spine tingles at the gobbling of a tom turkey in the pre-dawn woods, but I marvel equally at the towhee calling from the oak, or the chipping sparrow on the neighbor's roof.

We scour the forests for elusive orchids or ginseng or morel mushrooms, but we may miss the beauty in the feathery leaf of Dutchman's breeches or the soft greens of a maidenhair fern.

And just what is beauty? Is there not grace, and delicacy – and beauty – in a simple garden spider?

Could we dare to call even a toad beautiful, with its richly textured brown back and its mottled-yellow belly?

What about poison ivy? There's a certain attractiveness in its neatly-arranged trios of leaves and clusters of creamy white berries.

And ponder, please, the fox snake. What fluid grace in its movements, what beauty in its forest-floor-brown skin.

Run your hand over the coarse bark of a bur oak. Sniff the dank mud of a cattail marsh. Gaze at the crescent moon hanging among pin-pricks of starlight in the night vastness.

Smile at the black-eyed Susans dancing by the roadside. Treat yourself to the taste of a red, ripe wild strawberry. Listen, some calm night, for the "jug-o-rum" of the bullfrog chorus on the neighbor's pond.

Bundle up next winter and walk in the new-fallen snow. Watch as Nature the Artist carves ice sculptures along the creek.

Yes, Iowa boasts a few scenic spectacles, but most of her natural marvels aren't one-dimensional.

Beauty is in the eye – and ear and nose and touch and taste and even the mind – of the beholder.

Nature is at her prettiest when we're drinking deeply of her smallest wonders.

June 12, 1988

146

Pool 10 – McGregor   © Larry Stone

CHAPTER 11

MISSISSIPPI RIVER

The more things change . . .

For decades, conservationists and developers have feuded over the Mississippi. Create a refuge. Build locks and dams. Stop dredging. Clean up the water. Why not a park? Regulate construction on the bluffs and floodplains.

The same old drama – or tragedy? – with a slightly new cast of characters, unfolds regularly, as it has for a century.

The Mississippi remains a unique, incredible, diverse, heavily-used, seriously-threatened resource. Bureaucrats call for more studies, environmentalists lament increasing destruction, commercial interests quarrel over pieces of an ever-shrinking pie. Pleasure boaters crowd marinas and beaches. Fishermen race to coveted honey-holes. And, despite it all, bald eagles thrive in the valley, and the river corridor remains a magnet for other wildlife.

How long can the theatrics continue? We all will decide.

Upper Mississippi can be saved, says group after 5-year study

Is the upper Mississippi River destined to become nothing but a barge canal, a silt trap and a sewer? Environmentalists sometimes have nightmares to that effect – but a nearly completed study says it doesn't have to happen.

The Great River Environmental Action Team (GREAT), a group of representatives of state and federal agencies, has prepared a list of recommendations on how the river could be better managed for wildlife, recreation and commerce, while still protecting the valley's resources.

The plan incorporates ideas from the group's 50 scientists and planners, with input from dozens of public meetings held since the project began in 1974. One public meeting to review the draft report was held last week in McGregor.

The final report, which will be forwarded to Congress and to involved public agencies, is due next March.

Downstream Project

This GREAT report covers only that part of the river north of Guttenberg, but another team is working on a similar project downstream along the Iowa border. The second study is scheduled for completion next year.

The task force has proposed some far-reaching recommendations. Among them is the suggestion that Congress amend U. S. Army Corps of Engineers regulations to include fish and wildlife and recreation in river management. Under present laws, the Corps has legal authority only to maintain a nine-foot river channel for navigation.

And environmentalists complained that the Corps often dredged out the navigation channel and disposed of the spoil with little regard for environmental considerations. Wetlands and backwaters – prime fish and wildlife habitat – often were filled with dredged silt and sand.

Under GREAT proposals, the Corps would be given the authority to correct some of the damage with backwater dredging projects, and to spend more money to transport dredge spoil out of the floodplain of the river. GREAT suggested using dredge spoil for construction, highway sanding, beaches and other projects.

Railroad Spurs

One recommendation called for building railroad spurs near sites of frequent dredging, so spoil could be easily hauled away in freight cars. Another cited the need for improved dredging equipment.

Even without full adoption of the plan, it should be possible to reduce damage from dredging, GREAT members said. The group outlined an ambitious plan for dredging and spoil disposal through the year 2025.

The GREAT report also says the need for dredging could be greatly reduced by controlling erosion on farmlands in the watershed. The report calls for more funds for a variety of erosion control projects.

Erosion control was a high priority of fish and wildlife members of the team, as well. They noted that many backwaters are filling in rapidly, due to silt runoff from farmlands. The character of the river will be irreparably altered if this trend is not reversed soon, they said.

The GREAT report also contains a number of recommendations on management of the river's recreational and economic resources. A major proposal calls for the adoption of uniform flood-

148

plain management standards by the states, to prevent encroachment along the river. State and federal agencies also should better coordinate their permit procedures for river-oriented development, the report said.

Barge Fleeting Areas

Barge fleeting areas also should be carefully studied, the report said. It called for an inventory of fleeting sites and industry needs. (McGregor area residents are embroiled in a dispute over possible location of barge "parking lots" near there.)

The report also stresses the value of the river for esthetics and recreation. GREAT members called for careful development of recreation facilities and acquisition of scenic easements in the river corridor.

The quality of river recreation also should be considered, the report added. It called for noise limits on recreational boats, zoning to keep large boat accesses away from wildlife areas and restrictions on houseboats "to prevent extended residency, sanitary discharge and esthetic impacts."

Other GREAT recommendations included:

• Coordinating lock and dam operations to minimize water fluctuations that adversely affect fish and wildlife.

• Phasing out private leases of federal lands for cabins.

• Studying techniques to improve re-vegetation of dredge spoil sites.

• Identifying and protecting primitive and natural areas and islands.

• Providing better management of bottomland forests.

• Improving the monitoring of hazardous materials carried by barges.

• Managing the Upper Mississippi River Wildlife and Fish Refuge area for all wildlife, rather than just a few target species like waterfowl and furbearers.

Dan McGuiness, a Hastings, Minn., environmental consultant who served as public participation coordinator for GREAT, acknowledged that some of the group's suggestions may be controversial, but he's confident the plan will benefit river users, if adopted.

McGuiness and other GREAT members hope for strong support from the public to institute the program. Public pressure will be required to gain approval of the measures that require congressional action, he said.

The GREAT report calls for an interagency task force to implement the plan and to assign responsibilities to appropriate agencies. Continued public support will be necessary to obtain the required funding, McGuiness said.

But even if the GREAT plan is virtually ignored, the project will have been a success, said Mark Ackelson, Mississippi River coordinator for the Iowa Conservation Commission. The study has instilled in state and federal agencies the philosophy of working together on river resource problems, he said, and that cooperative spirit is likely to continue.

December 12, 1979

Proposed paths could provide
trail of enjoyment along rivers

HARPERS FERRY, IA – The October sun warmed the bluff-top prairie and burnished the russet oaks down the slope.

Over the valley, a migrating red-tail soared on the afternoon thermals.

Far below, a great blue heron flapped over the shimmering waters of the Mississippi.

"There's poetry in that," Bill Witt said with a sigh as he gazed across the mighty river.

"It is our most spectacular visual asset," he said. "It's world-class."

But that river, with its rocky bluffs and rugged valleys, should be more than just a scenic delight, Witt said. The corridor along the Mississippi could become a resource to rebuild Iowans both spiritually and economically.

As chairman of the Iowa Chapter of the Sierra Club, Witt is promoting a plan to develop a hiking trail along the river from New Albin on the Minnesota border, southward to Dubuque or Bellevue.

Linking Lands

The trail, Witt said, could link a series of public lands along the river. Yellow River State Forest near Harpers Ferry, Effigy Mounds National Monument near Marquette, Pikes Peak State Park near McGregor, the Mines of Spain Natural Area near Dubuque and Bellevue State Park near Bellevue already preserve significant tracts in the valley. Several county parks and wildlife areas add to the public lands, he said. And Witt suggested acquisition of a large preserve at the junction of the Mississippi and Upper Iowa Rivers.

The Upper Iowa, which was considered for inclusion in the National Wild and Scenic Rivers Program in the early 1970s, should again be proposed for that recognition, Witt suggested. A trail system running along the Upper Iowa could complement the stream's current popularity as a canoe route, Witt added.

Eventually, other "feeder" trails might be developed to follow the Turkey or Yellow rivers or other tributaries, Witt said.

The Upper Iowa Trail, through sparsely populated areas along the rugged stream, would offer a wilderness-like experience, Witt said. If necessary, limits on trail use could help preserve that primitive character.

The Mississippi trail, on the other hand, would pass through or near many small communities along the river. Along with parks and natural areas, hikers might find bed and breakfast stops, historic buildings, craft shops and other facilities.

Trail users would give a tremendous boost to local economies, Witt noted. And the trail could draw attention to the region, increasing tourism even more.

"There are any number of [tourism] possibilities," Witt said, "if we're willing to see what we have and recognize it as an asset, rather than see it as just a bunch of trees."

Trail or Park?

State Senator Dale Tieden (Dem., Elkader) agreed that the tourism benefits of a Mississippi Trail would be immense. He called the trails concept a great idea.

Witt said other legislators and citizens he's talked to also have been enthusiastic about the trail idea.

The Mississippi also has received national attention, with several proposals for a national park along the river, Witt said. But he believes a trail corridor might be a more practical way than a full-fledged park to recognize the natural heritage of the area. A trail would require less land acquisition, and could embrace many states in a cooperative system.

Witt hopes the trail concept can be endorsed by the Iowa Legislature's Open Spaces Task Force, of which he is a member. That group will advise the Department of Natural Resources in preparing a plan to protect Iowa's remaining open spaces.

"Sense of Vision"

Legislators see resource protection as an aid to tourism, but Witt hopes to sell the trail concept on its own merits and not solely as an answer to economic problems.

"Our job is to touch people's spirits," he said.

Iowans are ready, Witt said, to care about their land, and their state, without expecting any monetary return; "to sit and listen to the wind in the trees and see the sunlight filtering through the leaves."

"We've got to have a sense of vision," he said, "a sense of loving something and caring for it."

Everybody has a vision of the Mississippi, Witt said.

"In the corner of their mind," he said, "is a feeling for the magnificence of the Mississippi River."

Where better to capture that vision than on the upland forests, rich wetlands and ridgetop vistas of a Mississippi River Trail?

October 25, 1987

Keeping eagle eye on eagles as they face modern peril

LANSING, IA – Like sentinels, bald eagles once again are watching over the Mississippi River.

Soaring above the bluffs, perched in stately cottonwoods or tending eaglets in secluded nests, the awesome birds are at home on the awesome river.

But human sentinels also are watching the eagles.

Biologists are studying the birds to see how they're coping with man's dramatic alteration of a once-wild environment.

John Lyons, manager of the McGregor District of the Upper Mississippi River Wildlife and Fish Refuge, said the project may help predict whether the river system can survive man's use and abuse.

"We're loving it to death," Lyons said of the river.

"We've got people coming from everywhere to have their chunk of it.

"We have walleye clubs, bass fishing tournaments, gambling boats, the general users, hunters, trappers, fishermen, sightseers. There's constant pressure on our borders for development, marinas, increased boating and increased kinds of surface use . . . jet skis, hovercraft . . .

"It's just incredible."

Even in winter, the river ice may swarm with snowmobilers, fishermen and other people.

The Upper Mississippi Refuge, which stretches 260 miles from Wabasha, Minn., to the Quad Cities, was created in 1924 to protect a rich habitat for fish and wildlife, Lyons said.

"We have a refuge of international significance here," he said, but the resource can handle only so much.

"At some point in time, we're going to essentially trade off the biological significance of the migratory corridor if we give in to these incremental things."

Those fears led Lyons to coordinate the eagle study with the U.S. Army Corps of Engineers and the Midwest Raptor Research Fund. Eagles, which are recovering rapidly from their pesticide-related die-off of the 1950s and 1960s, could demonstrate how nature adapts to human interference.

Jon Stravers of Pella, director of the Midwest Raptor Research Fund, is leading teams of observers who have monitored eagles' reactions to people, boats and other disturbances.

The researchers hope the data will show whether people affect where the eagles nest or how successful the birds are at raising young.

The work includes 10 of the 26 or more eagle nesting sites in three river pools between Dubuque and the Minnesota border.

Kelly McKay, of Moline, Ill., who has studied eagles as a hobby and as a Western Illinois University student for at least 14 years, said initial results show the birds to be fairly tolerant of people. But he's also seen evidence that heavy boat traffic may drive the birds from nests, and reduce the care they give their young. That could reduce the chicks' survival, he said.

Lyons said it's too early to draw any conclusions, however. And he sees the results of the eagle research as just a small part of a broader look at how people affect the refuge.

"Eagles are not our sole consideration, and maybe not even our most important one," Lyons said.

He would like to see more studies on other species, such as black terns, rails, bitterns, herons, soft-shelled turtles, mink, songbirds and a host of other refuge inhabitants.

At the same time, biologists should examine how siltation, bank erosion, boat traffic, pollutants, industrial use and other factors are permanently altering the river, he said.

"The qualitative, incremental, insidious changes that are taking place almost defy analysis," Lyons said.

Stravers hopes eagles may be a catalyst to stir more interest in protecting the river. He said concern over the bald eagle's decline helped bring a ban on some pesticides more than 20 years ago.

"They really are an important barometer of the environment," Stravers said.

Native Americans even viewed eagles as messengers from the Great Spirit, he noted.

"They've showed us some things before," Stravers said, "and they could be valuable indicators again."

June 5, 1994

A Mississippi rookery

River nurtures egrets, herons

NEW ALBIN, IA – Like greedy piglets, the gangling creatures chatter, squeal and grunt as they struggle for a prime spot in the nursery, awaiting the signal that it's meal time.

But the similarity to a farrowing house ends there, since these youngsters have two legs, feathers and a beak – and their nursery is 50 feet above the Mississippi River bottoms.

About 600 pairs of great blue herons and 200 pairs of common egrets nest together in the huge rookery north of here. The gregarious birds build as many as 20 nests per tree in some big elms, maples or cottonwoods — sometimes killing the trees with their foul-smelling excrement.

The nesting season begins in April when the birds return from wintering grounds in the southern U. S. and along the Gulf Coast. They build large, flat nests of sticks, or remodel last year's nest. Ornithologist A. C. Bent observed that old nests become more sturdy as "accumulated filth helps to cement the material together."

The adults share the incubation chores and keep constant guard to save the eggs from crows. Very young birds also need continuous protection from hawks, owls and crows.

The rookery is a din of activity, as adults on food-gathering missions come and go, feed the noisy youngsters and manipulate their 6-foot wing spans among the tree branches.

As the young grow older and stronger – nourished by regurgitated "fish chowder" furnished by their parents – they begin to exercise and explore their treetop surroundings.

This probably is the most critical time in the birds' lives, since one careless step, a nudge from a nest mate or a violent windstorm can plunge a flightless youngster to the ground. A bird might survive the fall, but it would surely die soon, since the parents will not feed their offspring on the ground.

Doug Mullen, Lansing district manager for the U. S. Fish and Wildlife Service's Upper Mississippi River Wildlife and Fish Refuge, said foxes and other predators patrol the rookery to "clean up" such unfortunate young birds.

The weather and food supply probably regulate the heron and egret numbers in the rookery, Mullen said. The breeding population there peaked at 1,000 pairs in 1973, but has remained stable at about 600 pairs of herons and 200 pairs of egrets from the past three seasons.

Mullen monitors the bird numbers by counting nests in winter and by sampling the number of young per nest during the breeding season.

The adult birds are hard to count, he said, since their feeding territories extend some distance up and down the river. The big birds spend most of their time hunting frogs, fish, salamanders or other small prey in marshy areas.

People most often see herons or egrets when the birds are traveling to and from these feeding areas, or stalking a meal in the shallows. A hunting heron may stand motionless for hours, waiting for just the right instant to spear the prey with its sharp beak.

Adults and young leave the rookery by mid-summer and seem to scatter out before starting a leisurely trip south.

Most have left Iowa by early November, but herons occasionally winter here when they can find open water.

154

Egret population became very low in the early 1900s after pressure from plume hunters decimated many rookeries.

In 1903, egret plumes were worth $32 an ounce, or twice as much as gold. One adult bird yielded one ounce of plumes. The plumes – which were used in decorating women's hats – were most desireable when taken from live birds in breeding plumage, so many egrets were shot on the nest, and the young left to die.

The egret population began a comeback after killing them was outlawed, and the white birds now are relatively common.

Mullen said nearly every pool in the Upper Mississippi River has some nesting herons and egrets – but the rookery above New Albin apparently is the largest. Herons also have nested near the Red Rock and Rathbun Reservoirs in south-central Iowa. The rookery at Rathbun has produced a number of young in recent years, but nesting failures have plagued the Red Rock birds.

Scientists believe their reproductive problems are related to high pesticide concentrations.

June 19, 1977

When it's cold, he rows the Mississippi for walleyes

GUTTENBERG, IA – Stroke, squeak. Stroke, squeak.

Tirelessly, Irvin "John" Muench's practiced shoulders worked the oars on his rock-scarred, 14-foot, army-green, aluminum johnboat.

No need for a motor – even if this was the mighty Mississippi River.

"I've done this oaring for years and years," said Muench, 69. "It's good exercise for me.

"I can control a boat better with oars than I can with a motor."

Deftly, he worked the boat through the swirling current downstream from Lock and Dam 10 at Guttenberg. Almost instinctively, he felt for just the right spot, then dropped a "sonar" over the side in search of a hungry walleye.

"Sometimes they'll be here and sometimes they'll be over there," said Muench, nodding across the channel. "You've got to try and hunt 'em out."

Muench knows where to hunt. He grew up along the Mississippi near Buffalo City, Wis., and has fished the river all his life. He has been a commercial fisherman, trapper and duck hunter. For more than 40 years, he worked for the U.S. Army Corps of Engineers. He retired in 1984 from the Lock and Dam 10 maintenance staff.

Even in retirement, Muench can't stay away from the river. He loves fishing – mostly for walleyes and sauger.

"I usually go out once or twice a week to sample it, if the weather's right," he said. "I like cold weather fishing."

He fishes most of the winter, through the early spring spawning run. His biggest walleye – a 12-pounder – came one blustery March, just as the ice was going out.

"But when it gets to be April 15, I quit," Muench said, "And I don't start again until November.

"It seems like you catch bigger ones in cold weather," he said.

How cold?

"If it's 10-below, I'll get out here if there's no wind," Muench said. "But if it's 20-below, I might wait until afternoon when it warms up to zero.

"I have been rowing around here in the ice chunks," he said with a chuckle.

He keeps his boat on shore, just downstream from the locks. If the water freezes too much to launch the boat, he may slide it across the frozen river like a sled, then fish through the ice.

Whether he's battling ice or enjoying last week's January thaw, Muench uses the same fishing technique. All he needs is his battered spin-casting rod and a small plastic box with a half-dozen "sonar" lures.

He fishes the flat, minnow-shaped, metal lure by jigging it near the bottom as he drifts in the eddies.

"Just let it down 'til it hits the bottom, then give it a little jerk," he instructed.

Muench doesn't worry about snags.

"I kind of know where they are," he said, gazing across the water as if he could see every stick and boulder hidden under it.

And even if he does catch a rock or sunken limb, he can almost always free his lure with a homemade hook retriever he slides down the line.

Muench has fishing down to a science, but there's still one variable: the fish.

156

"About as soon as you think you've got figured out what's happening, they prove you wrong," he said with a laugh.

On last week's outing, Muench and a companion caught plenty of small saugers – but no keepers. (The largest, naturally, was the one that got away – a five-pound walleye hooked and lost by a fumble-thumbed journalist.)

Unlike some Mississippi River anglers, Muench throws back any walleye or sauger that doesn't weigh at least a pound or a pound-and-a-quarter.

He catches enough larger fish to get plenty to eat, however.

"I'd just as soon eat them as center-cut pork chops," he said.

"I eat them three or four different ways," he said. Baked, pan-fried, deep-fried or dipped in batter, fresh walleyes just can't be beat, Muench said.

January 22, 1989

CHAPTER 12

SPECIAL SPOTS – "GEMS"

With most of its prairies and woodlands plowed, planted or pastured, Iowa has earned the unofficial title of the "most altered state."

Perhaps that's why we cling so jealously to those special spots that have remained relatively unspoiled, or to the unique natural treasures found nowhere else.

Viewed from the Missouri River bottoms, the Loess Hills feel and look like mountains. They're gentle, friendly slopes – not "real" mountains – but The Hills, with their unique soils, plants, vistas and people, are almost exclusively Iowa's.

Likewise, Hayden Prairie's May carpet of shooting stars recalls the beauty of the virgin, pre-settlement Iowa flatlands. The surprising "driftless area" of northeast Iowa, with its forest, cliffs, trout streams and colorful history, reminds us not to stereotype our mostly agricultural state.

Finally, lest we become too egocentric about our place in Iowa history, the mysteries of Effigy Mounds lay buried atop Mississippi bluffs that have lured generations of nature worshippers.

Getting a 'feel' for nature in the Loess Hills

CASTANA, IA – Sculptured by the ages, the Loess Hills march eastward from the Big Muddy. Here, 200 centuries ago, these giant drifts of flour-fine soil were born of wind-whipped glacial silt. Like snow behind a fence, they were dumped along the valley edge.

Bluestem, Indiangrass, blazing star, puccoon and a hundred other prairie plants gradually swallowed up those drifts, smoothed out the ridges and stabilized the erodable loess soil.

Bur oaks, sumac and other trees and shrubs sought moister valleys. And thus evolved an ecosystem unique on this planet.

"The Hills," as natives call them, have sheltered Indian tribes, grown bison forage and discouraged pioneer plowmen.

Iowa Heritage

What's more, they've preserved a part of Iowa's heritage – the native prairie – that has all but vanished in other, less forbidding terrains.

The hills and their prairies hosted a "beautiful festival" near here recently when 200 naturalists and educators convened the fifth annual Loess Hills Prairie Seminar at the Iowa Conservation Commission's 2,700-acre Loess Hills Wildlife Area.

The first seminar was the brain-child of Carolyn Benne, an environmental education consultant for the Western Hills (Sioux City) Area Education Agency. This year's conference, organized by her husband Larry, was a tribute to Benne, who died last year. Moreover, it was a tribute to the Loess Hills and a call for protection of their natural areas.

Flo Krall, a University of Utah associate professor of educational studies, traveled widely with Benne. She recalled Benne's ability to "always be excited" about her environment, and she urged other environmentalists to cultivate that "sense of wonder" that Benne exuded.

"Feeling" Environment

Krall told of Benne's fondness for the nature writings of Rachel Carson, who believed "it's more important to feel than to know." What better place than the Loess Hills to "feel" your environment? Krall asked.

Indeed, what a feeling! By the light of a waxing moon, we pitched our tents in a grassy valley and drifted off to sleep to the frantic warbles of a dozen dueling whip-poor-wills.

The next morning, we hiked the prairie ridges and bur oak slopes, drawn by that "feeling." Turkey vultures and red-tailed hawks soared overhead, while orioles, bobolinks, brown thrashers and mourning doves serenaded us.

We paused briefly where a prairie knob broke above the timbered valley, and each of us found a secluded spot to sit and think and to "feel."

I flopped on my back in the little bluestem, and stared up at last year's dry seed heads swaying in the breeze. This season's shoots were just poking their green blades from the litter. Spring comes late to the prairie.

When I drew a deep breath, I was startled at the richness of the scents: flowering oaks, musty dead prairie plants, warm soil, greening grass, a dainty puccoon, the hint of approaching showers.

What other dreamers had lain here, I wondered? How long have people marveled at these hills and their beauty?

159

Open Cathedral

When our group reassembled, one hiker remarked that he found himself speaking in a hushed voice, like he was in a cathedral.

Another expressed awe at the texture of a prairie dandelion, the design of a spider's burrow and the diversity of the hill country.

Despite the nearby interstate highway, campground and farms, the hills fostered a sense of "aloneness," one man observed.

To come here and sit is "like restoring your soul," sighed another.

Can we take this feeling back, someone asked? Can we communicate our emotions, our wonder about these magnificent hills, to those who might have the power to help save more of them for our grandchildren?

"We can take back the surface, but we can't take the depth," one hiker philosophized.

Imagination Takes Over

Later, as gray clouds churned across the horizon, we ascended again to the peaks of these Iowa mountains, and stood there leaning into the gale. It was easier, then, to imagine the ice-age storms churning up the great clouds of river-bottom dust that built these drift-hills.

Once again I stretched out at ground squirrel level and felt how the prairie grasses tamed the winds, sheltering the plants nearest the earth. A slender stalk of blue-eyed grass barely waved – while the big bluestem four feet above it quaked and thrashed.

The next day, the hills lured us once more to their summits – and once more we were alone. The rains had brought a somber, yet serene, mood to now-familiar ridges. The freshly washed bur oak leaves hunched their silvery backs against the wind, and distant bluffs floated in the mist.

Our thoughts returned to eulogies from Carolyn Benne's friends. In their tributes, they had renewed vows to assure, somehow, that her beloved Loess Hills would remain unspoiled.

"If you would see Carolyn's monuments, look about you," exhorted Des Moines naturalist Sylvan Runkel.

We looked, and we felt, and we wondered. And we saw the Loess Hills, as Benne had, as "one of the most beautiful places on Earth."

May 24, 1981

'Swiss bliss' in N.E. Iowa

DECORAH, IA – Call it "Little Switzerland," the "Driftless Area" or just "the hills" – northeast Iowa's rugged, rocky, forested terrain stands out in a state better known for its expanses of crop fields.

But the region is more than just a curiosity. And, despite the area's popularity with sightseers and outdoor recreationists, it's also more than just a tourist attraction.

The scenic area actually comprises a unique environment that shelters rare species, serves as a geological laboratory, yields archaeological treasures and boasts a diversity of plant and animal life found nowhere else in Iowa.

When the Iowa Academy of Science recently held a Driftless Area symposium at Luther College, speakers called for a better understanding of northeast Iowa and for efforts to preserve the natural character of the region.

Geologist George Hallberg, of the Iowa Geological Survey, said the term "Driftless Area," referring to a lack of glaciation, actually is incorrect, since glaciers did cover northeast Iowa prior to 500,000 years ago. Geologists prefer to call the region the "Paleozoic Plateau," citing domination of the landscape by Paleozoic bedrock more than 400 million years old.

Overlaying those ancient rocks are characteristic landforms, which really are quite young, Hallberg said. Most of the deeply cut valleys probably were formed within the last 30,000 years by water from melting glaciers north of Iowa, he noted.

Another feature of the Paleozoic Plateau is the presence of sinkholes, caves, and springs, which form in "karst" limestone topography. Water seeping through rock fractures may dissolve the limestone, forming caves. When caves collapse, sinkholes may appear. If the water reaches a layer of shale or other impervious rock, the trickle may be diverted to emerge from a hill as a spring.

If cold air sinks into crevasses in the winter, underground rocks may get cold enough to freeze spring meltwater, forming ice caves. Occasionally the ice may linger well into the summer.

Cold air seeping from north-facing ice caves may create a microclimate that hosts some of Iowa's rarest plants and animals, said state ecologist Dean Roosa. Certain cold air slopes may simulate an environment near a glacier, allowing the survival of ice age relicts or northern species.

The Iowa Pleistocene snail exists only on a handful of such slopes. The northern monkshood, a flower on the federal endangered species list, also grows on cold air slopes. Several other species are restricted to such sites.

Other plants and animals survive in northeast Iowa because of the region's forest cover, rocky streams and relative lack of intensive farming. The river otter and bobcat, rare anywhere in the state, still hang on in a few northeast hideaways. Pileated woodpeckers and ruffed grouse thrive in some woodlands.

Surprisingly, the Paleozoic Plateau even boasts some prairies. On dry ridges or slopes, small "goat prairies" cling to the rocks, with many species normally found on flatland, tallgrass prairies.

This diverse environment, with its rich natural and scenic resources, has attracted people to the Paleozoic Plateau for 12,000 years, said Luther College archaeologist Dr. R. Clark Mallam.

The earliest Indian artifacts date to 10,000 B.C., and native habitation continued until white settlement.

Even today, the region has a special lure for people. Anyone who fishes or canoes northeast Iowa streams, who harvests timber in the forests or who builds a home or flies a hang glider on the hilltops, is capitalizing on the resources of the Paleozoic Plateau.

But too few people recognize what a "gem" this region is, Roosa said. While the area is rugged, it's also fragile, he noted. Improper land use could destroy its unique blend of forests, streams and natural areas, he warned.

Roosa challenged naturalists to lead an effort to protect large forest tracts, cold air slopes, archaeological sites, special geological formations and river systems in northeast Iowa.

But Roosa stressed that the preservation plan need not emphasize land purchases. In fact, private ownership might provide better protection, he said.

"The best possible conservation is caring people on the land," Roosa said.

He suggested that private and public conservation groups, coordinated by the Iowa Conservation Commission, begin planning preservation strategies.

Guided by the plan, conservationists could use easements, preserve dedication, natural area registry, acquisition or other techniques to ensure preservation of the best features of the Paleozoic Plateau, Roosa said.

"We have a great moral responsibility to protect what we have remaining in this part of the state," Roosa said. "We must be guardians of this treasure."

May 1, 1983

Northeast Iowa's 'Mines of Spain' steeped in history

DUBUQUE, IA – Perched on the hills south of Dubuque, overlooking Catfish Creek and the Mississippi River, lies a 2,000-acre tract of woods and prairie ridges that is steeped in the history of both Native Americans and Iowa's first settlers.

As a natural and historical site, the area is unique in Iowa, the Midwest and perhaps even the nation.

The loosely defined area is known locally as the "Mines of Spain" site, after a 200 square-mile land grant given by the Spanish government to Julien Dubuque in 1796. The pioneer Iowan and founder of the city of Dubuque acquired the tract, roughly where the present city sits, mainly for lead mining.

Civilization has gradually obscured visible evidence of much of the original Mines of Spain tract, but rugged terrain and benevolent landowners have spared several square miles from development. Conservationists and historians, led by the Iowa Natural Heritage Foundation, have launched a major effort to preserve the land as an historic site and natural area.

Archaeologists are enthralled with the plan, because of the site's rich history of Indian cultures, pioneer settlements and lead mining. There are numerous archaeological sites on the property.

Naturalists are equally excited because of the area's splendid biological communities. Several rare plants and animals have survived here.

The cultural history of the site dates back to at least 5,000 B.C., when Indians built burial mounds on the bluffs. Anthropologists believe the region has been inhabited more or less continuously since then.

Indians discovered and mined lead in the area for years before Julien Dubuque persuaded the Spaniards to grant him the prime lead mining lands. There are remains of an Indian lead smelter near Dubuque, and stories persist that George Washington's soldiers used Dubuque's lead shot in the Revolutionary War.

The natural communities of the Mines of Spain area have changed since Julien Dubuque's day – but that's part of its appeal to biologists.

State ecologist Dean Roosa said the site is a "wonderful interpretive area," showing the natural evolution of woodland and prairie communities. Trees have taken over a number of former hill prairies in the area, he said, while other prairie remnants persist as evidence of the sequential process.

Other trees on the site are more than 200 years old, Roosa said. Some of the largest white oaks in the state are found here. Huge red oak, white birch, black cherry and walnut trees also grow in fertile ravines. Some walnut trees were cut in the 1950s, but there has been no other apparent logging since the 1800s. Grazing also has been minimal.

Roosa said the oak forests on the site "are perhaps the most classic remaining in Iowa." Foresters are intrigued by their unusual tendency to perpetuate themselves, rather than evolve into a maple-basswood community.

The unspoiled forest ecosystem hosts rich growths of mosses and ferns, including several rare and unusual species.

Wildlife also thrives on the site, Roosa said. The plot along the Mississippi River and Catfish Creek has vitally important winter roosting spots for bald eagles. Red-shouldered hawks, an endangered species in Iowa, also may nest there.

River otters, a threatened species in Iowa, also inhabit Catfish Creek and other streams on the property. Deer, raccoons and other woodland wildlife species are abundant.

The combination of wildlife, plant life and historical values of the Mines of Spain site make the property "perhaps the most significant tract in Iowa," Roosa said.

But he voiced concern over past damage to the site by off-road vehicles, and potential encroachments from housing developments or industry.

Other officials share the assessment that the Mines of Spain area should be preserved. The U.S. Fish and Wildlife Service and the Iowa Conservation Commission have studied the project, but neither could tackle the $2-3 million acquisition.

Dubuque County has recognized the significance of the region with its 600-acre Swiss Valley Park, while the city owns a nearby park, the E.B. Lyons Nature Center and the Julien Dubuque Monument.

If the Natural Heritage Foundation, a non-profit organization, can acquire the Mines of Spain area, the group probably will transfer management of the land to an appropriate government agency, said foundation spokesman Mark Ackelson.

Whatever the mechanics of preserving the site, there's little disagreement that the Mines of Spain region should be saved as an irreplaceable part of Iowa's natural heritage.

"It's a precious gem," Roosa declared. "I think it's so priceless we shouldn't even consider the option of not, somehow, protecting it."

June 29, 1980

Massive monuments to Iowa's ancient past

MARQUETTE, IA – Hiking the wooded bluffs that tower above the Mississippi, with soaring eagles overhead and rugged limestone underfoot, a 20th-century visitor can "walk right back into the past."

More than a thousand years of history are laid out there along the path where, with a little imagination, you can take wing with a mystical bird rising from the ridge, or march with a symbolic bear whose form is one with the earth.

Early surveys documented 374 effigy mounds in northeast Iowa, along with more than 1,000 simpler mounds. Most have been destroyed by farming or development, however.

Of the effigies, only 48 remain, many preserved at Effigy Mounds National Monument, Pikes Peak State Park and a few other sites where archaeologists and amateur historians can still marvel at earthen forms of birds, bears and other creatures – and at the culture that shaped them.

R. Clark Mallam of Decorah, director of the Luther College Archaeological Research Center, has counted, measured, photographed, puzzled over and hypothesized about effigy mounds for more than 15 years.

From his scientific research have emerged some admittedly not-so-scientific theories on the mounds and their builders. Despite "quite a bit" of criticism from some other archaeologists, Mallam freely speculates about the feelings and philosophies of the ancient people whose culture he's studying.

"Archaeology is an inventive process," he said. "It's not so much science but a literary achievement."

That said, Mallam shares his controversial – yet plausible – ideas on what may have motivated the mound builders.

Foremost, Mallam believes, the Native Americans did not think of themselves as "building" mounds, but as releasing a form that was inherent in the environment.

That revelation struck Mallam dramatically last fall when he was working near Marquette on a project to outline a bird mound with lime to make it visible for aerial photography. As he stood on the bluff, Mallam gradually saw the whole ridge take the shape of a giant bird. And the bird effigy was perched on the very crest of the bird-like hill.

"This was one of the most exciting things I've ever encountered in northeast Iowa," Mallam said with delight. It seemed obvious that the Indians had built the mound, and probably other effigies, in a ritual to emphasize their ties to the Mother Earth.

"When you build a mound, you're recreating the act of creation which establishes order in the world," Mallam said.

That close relationship to the earth was of utmost importance to the Native Americans – as it should be to modern man, Mallam said. As hunters and gatherers, the Woodland Indians of the mound-building period, from about 600 to 1,300 A.D., were highly dependent on their environment for their survival.

Their mound building, Mallam said, may have been a "world renewal ritual, a sacred activity humans entered into in order to ensure regular and consistent production of natural resources." The ritual – the arduous process of clearing the shape, hauling in tons of dirt and piling the soil in forms that might be more than 100 feet long and several feet high – no doubt was more significant to the Indians than their finished product, Mallam suggested.

With mounds, the early Iowans were attempting to "symbolize their relationships to the forces of life," said Mallam. "By the action of building the mounds, they were seeking to atone for the injury they caused to the environment."

That contrasts with former theories that the mounds were primarily for burials, or with other mound systems that archaeologists think were built to define social structures.

Northeast Iowa's mounds may be unique, Mallam said, because Native Americans came to think of the area as "sacred space." The so-called "Driftless Area," where eastern forest and western grassland meet in a rugged, stream-laced terrain, is especially rich in wildlife and other natural resources – a most productive region for people living off the land.

The mounds, Mallam said, embodied that close man-nature relationship.

He pondered that theory while sitting on a ridge not far from a bird effigy, admiring a pair of bald eagles wheeling on the thermals. He gazed out over Bloody Run Creek, frowning at the thought of a planned road in the valley.

He contrasted modern man's treatment of his environment with the stewardship of the Indians. "We make a decision before we reflect on the long-term impact," he said.

When native Americans killed an animal or harvested a plant, Mallam noted, they asked forgiveness of the essence of that object, hoping for its renewal.

"What do we do?" Mallam asked wryly. "We have an environmental impact statement!"

To lessen that clash between old and new, Mallam often carries a pouch of tobacco or pipestone dust to sprinkle about when he visits mound sites.

It's a token of respect for the "incredible heritage" of mound builders, he said. "And it's something you do for yourself to make you feel in tune."

The only better way to feel in tune, Mallam reflected, might be to hike to a remote effigy, "and lie in the armpit of a bear for awhile."

April 29, 1984

166

Hayden Prairie – Living history of grassroots Iowa

SARATOGA, IA – Not so long ago, in Earth time, June mornings rolled across pastel seas of shooting stars and puccoons and prairie phlox. In this stretched-out, glacier-scraped country people now call "Iowa," the prairie was king.

Frank Watson of Saratoga can almost remember that time. When he was born 77 years ago, Howard County still had many tracts of virgin prairie. He's watched the last bits of that prairie slip beneath the plow. He's seen corn and soybeans spring up where bluestem and coneflowers and compass plants once thrived in the rich loam.

Watson, too, once farmed that fertile prairie soil, so he knows first-hand that it's the richest ground on Earth. But, unlike some 1980s farmers, he also knew and loved the prairie that has made Iowa agriculture so bountiful.

Watson still loves the prairie – especially the prairie wildflowers. Every Sunday, throughout the growing season, he takes a stroll on Hayden Prairie State Preserve, near here, to see what's blooming. And he's never disappointed.

"There are many changes in a season," he said.

In April, he may find a few pasque flowers nestled next to the sod, their pale, lavender-streaked petals beckoning to the first spring insects.

By late May, the shooting stars, or nightcaps, have carpeted parts of the prairie. In years when biologists have burned the prairie to invigorate it, the pointed blossoms carpet acres of the preserve.

Yellow puccoons, or painters, join the Memorial Day floral show, along with yellow star grass and creamy vetch blossoms. Tiny prairie phlox flowers add patches of brilliant pink. With luck, Watson may find lady slipper orchids in early June.

As the summer progresses, the display changes constantly. Purple coneflowers sway in July breezes. Several kinds of sunflowers paint the prairie with summer gold.

Occasional compass plants bloom in August. Watson recalls chewing the plant's sticky resin, much as modern youngsters chew gum.

By September, the prairie grasses dominate the scene. Pioneers exaggerated only a trifle when they told of how the grasses grew tall enough to hide a horse and rider.

As the grasses ripen in the fall, the prairie takes on more subtle hues once again. The waving grasses glow with russets and browns and soft golds in the October sun.

When he hikes Hayden Prairie, where 240 acres have never felt the plow, Watson can imagine what much of Iowa looked like when his grandparents came here in a covered wagon 100 years ago. Out there, where the century-old wagon track still winds across the unbroken sod, Watson likes to tell the story of how his grandmother scalded a prairie rattlesnake with her boiling wash water.

The rattlers are long gone, but the story lives – part of Watson's prairie heritage.

He's also linked to Hayden Prairie by recollections of his father-in-law's haying operation here before the state bought the tract in 1946. The land was left unplowed, when other fields were tilled, because it was used for hay.

Watson sits on another piece of heritage: a boulder dumped by the glacier that molded the rolling plain 10,000 years ago. He admires the texture of the rock, and remarks at the multicolored lichens that are ever-so-slowly turning it to sand.

The bobolinks also appreciate the heritage. Where else could they find grasslands suited to their busy chattering and fluttering and soaring?

"Friendly little fellows," Watson chuckles at the noisy birds.

Watson pauses to study some blossoms, etching the image in his mind. He disdains the camera on his flower hikes, preferring to "remember them just as I see them."

As Watson wanders through the pages of this living history book, a huge tractor roars by on an adjacent road. Watson imagines that the farmer on it covets that virgin sod, seeing only a potential cornfield.

"For heaven's sake, leave it alone!" he counters a joking suggestion that the prairie COULD grow a lot of corn.

"We've made enough of a mess of the country as it is," he continues. "If we plow it up, it'll just wash away."

He turns once more to gaze at the shooting stars.

"Let's leave this as it is."

June 7, 1981

Sylvan T. Runkel   © Des Moines Register

CHAPTER 13

PEOPLE

The story of Iowa's natural heritage is best told by our people.

An understanding game warden teaches respect for the outdoors. A couple dedicates their lives to conservation education. Photography brings an ex-hunter closer to wildlife. A soft-spoken forester exemplifies citizenship in the natural community.

Wildlife professionals learn from a clever amateur researcher. An Iowa-born outdoorsman becomes the father of modern conservation. A western Iowa family uses their farm heritage to introduce others to the magic of the Loess Hills.

These selfless Iowans, and many others so dedicated to conservation, hold the vision of the future.

He loved things 'natural, wild and free'

"Like winds and sunsets, wild things were taken for granted until progress began to do away with them. Now we face the question whether a still higher 'standard of living' is worth its cost in things natural, wild and free. For us of the minority, the opportunity to see geese is more important than television and the chance to find a pasque flower is a right as inalienable as free speech."

– From "A Sand County Almanac" by Aldo Leopold

BURLINGTON, IA – If the environmental movement has a Bible, it is "A Sand County Almanac." And if there is a high priest of ecology, he surely was Aldo Leopold.

With his delightful little book of nature essays and conservation philosophies, the Burlington native probably did more than any other one person to introduce "land ethics" to Americans.

"Conservation is a state of harmony between man and the land,'" Leopold preached. "Harmony with the land is like harmony with a friend; you cannot cherish his right hand and chop off his left."

Leopold died in 1948, but he is well-remembered here. A documentary, "A Prophet for All Seasons: Aldo Leopold," was shown on the Iowa Public Broadcasting Network recently, and the Iowa Humanities Board and several Burlington civic groups are sponsoring activities in honor of Leopold through the rest of this month.

Eco-guru Role

But if Leopold were alive today, he might chuckle at his role of eco-guru for the environmentalism that swept the country in the 1970s. He was a scientist and a teacher more than an activist. And his "Almanac" reads more like a country philosopher's musings than the harangues of a zealot.

"Our children are our signature to the roster of history," Leopold reflected, "our land is merely the place our money was made. There is as yet no social stigma in the possession of a gullied farm, a wrecked forest or a polluted stream, provided the dividends suffice to send the youngsters to college. Whatever ails the land, the government will fix it."

Leopold's love of "things natural wild and free" began on his family's acreage overlooking the Mississippi River, where he was born in 1887. The site was developed in the 1870s by Leopold's grandfather, Charles Starker, a prominent landscape architect and businessman. Leopold's brother, Frederic, and sister, Marie Lord, still live in century-old homes there.

Outdoor Family

The Leopold family is proud of its long tradition as nature lovers. Leopold's father, Carl, and grandfather Starker were outdoorsmen, and Frederic has been acclaimed for his 40 years of amateur research on wood duck nesting. Aldo Leopold's five children all chose science- or nature-related careers. A grandnephew, James Spring, of Burlington, is an accomplished wildlife artist.

The Leopolds saw no conflict in their appreciation for nature and their passion for hunting.

They were proud to be sportsmen, reveling as much in the interaction with the game and their surroundings as with the kill. Aldo's "congenital hunting fever" pervades some of his most powerful essays.

As a youth, Aldo grew so fond of the outdoors that he forsook a chance to enter the family's successful furniture business, choosing instead to become a forester. He earned a master's degree in forestry from Yale University in 1909.

His first job, with the U.S. Forest Service, took him to the wilds of Arizona Territory's Apache National Forest.

For 15 years, he lived in the Southwest, studying and learning from the rugged country, organizing fellow sportsmen into conservation clubs and formulating wilderness philosophies.

Early in his career, Leopold began to make his mark in the conservation movement. He argued so persuasively for wilderness that the Forest Service in 1924 established New Mexico's Gila Wilderness – the first such area in the country.

In his enthusiasm for the region and its wildlife, Leopold campaigned for stricter enforcement of game laws and, initially, for predator control. But he gradually came to understand that predators, too, were an important part of the land "organism."

"Only the mountain has lived long enough to listen objectively to the howl of the wolf," the former wolf-slayer later conceded.

When Leopold returned to the Midwest in 1924, he brought an undying love of wilderness "in all degrees, from the little accidental wild spot at the head of a ravine in a Corn Belt woodlot to vast expanses of virgin country." He later helped found The Wilderness Society.

Leopold didn't last long in his new assignment with the Forest Service's Forest Products Laboratory in Madison, Wis. The emphasis on forest products, rather than on the integrity of the forest community, was foreign to him. In 1929, he took a job with the Sporting Arms and Ammunition Manufacturers Institute to do a wildlife survey in nine Midwestern states, including Iowa.

Classic Text

From those exhaustive studies came "Game Management," a 1933 text that still is a classic in the wildlife management field.

The University of Wisconsin later created the position of professor of wildlife management for Leopold, and he began a teaching career that lasted until his death.

His students affectionately knew Leopold as "The Professor," and they were captivated by his boundless energy and enthusiasm.

Clay Schoenfield, a joint professor of wildlife ecology and journalism at the University of Wisconsin, recalls inspiring field trips with Leopold. "It is a revelation to walk in the open with the professor," he said. "Every grass blade is a challenge, every bird a question."

Moonshiner

About the time he entered teaching, Leopold also acquired the Wisconsin farm that became the setting for the "Almanac." The land had been abused by previous owners and finally turned back to the government by a moonshiner who left without paying his taxes.

The plot became a family retreat, as well as a living laboratory where Leopold set out to prove it was possible to live on the land without destroying it. The Leopolds planted thousands of pines on their farm and Aldo apparently never tired of the task.

"I only know that a good file, wielded vigorously, makes my shovel sing as it slices the mellow loam," he said. "[The music] hums in my wrist as I plant a pine."

Leopold's observations from his sand farm immortalized the "sky dance" of the woodcock, the "goose music" of spring and the "smoky gold" of October tamaracks. "A Sand County Almanac" and other Leopold essays prick the imagination as much today as they did when they were penned four decades ago.

And his ecological philosophies are guideposts for generations of fellow land lovers: "We abuse land because we regard it as a commodity belonging to us. When we see land as a community to which we belong, we may begin to use it with love and respect."

April 22, 1980

Mr. Wood Duck nurses brood

BURLINGTON, IA – Frederic Leopold doesn't look like a nursemaid, but the amateur naturalist probably has watched over more baby wood ducks than anyone else in the country.

About 100 young woodies per year have hatched in the 22 nesting boxes in his yard overlooking the Mississippi River since Leopold began his hobby about 30 years ago.

He's kept up the boxes ever since – even though it means the 78-year-old must climb up and down a ladder about 700 times a year to check the feathered inhabitants. He keeps careful notes on each nest, and has filled several notebooks with his voluminous notes.

"As a result," Leopold said, "I've found out a lot of things that the full time professionals haven't found out."

Leopold began experimenting with nesting boxes for woodies in the late 1930's, under the guidance of a student of his brother Aldo, who was one of the country's leading conservationists.

Fred rapidly gained fame for his work and became known as "Mr. Wood Duck" to Burlington residents.

Largely because of his influence, many other Burlington residents have put up wood duck boxes, and the Des Moines County Conservation Board annually makes and distributes boxes.

Leopold estimates that more than 1,000 wood duck boxes now adorn trees in and around the town.

Leopold built most of his boxes from rough hewn cypress – and several of the original boxes are still intact and sheltering wood duck families.

The boxes are a foot square and two feet high, with an oval hole three inches high and four inches wide near the top. The top is removable to permit cleaning and inspecting the nest.

On some of the boxes, Leopold made a series of sawcuts under the hole on the inside to serve as a "ladder" for the ducklings to climb out.

The activity in the boxes begins in late March, when pairs of wood ducks come to Leopold's yard to choose a nest site.

After several days of exploring, they finally pick a box, and the female lays one egg a day for 12 to 14 days. She then incubates the eggs, for 30 days.

Leopold inspects the nest frequently to check the duck's progress, but the really entertaining part comes the day after the ducklings hatch.

In their second day of life outside the egg, the ducklings – with their mother's coaxing – climb the inside of the box home and leap 20 feet or more to the ground below.

The hen then leads her youngsters over the 120-foot bluff and across a set of railroad tracks to the river. If there is not adequate cover on the near side of the river, Leopold said, the duck may lead her family across half a mile of open water to the opposite shore.

Leopold tried to predict when might be a good time to wait in a blind to witness the "coming out," but he wouldn't guarantee when the big event would take place.

"You can't think just like a duck," he laughed.

We entered the canvas blind shortly after 6 a.m., and then waited nearly two hours before the hen emerged to look for danger. Apparently she wasn't satisfied, because she returned to the nest for another two hours before she came out again and called her babies to join her.

The fuzzy, yellow balls soon began to appear at the box hole one by one, where they perched and peeped for a few seconds before leaping to the ground.

The mother did not join her youngsters immediately – probably because a curious neighbor was watching from a nearby window. But we resisted the temptation to pick up the bewildered ducklings.

"That's the nearest thing to a death warrant that you can give them," Leopold said.

Instead, we retreated to the house for a few minutes. When we returned, we caught a glimpse of the reunited family scampering through the bushes to the river.

When separated from her young, all the mother wood duck usually needs is to be left alone to have time to get the family together again, Leopold said.

We drove to the railroad tracks at the foot of the bluff, then watched from the bushes as the family crossed the tracks, then reached the river. We received an added treat when another hen and her brood appeared almost simultaneously.

The two families entered the river about the same time, and the water came alive as two dozen ducklings swam along the flooded trees to follow their mothers to cover.

Leopold breathed a sigh of relief as he watched "his babies" swim away.

"I get kind of a kick out of it – even after having done it so many times."

June 3, 1973

Friend of nature, friend of man

STRAWBERRY POINT, IA – When kids take a nature hike with Sylvan T. Runkel of Des Moines, they get more than just exercise.

For 40 years, Runkel has taught young Iowans to have fun in the woods.

If they enjoy the natural world, they'll feel at home there, Runkel figures. And if their environment feels like home, they'll want to protect it.

Runkel, 84, began interpreting nature at teachers' conservation camps about 1950. He has since led thousands of hikes with countless teachers and students.

A gentle man with a walking stick, battered ranger hat and stiff-kneed limp, Runkel has charmed a generation of naturalists.

A Remarkable Person

Duane Toomsen, environmental education consultant for the Iowa Department of Education, praised Runkel's sincerity, determination, enthusiasm and love of the outdoors.

"He's a remarkable person," Toomsen said. "He's done so much."

But Runkel's deeds aren't the kind that draw headlines. He doesn't move mountains – he merely motivates kids.

He recently roamed with sixth-graders from Dubuque's Kennedy School, during the students' three-day stay at Camp Ewalu near Strawberry Point.

"When the first people came here, they saw a beautiful community in good condition," Runkel told the restless 12-year-olds. "What we're going to do today is meet some of the citizens out here."

Captures Attention

Citizens? Community? BORING!

The kids didn't have to say it. The looks on their faces revealed their thoughts.

But Runkel's yarns about some very unordinary "citizens" soon captured the youths' attention.

They were amused by one of the contributions birds make to the natural community. Seeds in bird droppings mean new crops of wild cherries, gooseberries and blackberries.

A limestone cliff isn't just a chunk of rock, Runkel pointed out. It's evidence that Iowa once was at the bottom of an ocean.

Beside a basswood tree, Runkel told how the wood is used by beekeepers because it doesn't taint the honey. He described the tree's tough inner bark, used by native Americans as cord and for basket making. This "bast" gave the tree its name.

You can't judge nature on first impressions, Runkel said, pausing near a foul-smelling carrion flower that will produce edible berries.

"It starts out with a flower smelling like a dead rat, but it ends up with something good to eat," he said.

Runkel cautioned students to beware of stinging nettles. He explained how the plant's stiff hairs act as tiny hypodermic needles to inject an irritant into the skin of careless hikers. And, to a chorus of "yuck," he praised the spinach-like taste of cooked nettles.

When someone snagged a sleeve on a prickly ash, Runkel defended the thorny brush as habitat for swallowtail butterflies.

Recycling

An oak tree triggered a tale of how squirrels plant acorns, hunters shoot squirrels and unfound nuts grow into more trees.

A fungus on a rotting log prompted a talk on recycling. A natural community returns all its components to the system, Runkel said. When one organism dies, another grows.

"This natural community gets better as it gets older," he said. "What this tells us is if we want to have a community that gets better, we need to recycle everything we use."

Runkel also teased his charges.

"Rattlesnake!" he yelled, spying a rattlesnake fern along the trail. The kids just giggled.

He plucked a burdock seed, then stuck it on a boy's shirt. As the surprised youth pulled the bristly ball loose, Runkel grinned and talked about how animals carry seeds.

The hour-long hike covered only a couple of hundred yards – partly because Runkel found so much to talk about and partly because he doesn't get around as well as he used to.

"I've been in the woods a long time – some people say too long," Runkel said with a chuckle. "I'm an old forester."

Colorful Career

Runkel's career is as colorful as it is long. His mother was born in a log cabin near Jacksonville, Ill. He still has the muzzleloading Kentucky rifle owned by his great-grandfather in 1850.

As a youth, Runkel worked with clammers on the Mississippi River and on a cargo ship that sailed from San Francisco to New York through the Panama Canal. He hitch-hiked and rode freight trains across the country, looking for jobs fighting forest fires.

Before graduating from the Iowa State College School of Forestry in 1930, he was a fire lookout in national forests in Oregon, California and Montana. He later became an extension forester.

In 1933, Runkel headed Iowa's first Civilian Conservation Corps camp at Albia. He still proudly wears the ranger hat that came with the job.

Runkel became a glider pilot in World War II. But wounds from a D-day crash near Normandy, France, and an attack by a German patrol left him with a useless knee joint.

Despite the injury, Runkel worked for the U.S. Soil Conservation Service until 1972. He was a forester and biologist, always promoting natural areas and education.

Also an Author

Runkel also has backpacked in several wilderness areas and led dozens of nature hikes and Boy Scout outings – bum leg and all.

"I walk so far and then say 'What do you know; here's a flower,'" Runkel joked. "Then everybody stops and I rest while I'm talking about the flower."

And when Runkel talks about flowers, people listen. He co-authored "Wildflowers of Iowa Woodlands" and "Wildflowers of the Tallgrass Prairie." Runkel and State Ecologist Dean Roosa now are writing a book on wetland wildflowers.

Always, citizenship is the theme.

"Maybe these natural communities are doing something we ought to know about to do a better job in our people communities," Runkel said.

June 21, 1991

Rural Turin couple share love for adventure, outdoor activities

TURIN, IA – Thirty years ago, when Don and Luella Reese packed their four young children in the old Kaiser automobile and headed west on a camping trip, they were following a family tradition.

The wanderlust carried back to Reese's parents, who spent three months in 1915 roaming the western U.S. in a 1909 Jackson automobile and living in a one-pole canvas tent. Reese was born the next spring – and went on his first camp-out just a little more than a year later.

That pioneer spirit may have been passed down from Reese's grandfather, who came west to Iowa from Ohio in 1855, bringing his 16-year-old bride and two sons to homestead on the frontier.

In some ways, the Reeses still are pioneers.

Reese, 69, a retired farmer and rural mail carrier, and his wife, Luella, 68, live on the farm that Reese's father settled 130 years ago. The original house, now occupied by a tenant, still stands. The Reeses live nearby in a rustic home built around the frame of a cattle feeder. The cozy rooms are jammed with striking clocks, pipes, books, maps, wooden furniture and camping gear.

Love Exploring

Never tired of exploring, the Reeses camped extensively with their four children in the 1950s and '60s – often in that same, one-pole tent Reese's parents had used. They began backpacking in 1969 after a stranger in California's Lassen National Park loaned them some gear.

Now the Reeses plan a backpacking trip nearly every summer. This year they're headed for Wyoming's Bridger Wilderness, undaunted by the slight stroke Luella suffered late last year. The ailment hasn't slowed her noticeably.

The couple also biked across Iowa on four consecutive RAGBRAI trips in the 1970s.

But when the Reeses return from their travels, they come home to a site that's unique. Behind their shady yard loom the Loess Hills – those towering 14,000-year-old drifts of wind-blown soil found only on the eastern slope of the Missouri River Valley.

The Reeses now are active in efforts to protect the hills for their natural qualities – but Reese admits that's a relatively new attitude.

"I lived in the Loess Hills for 50 years before I knew it," he said. "They were always just kind of a barrier to climb over to go get the cows.

"I used to lie awake nights trying to figure how to get the loess soil down on the bottoms where we could farm it," he said.

He Scoffed

Only a decade ago, Reese confessed, he scoffed when environmentalists asked how the Loess Hills could be protected.

"I laughed at them," he said. "'You don't need to do anything,' I said. 'They're rugged enough to take care of themselves.'"

"But I was wrong," he laments. Now the Reeses worry about soil erosion, land clearing schemes and housing developments marring the hills.

Reese admits he was "never much of an organization man," but he's become chairman of the

Monona County Soil Conservation Task Force, a volunteer group that promotes soil conservation. His wife is a former secretary to the Monona County Soil Conservation District Commissioners.

The Reeses also have been active in the Sierra Club. Reese has served on the club's state executive committee and as state outings chairman, and his wife is a former state treasurer of the organization.

Behind-the-Scenes Force

The couple also is a behind-the-scenes force in the popular Loess Hills Prairie Seminar, a naturalists' workshop held annually at the state-owned Loess Hills Wildlife Area near Turin. The Reeses became involved when they met the seminar's founder, the late Carolyn Benne of Sioux City, in 1977.

At this year's seminar, the Reeses received an award for their conservation efforts.

"It's a little embarrassing," Reese confided later. "We get credit for a lot of things that other unheralded people have done."

Luella Reese suggested the recognition came because "we're fixtures."

"We get to a lot of [conservation meetings]," Reese said. "We show up."

Indeed, the Reeses are familiar faces at environmental events in the Loess Hills and elsewhere. Reese's slight build and short stature can't hide him. His goatee, walking stick, pipe and green-visored cap distinguish him in a crowd.

Not Afraid to Act

But the Reeses aren't afraid to act, either. In 1982, they spoke against a controversial plan to improve a road through the Loess Hills Wildlife Area. That project later was shelved by the Monona County Board of Supervisors.

Reese also frequently voices his opinion in letters to the editor. Readers of The Des Moines Register may recognize him as one of the most prolific contributors. His brief, sharp-witted essays on politics and conservation have appeared 48 times since 1951.

In a tribute at the Loess Hills Seminar recently, Sylvan Runkel of Des Moines, the Reeses' long-time friend and hiking companion, called the couple "dedicated conservationists who love and respect people. They're making a difference about how people look at their natural environment."

Reese responded with typical modesty – and humor.

"I would *like* to believe all the nice things [Runkel] had to say about us," he said. "And since I'd *like* to, I guess I *will* . . . but the rest of you certainly don't have to."

June 9, 1985

Iowa outdoorsman shoots his prey with camera

HALSEY, NEB – As a hunter, Roger Hill was one of the best.

For 20 years, he traveled most of North America, stalking brown bears in Alaska, moose in the Yukon, coyotes in Kansas, pronghorns in Wyoming, Stone sheep in British Columbia and deer in several states.

He worked at the sport, and never failed to bag the species he was after.

"But once you accomplish what you want, you look for something else," Hill said.

That "something else" turned out to be wildlife photography.

Hill always had taken a camera on his hunting trips, and he compiled slide shows of camps, scenery and hunters with their game. Eventually, he decided it was more of a challenge to get good photographs than to kill a trophy.

He sold two big game rifles, two handguns and a spotting scope, and used the money to buy camera gear.

Since that day almost 10 years ago, Hill has shot thousands of animals – on film. He's seen dozens of his photos published, and has given away scores of others to conservation groups.

Photography has become an obsession.

"I photograph seven days a week," said Hill, 46, who lives on an acreage near Roland. "There are spells when I don't miss one day in six weeks."

He's out with a camera at daylight, before reporting to his job as a materials shipper at 3-M in Ames, where he has worked since 1971. In the evening, Hill roams the Skunk River Green Belt, prowls fencerows and woodlots or sits in a blind waiting for foxes or pheasants.

A favorite photo site is the family farm near McCallsburg where Hill and his brothers, Jerry and Randy, who also are accomplished photographers, have developed several wildlife areas. Hill's father, Walt, began the conservation effort more than 30 years ago.

The only thing that interrupts Hill's photography is darkness. When the light is gone, he retreats indoors to sort slides, to prepare photos to send to publishers or to plan slide talks for service clubs, youth groups, conservation organizations or schools.

On the weekend, Hill may drive all night to reach a new photo haven. Earlier this month, he left Roland about 7 p.m. for an eight-hour drive to west-central Nebraska, arriving in time to erect a blind and photograph sharp-tailed grouse on their mating grounds at dawn.

Each September or October, for the past 19 years, Hill has spent part of his vacation in Yellowstone National Park, photographing animals.

On trips, he usually drives all night, munching on Frosted Mini-Wheats, drinking Mountain Dew and listening to music on the headphones of a portable cassette player.

While at his destination, the rugged, 6-foot 6-inch Hill rests on a foam pad in the back of his Nissan pickup. He slept 31 nights in the truck last year to avoid losing precious photography time driving to motels.

During the mid-day lull, when the light is too harsh for good pictures, Hill often scouts for new areas or scenic vistas.

"It never hurts to snoop," he said. He's perpetually searching for better backgrounds, interesting animals or people with advice on where to find wildlife. Hill thinks nothing of marching up a sand dune – or a mountain – carrying a photo blind, a tripod-mounted camera and 600 millimeter lens and assorted other gear.

Photography may be a hobby, he said, but that doesn't mean it's easy.

"Any time you want good pictures, you've got to work at them," he said.

Hill disdains "set-ups" – pictures of tame animals shot in a wild setting. Instead, he relies on persistence and his knowledge of wildlife to photograph free-roaming creatures. He's learned to anticipate how certain animals behave.

"Patience is the main thing," he said. "If you wait, something else always happens.

"I never give up until I'm out of light."

That determination pays off. Last year, Hill's photos were printed on the covers of three national magazines – "Rocky Mountain Game and Fish," "The Wild Sheep" and "Deer and Big Game Hunting Annual" – in one month.

But Hill isn't about to rest on his laurels. He never tires of searching for new images. After photographing 49 different grizzly bears, he can't wait for No. 50. With pictures of 100 different Iowa white-tail bucks in 1989, he's eager to beat that record this year.

"Every one is a different challenge," Hill said. The light, pose or behavior of each animal is unique. A photographer always has a new angle to try."

April 29, 1990

A rich life as 'keeper of outdoors'

Harvey's 40-year career as a game warden had risks and rewards

MARSHALLTOWN, IA – He was a cowboy, ironworker, restaurateur, spy, timber buyer, newspaper columnist and – when he had to be – a tough cop. But most of all, Walter L. Harvey figures he was a public relations man.

Harvey, 89, was an Iowa game warden from 1933 to 1973.

Sure, he made arrests and confronted criminals, Harvey said.

"But my philosophy was to prevent a violation whenever I can," he said. "You don't scare people very much by arresting them."

After filing his job application on a penny postcard, Harvey learned his trade on the job.

Learned From Experience

As a rookie, he almost caused a riot when he accosted commercial fishermen near Keokuk. He decided to try another approach.

"If we could talk to somebody and show them a different way . . . " he said.

Harvey eventually became one of the Iowa Conservation Commission's better public relations men, said Ken Kakac, a former law enforcement superintendent for the agency.

"He really was kind of a striking person," Kakac said. "He was always very well dressed. He wore a necktie long before most people thought they were invented."

And there was substance behind that dashing image, said Larry Runneals of Marshalltown. He met Harvey in 1938, and their paths crossed often.

"I was kind of a wild guy," Runneals admitted. "But Walt was the type of fellow who made me feel that if I committed a game violation, it'd be a personal affront to him and to society.

"That became his methodology, educating kids in school to be a citizen and a sportsman and to have morals."

Often Visited Schools

Harvey often visited schools to teach hunter safety or show slides and talk about conservation. He took youths on field trips to rescue stranded fish or to see pheasants being raised.

Evenings and weekends, Harvey helped conservation groups, such as the Marshall County Wildlife Club. He kept the clubs family oriented, with nature programs and no gambling or swearing.

An avid reader, Harvey also gathered outdoor oddities for a column in the Marshalltown Times-Republican.

Escorted 'Skunk Wagon'

The personable warden made a good escort for the state's mobile wildlife exhibit, fondly known as the "Skunk Wagon." He traveled with it for two years.

Harvey also takes some credit for Iowa's thriving deer herd. In the 1930s, he proposed transplanting animals from a herd near Boone.

"You're nuts!" a supervisor responded.

Undaunted, Harvey went to higher officials and got the OK to trap deer. For three years,

Harvey and his wife, Mary, used horse trailers to haul white-tails throughout Iowa

"He lived his work," said Harvey's adopted son, Ralph Harvey Welch of Storm Lake. "Everything we did was related to it."

Welch rode with his dad, counting pheasants and noting license numbers of suspicious vehicles. Once, he watched his father wrestle and arrest two fleeing suspects.

"He was a very brave man," Welch said.

Maybe a little lucky, too, Harvey conceded. He remembered being shot at more than once.

He was not easily intimidated, however. One of the first people he arrested was a county attorney.

But Harvey also was compassionate, Welch said. He'd bring home orphaned wildlife – such as raccoons or flying squirrels.

And Harvey – despite yearning to sleep late – got up at 5 a.m. to help his son deliver The Des Moines Sunday Register.

If Ralph's customers could not pay their bills, Harvey came up with the money. And when the boy failed to sell enough papers to win a bicycle, his dad paid for the prized bike.

His Own Boyhood on Farm

Perhaps Harvey recalled his own boyhood on a farm near Harvey, Ia.

Too poor to own a shotgun, he borrowed a neighbor's weapon to go hunting.

At age 14, Harvey ran away from home. He got as far as Douglas, Wyo., where he worked as a cowboy for a year before he became homesick for Iowa.

The strapping youth returned to high school, where he played football and basketball. He also was a good athlete at Central College in Pella and Simpson College in Indianola. Academics were not his strong suit.

Later, he bought and sold walnut logs, built bridges and owned cafes in Pella and Harvey.

Then, during the Depression, he penned a postcard to the State Fish and Game Department, asking for a job.

Harvey's career as a game warden was broken only by World War II, when he was an undercover agent testing the security of military facilities in the United States. As cover for the spying, he posed as – what else? – a game warden.

He has few regrets.

"I sure loved my work," Harvey said.

But he'd rather not be called a game warden.

He prefers the German title: Keeper of the outdoors.

January 2, 1994

Iowa couple has spent lives living, teaching about the environment

STORM LAKE, IA – The first clue is their back-yard garden "jungle" of bird feeders, sunflowers and highbush cranberry bushes.

Then come the prints of warbler, whooping crane and wolf art on the living room walls, the tables piled with nature books and the window bench packed with blooming flowers.

If any doubt remains, read the annual Christmas letter, with news of Izaak Walton League conventions and birding safaris – and a pitch for environmental protection.

Ed and Virginia Crocker live conservation.

The Storm Lake couple has taught grade-school nature classes, counted birds for the Iowa Ornithologists' Union, built fences on Nature Conservancy preserves, chaired environmental education committees, led Soil Conservation Society of America meetings and conducted scores of conservation programs all over northwest Iowa.

"We're just two people who are interested in our natural resources," Ed said modestly.

Izaak Walton Leaguers

But 40 years of being interested have earned the Crockers accolades from their peers.

Ed was elected a fellow in the Soil Conservation Society of America and received the 1977 Award of Merit from the Iowa Chapter of the Wildlife Society. He was named an outstanding alumnus of the University of Delaware, and he received a conservation service award from the Sioux City Journal.

The couple has worked particularly hard for the Izaak Walton League. Ed is a perennial leader of the Storm Lake (United Counties) chapter, and he has been a national director. In 1985, he was honorary president of the league's Iowa Division. League members honored the couple again last month at Storm Lake.

The Crockers also have been cited by both the Iowa and Maryland chapters of The Nature Conservancy. And the couple's financial contributions to conservation have earned them life memberships in a half-dozen or more organizations.

"Everybody thinks so much of them for the unselfish work they have contributed," said Sylvan Runkel of Des Moines, who has known Ed since both were U.S. Soil Conservation Service employees in the late 1940s.

Naturalist's Daughter

The Crockers' conservation interests run deep. Ed's father was a vocational agriculture teacher in Delaware in the 1920s. Ed earned a degree in agriculture education, soils and agronomy from the University of Delaware in 1936. He taught agriculture in Snow Hill, Md., before joining the Soil Conservation Service.

In Snow Hill, Ed met Virginia, a teacher of chemistry, science, math and music who was the daughter of a country doctor. Her father also was a naturalist who taught her a love for the outdoors and for books.

It was with some trepidation that the couple accepted Ed's job as an SCS soil scientist in Storm Lake in 1947. Compared to the wetlands, forests and beaches of the Maryland coast, Iowa "looked pretty barren to me," Virginia said. A rip-snortin' January blizzard welcomed them to Storm Lake.

But 40 years later, the couple views the move to Iowa as the best thing they ever did.

Ed figuratively immersed himself in Iowa topsoil, working as a soil scientist and district conservationist until his retirement in 1973. He preached soil husbandry on and off the job, to farmers and non-farmers.

Won't Slow Down

To demonstrate their commitment, the Crockers also became farm managers. They bought 40 acres near Alta and have built its soil with 30 years of terracing, crop rotation and chemical-free farming.

It's all part of the Crockers' conservation message. An avid nature photographer, Ed regularly gives free slide lectures on conservation. Virginia, too, frequents the lecture circuit, using Ed's slides in programs on birds and birding.

She's also headed the General Federated Garden Clubs of Buena Vista County.

The couple's busy schedule has been slowed only slightly by Ed's treatment for bone marrow cancer, his 1986 heart attack and Virginia's pacemaker replacement.

The Crockers are especially eager to share nature's wonders with children. Ed and the late Frank Starr started an Izaak Walton League youth conservation camp in the late 1940s.

Ed and Virginia still teach in outdoor classroom sessions in Storm Lake grade schools.

Ardent Speaker

But conservation education need not be limited to schools, Ed emphasized. "There are 3 million Iowans and they're all teachers and all students," he said.

"Ed believes conservation and understanding of the outdoors are a part of everyone's life, whether they recognize it or not," said Dale Brentnall of Ames, president of the Izaak Walton League of America. "He was a floor fighter for basic conservation issues," Brentnall said.

Ed became a familiar figure in policy debates at both state and national Izaak Walton League conventions. He often prodded the group to address more issues concerning soil and resources, and fewer local matters, such as dove hunting.

He chided conservation groups that met at plush hotels, arguing that they could save money for their cause and attract more grass-roots members by meeting on college campuses or parks.

"I've been controversial," Ed acknowledged. "I'm not a yes-man . . . . I take pride in standing up for what I believe."

Frequent Travelers

One of those beliefs is the need for natural areas.

"Preserving the remaining . . . prairies and forests to at least have a gene bank is critical for the future," Ed said. He shudders at people who still ask, "What good is the whooping crane?"

"It's another species in the labyrinth of chains that link us all together," Ed said. "Losing the whooping crane is fraying that chain."

The Crockers have seen their share of that chain, camping and traveling in 48 states. They visit Arkansas each fall, and spend part of the summer enjoying the swamp, jewelweeds and hummingbirds around Virginia's family home near Chesapeake Bay.

And wherever they go, the exude love for their planet – and the people who must preserve it.

"We're all on the same spaceship," Ed said.

February 8, 1987

184

Motor Mill – Turkey River

© Larry Stone

CHAPTER 14

HISTORY

To respect Iowa's outdoors, you first must understand our past. Most of us owe our lives and livelihoods to the state's rivers and prairies and hills and woodlands. And those resources can't be separated from the people – Native Americans, trappers, traders and settlers – who were shaped by the land.

A pioneer farmstead, an Indian campsite or history lesson can transform a familiar landscape into a more vivid image of our natural heritage. A cottonwood tree becomes a sentinel for weary travelers. A hilltop once hosted a thriving Indian village. River highways led explorers throughout the new land. Abundant game and diverse plant life sustained the first Iowans, as bountiful crops support today's people.

As we learn to love and revere our past, we gain a deeper affection for the land.

'Frontiersman' teaches unique history lesson

GUTHRIE CENTER, IA – With buckskin clothing, moccasins, flintlock rifle, powder horn and bundles of furs, French trappers and traders explored Iowa by canoe 300 years ago.

Today, that same frontier gear and garb helps young Iowans explore the state's frontier in their imaginations.

Mark Wagner, an amateur historian and a naturalist for the Jasper County Conservation Board, wears a buckskin shirt and moccasins, teaches fire-building with flint, and demonstrates his hand-made flintlock rifle as he portrays a 17th century fur trader.

He gives the unique history lesson at Jasper County grade schools or at environmental education workshops such as one held recently at Springbrook State Park near Guthrie Center.

Most people think of northern Minnesota and Canada when they think of the fur trade, Wagner said. Recreational canoeists now flock to the same northern lakes and rivers that 200 years ago were highways for fur traders penetrating the interior of the North American continent.

But Iowans needn't go north to find waters traveled by early voyagers, he said. Similar history flows along many of the state's rivers and streams, which were heavily used by trappers and traders even before the heyday of the Canadian fur trade.

Marquette and Joliet

Wagner said the fur trade in Iowa began soon after Father Marquette and Louis Joliet reached the Mississippi at the mouth of the Wisconsin River, just south of present-day McGregor. That was in 1673. Marquette and Joliet came through Green Bay, Lake Winnebago and the Fox River, and then over a portage to the Wisconsin River, which they followed to the Mississippi. That water thoroughfare within a few years became an important trade route for Iowa furs bound for Montreal.

In 1685, French explorer Nicholas Perrot established Fort St. Nicholas at what is now Prairie du Chien, Wis. The site, opposite Marquette, was a wilderness outpost with good access to the fur riches of the Mississippi and its tributaries. Wagner said early reports told of up to 130 large birch bark canoes beached at the fort while Indians and French traders did business.

Indians did much of the trapping, but white traders also paddled the rivers with guns, knives, steel traps, blankets and other goods to exchange for furs, Wagner said. The Frenchmen also may have set up some winter trading camps along Iowa rivers.

These early Iowa travelers probably visited the Des Moines, Skunk, Maquoketa, Turkey, Wapsipinicon and nearly every other river or stream that joined the upper Mississippi.

Beaver pelts were the most highly sought-after furs, but trappers also took otter, muskrat, mink, wolf, skunk, ermine and other fur-bearing animals, Wagner said.

The prized beaver pelts set the trading standard. A flintlock rifle might cost 12 beaver pelts. Deer hides were so common that it might take six to equal the value of one beaver.

Most of the beaver skins ultimately were shipped to France for hat-making, Wagner said. The pelts were sheared, and the thick underfur was processed into felt for hats.

By the 1830s trapping had nearly wiped out beavers in much of their range, Wagner said. It took more than 100 years and restocking efforts by wildlife biologists to bring the animals back.

Lead, as well as furs, played a key role in the early history of Iowa. When Perrot moved downstream from Prairie du Chien to establish a fort at Dubuque in 1690, he was lured not only by furs but also by rumors of the rich lead deposits. His trade for lead and early attempts at lead

186

mining helped develop the market for the valuable mineral.

Lead for Colonists

At first, the lead was carried over the usual fur trade route to Montreal, but by the time of the American Revolution much of the lead was sent down the Mississippi to St. Louis and on to New Orleans. Spanish traders then shipped it to the East Coast for use in the guns of freedom-fighting American colonists.

Julien Dubuque arrived on the scene in 1788 and soon had persuaded the Indians to give him a contract to mine lead in the area. In 1796 he acquired a Spanish land grant stretching 21 miles along the Mississippi near Dubuque.

After Dubuque died in 1810, the Fox Indians regained control of the area until 1832, when the Black Hawk Treaty officially opened the Iowa Territory to white settlement.

The rest, as they say, is history. But it's history that might have taken a different turn if it hadn't been for the pursuit of some soft-furred animals.

January 26, 1986

Iowan reaps respect for past

ROWLEY, IA – To Michael Andorf, the spirit of the prairie still rides on March winds.

Wandering the hills and valleys along Bear Creek, Lime Creek, Mud Creek and the Red Cedar River, Andorf sees campfires among the cornstalks, buffalo hunters along the fencerows.

He stops to caress a smooth boulder, or to study a flint chip – and he drifts into the past. He's there with the brave, chipping a new arrow point, or the squaw pounding acorn flour.

As a boy, Andorf always let the Indians win whenever he played cowboys and Indians.

He loves the Indians' revered Cedar River, not far from where he and his wife, Beverly, operate Willow Creek campground and bed and breakfast along the Cedar Valley Nature Trail.

Andorf also farms with respect for the land. He has quit using chemicals, and has gone back to crop rotation and spreading manure to maintain fertility and control weeds.

In fact, Andorf cringes at the word "weed." He quotes a Mesquakie friend who told him there are no weeds, only plants that we don't know the use for.

Andorf laments the timber clearing, stream straightening and wildlife habitat destruction that have become a part of modern agriculture. There's no concern for the integrity of the earth, he fears.

Sometimes, following his dreams over the muddy fields, Andorf may find a stone arrow point, a flint chip, or a rock scraper. He cherishes such discoveries, and the links to those lost people he admires.

"But it's more than just being out hunting arrowheads," Andorf said. He doesn't just look at the ground for a glint of flint or an out-of-place rock. He watches the clouds, the crows, the sky, the trees, the creek.

"Most of the time you're out there, you do a lot of thinking," he mused. "And you get out on those hills and listen to the silence."

Gradually, inspirations become words, and words flow into poems that honor the Indians and their land.

"lay your hands
on her tender breast
and feel
"she who gives so freely
asks only to be treated
with kindness"

On Turkey Ridge, Andorf stops to gaze across the Cedar River Valley, and to imagine the people, wildlife and wilderness here thousands of years before the white man's plow and cattle and ax.

"It makes you feel pretty insignificant," he reflected.

He scans bare patches of dirt, looking for a bit of rock that might be a stone tool or arrow point. But it's a casual search.

"They always find me," he said of the elusive artifacts. "I never find them."

A companion digs up a smooth, pinkish, pitted stone the size of two fists. Is it just a rock? Or perhaps a centuries-old pounding tool? Andorf unrolls a pouch of tobacco, offering a pinch to sprinkle on the ground where the rock had lain.

"When you find something, always give something back," he said. That's the Indian way.

188

"Anything you pick up is special. It's a gift to you."

But, much to the consternation of professional archeologists, Andorf views his artifacts as symbols of a culture he esteems, rather than scientific specimens. He doesn't bother with site records and cataloged displays, preferring instead to give away stone points to special friends or interested school children. As his Indian friends would say, "You only get to keep what you give away in life."

"spring
on the prairie
was made for
a warrior
wearing a buffalo-skin robe
mounted on a painted pony . . .
"he had no time for time
he ate when he was hungry
he slept when he was tired
he traveled when he had a place to go . . .
"he braved the outdoors
because he was one
with the earth
sky
rain
wind . . ."

Michael Andorf

March 28, 1988

Warren County man sees artifacts as art

"A broken piece has got just as much history in it as a full piece"

– Bernard Ripperger

INDIANOLA, IA—High above South River, on a ridge jutting out to the valley, Bernard Ripperger was studying history.

Strolling a freshly worked oats field, poking at the clods with his walking stick, Ripperger probed for clues to the ancient people that once called this place home.

He rolled over one dusty rock, then another.

"Camp rock," Ripperger declared. The crumbling surface and dirty-pink color of the granite betrayed cooking fires that had heated these stones centuries ago.

Toward the point of the ridge, two gentle humps rose against a background of forest. Decades of farming still hadn't entirely erased the unmistakable shape of the Indian mounds.

Such traces of early man abound in the South River valley, Ripperger said. He has found Indian artifacts on dozens of sites overlooking the river.

"I think they enjoyed the scenery, too," he said, nodding across the wooded hills and broad floodplain.

For 30 years, Ripperger has roamed his native Warren County, hungry for knowledge about the first inhabitants. He grew up in the South River valley near Ackworth – but he didn't begin picking up Indian relics until later.

"We farmed all this and we never did find any arrowheads because we weren't looking for them," he said.

Now that he knows where and how to look, he regularly picks up remnants of an earlier civilization.

"You get above the river like this and find a field that's been plowed up and chances are you'll find some sign," Ripperger said.

But it's hard to find a plowed field when government programs encourage permanent seeding, Ripperger said. And many farmers have switched from plowing to reduced tillage.

The practices save soil – but less erosion means less chance of a buried stone or arrow point being uncovered. The drought has compounded the problem, Ripperger said. Relics may not show up until rain washes the dirt away from them.

Ripperger tries to go artifact hunting soon after a rain. On some of the best-known sites, he said, it almost becomes a race to see which amateur archeologist gets there first.

"If you don't get out there right away, all you find is footprints," he said.

But a careful, persistent hunter can find a variety of centuries-old relics, as Ripperger's collection attests. He has discovered grooved stone axes, wedge-like celts and hammer stones.

Ripperger has found numerous arrow or spear points, some of which he estimates are up to 10,000 years old. He marvels at the way the ancient craftsmen chipped flakes from the stones to sharpen the edges.

"They had to make do with what they had at hand," he said. "They couldn't go to the hardware store and buy it."

Many relics are works of art, Ripperger said, but they're even more important for their historical value.

190

With the encouragement of the late Jack Musgrove, former curator of the Iowa State Historical Museum, Ripperger has kept careful records of each item he has found.

He gives each piece a code number and records the place and date where it was found. He locates each site on a county map. The system once helped him piece together a broken spear point, after he had found the two halves three years apart.

"A lot of collectors don't bother to pick up broken pieces, but I do," Ripperger said. "A broken piece has got just as much history in it as a full piece."

Ripperger reads extensively to learn more of that history. He eagerly shares his knowledge, giving talks to school children or civic groups.

He also likes to imagine what the people and the land were like before the white man came to South River.

"Usually about everything you find has got a little different story behind it," Ripperger said. "You pick something up and you wonder what the story really is . . ."

April 30, 1989

His hobby: Paddling for history

BATTLE CREEK, IA – Kids gather pockets full of pretty rocks.

Roadside hikers pick up nickel deposit beer and pop cans.

Dennis Laughlin collects bones.

Or teeth . . . or arrow points . . . or pottery pieces . . . or petrified wood . . . or fossils.

By canoe.

Never is Laughlin more content than when he's pulling his canoe through the shallows of the Maple or Soldier River, heading for a gravel bar where he might find a bison bone, a petrified shark's tooth or an ancient elk antler.

Happiness, he jokes, "is having one billion rocks to look through."

It's like browsing through a history book. One rock might turn out to be a piece of fossil coral millions of years old; another could be a 12,000-year-old mastodon tooth; what looks like a chunk of mud might be a fragment of Indian pottery; and a mysterious bone could be the remains of a plow horse dumped into the river by a 19th-century farmer.

"You go with the idea you do not know what you're going to find," Laughlin said. "But I always find something."

On the Maple River last September, that something turned out to be an elk antler that obviously had been hacked from a skull with a hand tool. Was it the work of a native American 1,000 years ago – or merely the remains of a discarded 20th-century hunting trophy?

"Sometimes," Laughlin said, "the things you can't figure out are the most interesting."

There's less doubt about a bison skull he found on the Maple River, however. That animal's horns probably spread at least 36 inches, and the huge bull may have weighed 3,500 pounds, Laughlin said.

He's confident the skull came from a subspecies that died out at least 5,000 years ago.

Laughlin has found at least 34 other bison skulls or parts of skulls in the past four years. He and a friend also uncovered an elk skull, complete with massive antlers.

Such discoveries are more common in western Iowa than elsewhere in the state, said Art Bettis, a geologist with the Iowa Department of Natural Resources. The steep hills, frequent summer thunderstorms, unstable soil and past channelization make rivers there erode faster, he said. The erosion exposes fossil materials.

Laughlin makes 15 to 20 canoe trips each year. But the outings aren't for recreational paddlers or racers. Laughlin likes low water, when sand and gravel bars are exposed. That means hip boots or tennis shoes and lots of wading. The trips can be tedious, time-consuming and exhausting.

But it's not all work, Laughlin said.

Along the river, canoeists may see kingfishers, great blue herons, great horned owls, red-tailed hawks or songbirds. The shady river banks and cool water help take the edge off a hot July day.

Just enjoying the nature experience is incentive enough for the canoe trips, Laughlin said. Finding ancient animal bones or Indian artifacts simply adds a new dimension.

"It's fascinating," Laughlin said. "Just the idea we had somebody here 1,000 or 5,000 years ago . . ."

Laughlin's fascination with the outdoors began when he was a grade-schooler searching for petrified wood along the Raccoon River near his boyhood home in Sac City. He caught turtles, became an avid hunter, and dabbled in taxidermy.

Later, he began collecting wildlife skins, mounted game birds or animals, fossils, ancient animal remains and Indian artifacts.

But a collection is useless unless it's shared, Laughlin said. He regularly takes displays to Battle Creek grade school classes for lectures on Indian lore and natural history.

He recently bought an abandoned one-room school building in which he hopes to house a natural history museum adjacent to his restaurant along Iowa Highway 175 in Battle Creek.

"The whole thing may be angled towards kids," Laughlin said.

Young people especially, he said, need to appreciate the history of the land if they are to protect it for the future.

"We used to have bison here and we used to have elk here," he said. "Let's be keeping what we (still) have now."

July 23, 1989

Pioneer history alive and well

PALMER, IA – In an era of aluminum barns, half-section cornfields and 200-horsepower tractors, Iowa's pioneer history is alive and well on a century-old farmstead near here.

The Pocahontas County Conservation Board recently acquired a 30-acre prairie and a seven-acre homestead from the Harry Wiegert estate, with plans to continue to preserve the farm as Wiegert had done for 75 years.

Mark Peterson, executive officer of the county board, said the prairie has never been plowed. In fact, it had seldom even had a tractor driven over it, since Wiegert always used horses to cut and harvest his hay.

The prairie escaped the plow because Wiegert wanted the hay for his Belgian draft horses and his beef cows. It's the largest tract of virgin land left in the county, except for the 160-acre, state-owned Kalsow Prairie, a few miles away.

The dense, seven-acre farm grove also is somewhat unique in this heavily-farmed, relatively tree-less part of the state, Peterson said. The site is "a hub for a lot of wildlife in that area," he noted.

Deer and raccoon tracks dot the farm yard, and birds whistle constantly from the trees and thickets.

"It's interesting to come here and sort of lose yourself," Peterson said.

"It's like stepping into a different world."

Even the farm buildings are unusual for 1981 Iowa. The 100-year-old house has no electricity or indoor plumbing. The stately barn, with its cupola and weather vane, sheltered Wiegert's work horses until last year. Loose prairie hay is scattered about the haymow.

A well-kept windmill stands ready to pump water to livestock – or to wildlife seeking refuge in the farmyard. The aroma of charred wood hangs in the blackened smokehouse.

Wiegert's second cousin, Robert Peterson, administrator of the estate, said Wiegert was born on the farm in 1905, and died there last year. Until his death, Wiegert drew water with a hand pump, heated with wood from the grove and used kerosene lanterns for light.

"He just lived the way he grew up," Peterson said. "And he never threw anything away."

The result was a bonanza for antique collectors, when the estate sale was held in December. Some 1,500 people from several states bid on old kerosene lamps, children's toys, crocks, furniture, picture frames and other household goods accumulated by Wiegert and his family since the Wiegerts came to Iowa a century ago.

Robert Peterson couldn't bear to see the farmstead sold, however. He felt the site deserved a better fate than the probability of being bulldozed for another cornfield.

"It would be a dirty shame" not to preserve it, he declared.

Likewise, he didn't want to see the prairie sold and converted to crop land.

"That virgin ground is something you haven't got anymore," he declared. "Why plow it up?"

Working with the Iowa Natural Heritage Foundation and the Pocahontas County Conservation Board, Peterson arranged for several heirs of the estate to donate their share of the inheritance to the county. When the conservation board bought the prairie and the farmstead at auction earlier this year for $69,980, the heirs contributed 64 percent of the purchase price.

The land was donated by Lois Mosbach of Fort Dodge; John Peterson of Palmer; Glen Peterson of Rogers, Ark; and Mildred Spear, Rita Hoefling and Robert Peterson of Pocahontas.

194

Mark Peterson said the conservation board hopes to get cost-sharing money from the Iowa Conservation Commission's habitat stamp fund on the remaining $25,000 cost of the land, thus reducing the county's cost to less than $7,000.

The county plans to manage the prairie for wildlife nesting cover and to preserve native vegetation, Peterson said. The tract was burned this spring to discourage woody plants and invading bluegrass and brome.

Plans for the farm buildings are uncertain, Peterson said, but the structures definitely will be preserved. He said the county board may seek advice and financial help from the county's historical society.

But this much IS certain: Harry Wiegert left a historical and natural treasure for the people of Pocahontas County, and of Iowa.

June 14, 1981

Gary and Judith Wagner © The Des Moines Register

CHAPTER 15

AGRICULTURE

Before "agribusiness," farming was a way of life.

Rural people raised oats, hay, corn, chickens, hogs and cattle. Wildlife and wildflowers co-existed with pastures, crops and forgotten corners of the diverse landscape. Kids thrived on the hard work, fresh air and natural classrooms.

Economics, politics and progress have changed the face of the state – not always for the better. But some farmers still think first of their heritage, and live by the credo that the land is not inherited from our parents; it is borrowed from our children.

Iowans treat land with love

BURLINGTON, IA – When newlyweds Gary and Judith Wagner bought some land and started planting trees 34 years ago, their neighbors were puzzled.

"Nobody was doing that then," Judith said. "We were pioneers."

The Wagners also built their house and several ponds on their 40-acre tract near Burlington. They worked with a neighboring farmer to control erosion on their own land and nearby fields.

"Land is your most important machinery," Gary said. "You'd better take care of it, just like you change the oil in your tractor."

In the 1980s, the couple started buying more land to expand their tree planting and conservation efforts. The family now owns more than 1,500 acres in Des Moines, Johnson, Washington and Louisa counties.

The Wagners also own an elevator service business and are both family therapists – but they spend nearly every free moment working on their land.

They've planted more than 370 acres of trees, and another 200 acres are to be planted this year and next.

The couple, along with their son, Greg, and daughter, Laura Wagner-Ertz, who operate a prairie seed and forestry services business, has seeded 107 acres of native grasses. They plan to convert 75 more acres to prairie grasses and flowers this year.

Initially, people asked, "Why?"

"Because we want to," the Wagners would respond.

They also quoted the conservation credo: "We don't inherit the land from our parents, we borrow it from our children."

"When you borrow something, you should return it in as good a shape as when you got it," Gary said.

Gary also recalled advice he got from his father at age 12.

"Gary, you should buy some land and plant walnut trees," his dad said. "There's lots of money to be made in walnut trees."

But they've yet to get rich on the trees they've planted, the Wagners said.

"We've planted way more than we harvested," Gary said.

The Wagners also have made their land a showcase for wildlife habitat and forestry. They built a 38-acre marsh with 19 nesting islands, erected dozens of wood duck boxes and planted windbreaks around crop fields.

Gary says he likes to experiment. He's tried planting walnut trees between European black alder seedlings. In theory, the alders fix nitrogen in the soil, while crowding the walnuts to grow taller. Eventually, the alders will die from a chemical produced by the walnuts.

Gary and Greg also are perfecting an improved tree-planting machine, and they're testing ways to plant tree seeds, instead of seedlings, to simplify reforestation.

"They can't stand to use the same old thing," Judith said. "They have to keep improving it."

The Wagners' enthusiasm has not gone unnoticed.

Gary and Judith received both the Woodland Owner of the Year and the Wildlife Farmer of the Year awards for 1992 from the Iowa Department of Natural Resources.

Gary often speaks to forestry, civic and landowner groups, preaching conservation.

"Trees are the lungs of the earth and wetlands are the kidneys," Gary said. "But we've already cut out three lobes of the lungs and removed one of the kidneys."

Helping to renew that tired, old land can be very satisfying, the Wagners said.

"It kind of takes your breath away to stand under an 85-foot pine tree and remember your children helped plant them," Judith said. "It's special – different than things you buy."

Conservation also sends a message of confidence to the next generation, Judith added.

"It's saying we *do* care about your future."

April 25, 1993

Wildlife takes top priority with Armstrong

BOONEVILLE, IA – "There's nothing better than weeds for wildlife," declared Eugene Armstrong.

But that doesn't mean that the 1,000 acres Armstrong farms with two sons and a nephew are allowed to grow into a weed patch. Armstrong likes to think that modern agriculture and good wildlife habitat can co-exist.

So how does he find room for wildlife in his farming operations, given the economic pressures that lead many farmers to till every available parcel of ground?

It's philosophical, partly.

"If you're more interested in the out-of-doors than just in the almighty dollar, you see more than just a row of corn," he shrugged.

On his farm, Armstrong sees potential wildlife habitat in places many farmers might not think about – fencerows, for example.

"The mark of a good farmer is supposed to be how clean the fencerows are," he said, "but I don't agree with that."

He doesn't mow or spray fencerows, because weeds there don't harm crops. But the cover left along fences and field edges is a boon to small animals and birds.

Armstrong also has left some "odd areas" for wildlife habitat, where farming would be difficult anyway. One dense corner was established by his father, more than 15 years ago.

"How much does it cost you to leave a little area?" he queried, when asked how hard-pressed farmers can afford not to crop "fence to fence."

"If you're that close to going broke, you're not going to make it, anyway!"

Near an eight-acre pond, built as part of the Badger Creek watershed project, Armstrong has left an old hedgerow, built brushpiles, sowed prairie grass and planted trees and shrubs.

When the pond was being built, he made a special effort to leave a shallow end, with an island, for shorebirds. He also asked the contractors to save as many trees as possible, and to pile brush for wildlife cover.

The efforts paid off. The pond and surrounding area have attracted deer, waterfowl, pheasants, quail, rabbits and dozens of species of songbirds.

Armstrong and his wife, Eloise, are both avid birders, so they frequently hike around the pond, checking on the latest migrants and the active nesters.

During calving season, Armstrong must check on his cows in a nearby pasture three times a day, so he seldom fails to swing by the pond for a look at the birds, too.

In fact, he keeps his binoculars and spotting scope in his pickup, ready to aid in a quick identification of birds he sees while on farm errands.

Neighbors occasionally tease him about his preoccupation with birding, but the joshing doesn't dim his enthusiasm. Armstrong is nearing 300 species on his life list of birds seen, and he and Eloise often take weekend trips in hopes of raising their tally. Last winter they birded across the southwestern United States.

Armstrong realizes that all farmers don't share his enthusiasm about wildlife, but he believes they SHOULD take an interest in soil and water conservation practices – from which wildlife can receive fringe benefits.

For example, a good farmstead windbreak will protect livestock and decrease heating bills – while serving as ideal wildlife cover, if properly maintained. Field terraces prevent soil erosion, he continued, and the seeded backslopes make excellent pheasant nesting cover.

Ponds to control erosion or to water livestock are natural wildlife attractors, he added.

Financing conservation projects shouldn't be a stumbling block, Armstrong said, because in most counties the Agricultural Stabilization and Conservation Service offers aid for pond building, windbreak planting, wildlife habitat, erosion control and other conservation work.

Free cedar trees can be transplanted from some road ditches, Armstrong suggested, because they're often cut by road crews, anyway.

Some county conservation boards – like Madison County (Armstrong is on the board) – will furnish seedlings and plant wildlife habitat for farmers who agree to protect the site.

Such projects can be good insurance to help protect the land for future generations – and they can offer immediate pleasure to present-day wildlife lovers.

Just ask Armstrong – if you can pry him away from his binoculars.

April 9, 1978

The clearing of a fencerow:
Tale of tragedy for wildlife, hunters

When a 2,000-year-old redwood is felled, or a wild river is dammed or a marsh is smothered by industrialization, most people recognize that there has been some environmental damage.

But it's harder for us to see the smaller, day-to-day inroads being made into our dwindling number of natural areas.

Take the clearing of a farm fencerow, for instance. To a farmer, a tangle of shrubs, weeds and trees along his fence may be an eyesore, a nuisance and a hazard for his expensive machinery. Many landowners take advantage of a late-summer lull in farm chores and clean out these fence-rows or farm groves to make the place look neat.

But for wild birds and animals, there between the plowed fields and paved roads lies a natural sanctuary.

Pheasants, rabbits and quail seek the shelter of grasses left unmowed. Foxes and other predators use the fencerows in their search for meals.

Hawks sometimes hunt these strips of cover, knowing the attraction of fencerows for mice, ground squirrels and other morsels.

Some wise white-tail bucks lurk in fencerows, sensing the security of an isolated hideout in the midst of farm country.

Hunters who know the value of a fencerow send their dogs there in search of quail, pheasants and rabbits.

Berry pickers also are drawn to fencerows, where wild plums, grapes, chokecherries and elderberries often grow in abundance.

This rich food supply also draws hordes of birds, which eat the berries and scatter the seeds.

Fencerows also are home to an incredible number of insects. When driven out, they may move into crop fields, where their eating habits are more destructive.

The diverse habitat also may host insect predators, parasites or diseases, which keep pest numbers from exploding.

The rich variety of life in fencerows is out of proportion to the size of the areas. But biologists explain this with a phenomenon called the "edge effect." It says that the greatest diversity and numbers of plants and animals usually are found where two types of habitat meet.

Since fencerows are almost entirely "edge," they're some of our finest wildlife habitat.

But many farmers don't need fences, groves and sloughs anymore because they're working for more efficient production or because they don't own livestock.

Perhaps the landowner won't miss the brushy fencerow, but he'll surely be poorer when the birds and rabbits no longer are around.

And he may notice the difference when the March winds blow across the open field, carrying away topsoil from where the fencerow once served as a windbreak.

Fencerows may seem like tiny parts of our world, but it's a big tragedy when one dies.

August 31, 1977

Tiny grove of trees lets history branch out

RENWICK, IA – Like an island, the little grove of cottonwoods, walnuts, hackberries and ashes pokes above the wide expanses of rolling, black farmland.

Just 10 acres of trees among thousands of acres of row crops, the woodlot is a testimony to a century of conservation conscience – and to a long-dead dream to turn the Great Plains into a forest.

When Ernie Macha bought the 40-acre plot with its corner of trees 29 years ago, he saw the land as a good addition to his adjacent farm. To be sure, $325 an acre sounded like a lot of money, but he decided to take a chance.

What's more, as a founder of the Oakdale Chapter of the Izaak Walton League and a charter member of the Humboldt County Conservation Board, he recognized the woodlot as a real bonus for wildlife. It would fit in well with the honeysuckle and dogwood he'd planted along nearly a mile of fencerows.

Planted in 1890s

But Macha eventually learned the trees were special – they weren't just a ragged grove someone had neglected to grub out.

An elderly neighbor recalled to Macha about when the trees were planted in the 1890s. And Macha's abstract showed that one of the first landowners had acquired the property from the U.S. Government, under a law designed "to encourage the growth of timber on the western prairies."

Terry West, a historian for the U.S. Forest Service, said the Timber Culture Act of 1873 was passed by Congress in the belief that growing trees on the plains would attract rainfall to the dry region. The government agreed to give a section of land to anyone who would plant trees on one-fourth of the tract, and maintain the woodlands for eight years.

By 1886, Americans had applied to take over 31 million acres of these so-called "tree claims" – but many would-be tree farmers apparently failed. A 1977 U.S. Forest Service publication said only 10.8 million acres of land was transferred to private hands. The law was repealed in 1891.

Tree claims apparently were used mostly in western states, but a few were filed in Iowa. State and federal officials could not say how many still exist here.

New Owners, Old Trees

But this much is certain:

On March 3, 1895, Mathias Baumgartner received the deed to 40 acres in section 12, Vernon Township, Humboldt County, Iowa.

And 65 years later, when Macha bought the property, some of the trees were still there, despite a succession of several different owners.

Some timber had been cut in 1942, however. Macha recalled a portable sawmill working in the woodlot, and he'd even hauled away some of the sawdust for garden mulch. He also remembered county crews cutting several large cottonwoods along the road right-of-way.

Macha at first pastured the woodlot, but he later decided to keep it as a refuge for deer, pheasants and other wildlife.

"I figure they should have someplace," he said.

He also planted more trees and shrubs: white pine, tamarac, dogwood, honeysuckle, green ash, oak, hickory and butternut. The tree-planting brought back memories of his boyhood, when he tagged along as his father planted willows to slow erosion on the family farm above Bloody Run Creek near McGregor.

"I grew up with conservation," Macha said.

Macha has gathered blackberries and hunted mushrooms in his woodlot, and he once made maple syrup by tapping the soft maple trees. But mostly he's just content to know that his "tree claim" protects a bit of Iowa's heritage.

The resident red-tail, the squirrels, the wintering pheasants, the raccoons, the sapling-nibbling blankety-blank deer, the songbirds that flock to the forested oasis – they're all a part of history.

November 5, 1989

Wildlife also matters, farmer says

FORT ATKINSON, IA – Despite what you see in some parts of Iowa, farming need not be black-dirt barrens, endless rows of corn and dull expanses of soybeans.

Julian Kuhn of Fort Atkinson raises plum thickets as well as corn on his 280-acre farm . . . pheasants instead of soybeans.

Unlike many landowners who have grubbed out brush and fences so they can plow every last acre, Kuhn still has brushy fencerows, unpastured sloughs and scraggly hay fields where wildlife can survive.

"When you provide a place, [wildlife] will come and stay," he said.

Iowa has lost much of its wildlife habitat because "the dollar bill rules everything," Kuhn lamented.

Kuhn doesn't advocate letting his land revert to a weed patch, however. He believes it's possible to farm efficiently while still attracting wildlife.

"Farm it neatly, but leave these patches you never touch," he said.

Thus, he cooperated with the Iowa Conservation Commission more than 15 years ago to fence several acres near a sinkhole, then plant shrubs and trees for wildlife cover.

Kuhn also maintains a 12-acre hay field on rough land next to the plot. The hay ground, now seeded to sweet clover, was "really booming" with pheasants this spring.

A Bit More Woolly

The overgrown field, uncut for several years, looked terrible, Kuhn said, "but, by gol, that's where the habitat is."

Kuhn admits that his fencerows have grown a bit more woolly than some neighbors might prefer, but he still resists cutting the brush and trees. Those little strips of habitat can be life-saving winter cover for pheasants and other birds, Kuhn said. And the rows help check wind erosion.

When Kuhn does cut brush on his farm, he stacks it for wildlife cover, instead of burning it. Rather than burying rocks he picks off his fields, Kuhn piles the stones in the wildlife area to attract more critters.

"That provides a little habitat for something, too," he explained.

One of the best ways to create wildlife habitat is to "just leave it alone," Kuhn said. When he took his cattle out of a creek pasture about 10 years ago, the once-barren area quickly grew up into a "jungle" that's now a haven for deer, mink, muskrats and other wildlife.

Kuhn also maintains three small woodlots several miles from his home. One was a wedding gift from his father, who gave Kuhn the choice of the timber land or a new television set.

Kuhn still prefers trees to TV.

"If anybody ever got hold of one of those timbers and started grubbing, I guarantee I'd jump out of my grave and get 'em," he declared.

Weak Moments

Kuhn has had his weak moments, however. He, too, has given in to the urge to "get a little more corn." He's straightened a small creek on his farm and shaped a few waterways.

But after finishing the grading work, Kuhn has let the areas revert to natural cover, complete with cattails, willows, slough grass, trees and shrubs. The habitat value has returned.

"I watch red-winged blackbirds nest there," Kuhn said.

Some farmers might scoff at raising red-wings where there could be corn, but not Kuhn. He pointed to a corn field where the dry weather had nearly ruined the crop.

"I'm not getting anything out of it, but it's costing me $100 an acre" in fixed costs, he shrugged.

The creek habitat, on the other hand, will raise free deer, pheasants and rabbits, as well as wild plums, grapes and elderberries.

There are other, less tangible benefits, Kuhn said. He recalled mowing hay near the creek while he watched a heron.

"He made nice company that afternoon," he said.

Kuhn once spooked a small flock of mallards from a beaver pond on the creek. "The prettiest sight I ever saw," he mused.

He smiled as he again visualized a den of young foxes in a fence row . . . a flock of pheasants "boiling" out of a slough . . . jackrabbits loping across a field.

"And deer. I still stop and watch them until I can't see them anymore," he said.

Gave Up Hunting

But even with the abundance of wildlife, Kuhn harvests very few animals, only trapping a few mink, muskrats and raccoons. He's given up hunting.

"I can't," he said simply. "It's too pretty. I can't shoot it. But I still respect the guys who do." He welcomes a group of friends from Wisconsin that traditionally come for a fall pheasant hunt.

But for Kuhn, the satisfaction of just seeing wildlife as he works around the farm is all the reward he needs.

September 8, 1985

CHAPTER 16

EDUCATION

Too many kids these days are missing the *real* education that my generation of farm kids had. Video games and TV and even hikes with the daycare group are no substitute for getting your feet muddy in the creek, finding a red-winged blackbird's nest in the pasture or hearing a katydid's call.

Thoughtful Iowans long have recognized the importance of introducing our children to the wonders of the outdoors. We're weaving conservation education into all levels of our school systems. The smallest tots can recycle. Gradeschoolers understand the concept of "Spaceship Earth." Older students often monitor air and water quality, and make politicians squirm with pointed questions about environmental policies.

But we must not leave the task to the schools. We're *all* teachers, whose most important mission may be to show our children how to be good citizens of Planet Earth.

Class becomes fun when linked to nature

Ames environmental project, one of the oldest in the nation,
lets kids laugh while they learn

AMES, IA – What a perfect day for a convention of The Society of Sled Building Engineers!

The members fine-tuned their machines, nervously eyed the inclined plane, then prepared to test their scientific designs.

With shrieks and giggles and cheers and clouds of flying snow, the snow-suited engineers slid and tumbled down the hill after their home-made sleds.

Guess what? Engineering can be *fun!* Especially if you're a third-grader.

Fun and learning can go together, said Nancy Kurrle, director of Project ECO, an environmental education program in the Ames public schools. The curriculum, in its twenty-second year, is one of the oldest such projects in the nation, she said.

Kurrle recently led an outing of 23 students from Sawyer Elementary School to discover the wonders of winter at the Iowa State University/YMCA Outdoor Center.

"The kids just begged to come," their teacher, Lizz Bowman, said.

But the field trip is more than just a day in the snow, Bowman and Kurrle agreed.

To prepare for the zero temperatures and bitter winds, the youths discussed the principles of staying warm. They experimented with layers, thick and thin clothing, and different fabrics.

The students also had to build their own miniature sleds. Imaginations ran wild. The kids used pop bottles, milk jugs, aluminum foil, waxed paper, cardboard boxes, wood, plastic tubing and a host of other materials.

Some sleds were streamlined, some were highly decorated, a few had bells.

"All of you created something out of nothing," Kurrle said. "And if it doesn't work as well as you want it to work, steal the ideas of other engineers and go home and create a new design."

The youngsters also became M-A-D scientists.

Kurrle explained how animals get M-A-D in winter. They "migrate," they "adapt" or they "die."

To illustrate, the kids poured a mysterious liquid into film canisters to simulate an animal's body. They hid the containers in make-shift shelters, then returned later to see if the critter had survived.

The once-liquid gelatin had hardened. The "animals" were dead.

The cold can cause physical changes, as well, the kids learned. They blew up balloons, measured their circumference, then noted how they shrank after a day in the zero degree air.

The students also collected cups of snow, then marveled at how the volume decreased as the snow melted.

Kurrle said the students use the results of their experiments to do math problems, draw graphs, write essays and in other follow-up classroom work.

The recent outing is typical of the three days set aside each school year for students in third, fifth and seventh grades, Kurrle said. Counting single-day trips with other grades, about 2,000 students are involved in the ECO program annually, she said.

In fall, third-graders might observe pond life, study tree leaves or learn fishing skills.

Spring brings a geology session, with a visit to the Iowa Department of Transportation to learn

207

how gravel is tested and used in road building.

In fifth grade, classes explore streams and prairies, visit museums and study marshes and migrations.

Seventh-grade youths take a fall hike along the Skunk River Greenbelt to learn the area's history and natural history. In winter, they chop through the ice of a pond to measure water quality. In spring, they learn bird and wildflower identification and test their math and geography skills on an orienteering course.

"It's interdisciplinary," Kurrle said.

"We're not just science, we're not just environmental education."

Nearly all teachers welcome the outdoor classes – especially when they see the students' enthusiasm, Kurrle said.

"Some kids just blossom in the outdoors," she said. "It gives every child a chance to flourish in his or her own setting."

February 13, 1994

208

Packaged sunlight – that's YOU!

Jasper County kids study Nature

NEWTON, IA – "Think of yourselves as packaged sunlight – because that's exactly what you are."

If we'd all follow that suggestion, perhaps people would feel closer to their environment – and a truce could be reached in Americans' war with Nature.

Mike Gross, environmental education coordinator for the Jasper County Conservation Board, uses the "packaged sunlight" analogy with grade-schoolers in his outdoor classrooms. The comparison helps emphasize that the youngsters are part of the same natural cycles as the "critters" they've been studying.

"The most important thing is to teach them their relationship to Nature, and show them they are a part of their environment," Mike said.

Every fifth- and sixth-grader in the county has the class once a year, while Mike reaches about half the younger students annually.

The sixth-graders' one-day workshops usually begin with a field trip around the Mariposa Recreation Area, near Newton, where the youths observe a 17-acre lake and its watershed.

After analyzing the land use patterns, soil erosion potential and vegetation of the surrounding area, the kids check the lake to see how it's affected by its location.

With simple kits they measure the temperature, oxygen content and pH of the water to help in their eventual diagnosis of the lake's health.

To complete their examination the young "lake doctors" conduct a "critter hunt" in the aquatic patient.

With bare hands, dishpans, nets and a large helping of energy and enthusiasm, they sample the lake's inhabitants.

"You might catch stuff that you don't want to pick up," Mike warns. "If you do – pick it up anyway!"

Several wet feet and mud spatters later, the critters are studied, identified from pictures, and released.

Mike doesn't bother with much lecturing during the hunts, since the activity is basically an "experience program."

"They don't hear too much of what I say," Mike laughed. "They're pretty well engrossed in their buckets (of critters.)"

Occasionally, the youths are treated to another "experience" on a nearby prairie, where Mike leads them on a "fantasy trip" back through history.

The students all flop down in the tall prairie grass, close their eyes and let their imaginations run wild.

"Don't touch anybody else," Mike says. "Relax . . . let's go back to 1491, when everything was wilderness . . . listen to the sounds of the prairie . . . feel the warmth of the sun . . . feel the cool breeze in your face . . . and imagine the scene you see . . ."

With that prelude, Mike guides them through a short course on prairie ecology, the roles of fire, buffalo and Indians in its evolution, and the importance of the prairie to the Iowa economy today.

"We've lost half our prairie soil since the pioneers came," Mike reminds the day-dreaming youngsters.

"What can we do about that?"

Does the program reach the youths – and help them develop an environmental conscience?

Mike doesn't know. But he does know that the teachers are enthusiastic about the program. And it's obvious from the kids' excitement that they enjoy the nature study – and probably are cultivating more respect for their environment.

"If we can develop positive values and attitudes in children," Mike said, "then I don't see why they won't carry over when they're adults."

But Mike's real goal is best described by an idea he borrowed from another educator.

"Our most important function is to open the doors of perception."

October 17, 1976

Ms. Tornell and her sixth-graders take a 'Stone Park Walk'

Some of Iowa's best teachers are frogs, earthworms and prairie grasses – and some of the finest classrooms have dirt floors, no walls and the sky for ceilings.

That's the premise behind the "Stone Park Walk" – an annual encounter for Woodbury County sixth-graders since 1967.

The youths spend a day at Stone State Park near Sioux City poking in ponds, smelling flowers, sifting the dirt on the forest floor and getting closer to their environment than they've probably ever been.

Carolyn Benne, environmental education consultant for the Area XII Education Agency, said the students are encouraged to "look and find things on their own."

At a shallow pond, for example, the kids are given a plastic bag and told to see what sort of critters they can find.

In short order, most return with bags of whirligig beetles, freshwater shrimp, frogs and tiny aquatic insects – to say nothing of muddy feet and splattered clothes.

When the inquisitive pupils study drops of pond water under microscopes, they discover a whole new world of creatures – and they react with enthusiasm only 12-year-olds can muster.

"Ooo, neat!" yelled one exuberant boy, as he peered through the lens.

"Oh, cool!" shouted another.

"Aww-rright!" chimed in a third.

"Goll! There are so many neat things!"

After the youths study, marvel at and sketch their favorite animals, all are returned to the water.

Instructors stress the careful use and preservation of the environment throughout the field trip.

Virginia Tornell, an instructor at Sioux City's Bryant School, set the ground rules before turning loose her charges for a prairie hike.

"If you want to move a rock or stick to look at something, put it back," she said.

"Don't disturb anything. We're here as guests. We're visiting their homes."

Tornell interrupted herself with a gesture at a day-dreaming youth.

"You're stepping on a wild rose," she said calmly, as the boy searched in bewilderment for another place to put his feet.

The students learn to use all their senses: to smell the leadplant, listen to the birds and frogs, and look for animal signs.

On a "blind walk," they gain new respect for the sense of touch. Students lead their blindfolded partners on a "feeling" nature hike.

"You really see things differently when you're blind," coached Bryant schoolteacher Donna Roeper. "You have a different perspective. You have to FEEL things."

Last season's seed pod from an evening primrose is "hard and pointy," while dandelion seeds are fluffy and elusive. Even common objects like tree leaves take on a new fascination for the blindfolded naturalists.

A highlight of the day for many of the sixth-graders comes when the students have the option of handling garter and fox snakes. Few pass up the chance.

The students obviously enjoy the outing – but the day is educational, as well as fun, Benne said.

Most schools have orientation sessions before the trip, so the youths have an idea of what they'll see, she said.

"If they know why they're coming, it's one of the best days of their lives," Benne exclaimed.

During the outing, the classes have assignments – like reporting their observations on the drive to and from the park, drawing pictures of interesting things they find, and writing poems about their experiences.

With the outdoor "happening" comes an increased awareness of nature, Benne said. Students who immerse themselves in the Stone Park environment as sixth graders should appreciate and protect their natural surroundings as adults, she added.

September 24, 1978

Woman's stories enchant children

COLO, IA – A miracle?

What else could explain 18 exuberant first-graders sitting still as toadstools, eyes shining and mouths buttoned?

The children were transfixed – not by magic but by the soft voice, fur wraps and outdoor lore of Woman of the Woods.

"It's not the name my parents gave me," the gentle woman told the children, "but it's a name that suits me."

Clad in a deerskin cape and fox furs, wearing a hat adorned with rabbits' feet and pheasant feathers, Woman of the Woods (also known as Nancy Geske, volunteer naturalist) had come calling at Colo Elementary School.

"My Home is the Woods"

Woman of the Woods joined fellow naturalist Linda Zaletel, who frequently gives school programs for the Story County Conservation Board.

Although Woman of the Woods is a creation of Zaletel and Story County naturalist Cele Burnett, she becomes a very real person to many students, Zaletel said. And her stories have an authentic ring.

She said she wanders the Skunk River Greenbelt, eating wild fruits, nuts, greens and berries while learning about her environment.

"At night I hear the animals, and in the morning I see their signs," she said.

"Down along the river in an old silver maple covered with vines – that's where I sleep.

"You all have homes," she said. "My home is the woods. The woods give me food, water and shelter – that's all I need."

Zaletel seized the moment.

"We have a word for that," she said. "It's habitat."

Children Join In

Woman of the Woods explained how the fox has sharp eyes to help him hunt at night. The children cupped their hands at the sides of their heads to join her imitation of the fox's efficient ears.

Zaletel opened a battered trunk and produced a stuffed red-headed woodpecker. She flicked the bird's stiff tail, comparing it to a bicycle kick-stand.

She thumped the woodpecker's beak against her knee, wondering aloud how it would feel to pound your head against a tree trunk in search of food.

Woodpeckers don't mind the pounding, she said, because the birds' skulls have a built-in cushion. Football helmet designers studied woodpeckers to improve the protective headgear, she said.

Zaletel challenged the children to stick out their tongues as far as they could – then to imagine a woodpecker with a tongue "this long" probing deep into bark and cracks for breakfast.

Giving Clues

Woman of the Woods introduced another friend with a series of clues: sharp teeth, two kinds of fur, flat tail.

Too easy; everybody recognizes a beaver.

Woman of the Woods stroked a soft beaver pelt. She explained how the beaver uses its tail as a prop to stand beside the tree it is cutting, and how the tail slaps the water when a frightened beaver dives.

One boy volunteered to become beaver "food." He stood like a tree and then fell dramatically as Woman of the Woods pretended to cut him down.

They imagined a beaver's lodge, built of sticks – and laughed at the thought of a hungry beaver chewing on his own walls.

Grey Fox

From her trunk, Zaletel produced a spotted fawn skin. Once again, the children sat quietly, as they imagined they were fawns lying in the sun-mottled grass, camouflaged from a prowling coyote.

Woman of the Woods next stroked the soft feathers of a great horned owl. The children marveled at the sharp talons of the stuffed bird. Woman of the Woods told how its huge eyes and off-center ears help the owl locate prey by sound and sight in the dim light. They talked about the owl's diet: mice, rabbits, snakes, even skunks. "Oooooo."

Every creature fits into its own habitat, Woman of the Woods said.

"I kind of like to think of myself as a gray fox," she said. "I sit quiet and look and listen and people don't know I'm there."

Think of the woods as somebody else's home, Zaletel said. Shouldn't we treat outdoor habitat with the same respect we have for other peoples' homes?

Woman of the Woods nodded, and then bade farewell.

"If you're ever in the woods, go quietly and we might meet again," she said. "But if you're noisy, I'll probably just watch you go by."

February 18, 1990

Camp reveals things that go bump in the night

LUTHER, IA — Giggling kids roaming the woods at 2 a.m.; youths hiding along a dark path to scare their friends that walk past; teen-agers sleeping until noon; counselors leading midnight hikes.

Sound like chaos at summer camp?

Not quite.

More than 50 teens last week played "Invaders of the Darkness" at the Iowa 4-H Camping Center near Luther — but this time the kids had their leaders' blessings.

A sunrise bedtime, 1 a.m. cookout, 3 a.m. campfire and 1 p.m. breakfast were all part of the schedule, as the campers reversed their normal day and night schedules.

"The main theory is to discover what animals are out at night and what they do," said camp counselor Matt Durbala.

The youths discovered barred owls on a midnight "hoot" to a wooded bluff at the camp. Assistant camp manager Paul Torbert imitated the owls' eight-hoot call — and promptly was answered by real owls in the distance.

Set Dogs To Howling

Farm dogs also set up a howl, much to Torbert's chagrin and the students' amusement.

As the group sat listening to the night sounds, a bullfrog "chug-o-rummed" from the backwaters down by the river. Far up the valley, a whip-poor-will called. In the underbrush, small birds rustled and cheeped at the human intruders.

Then a dark shadow flitted over the clearing.

"What was that?" whispered one nervous youth.

"A bat!" another squealed.

"Oh, ugh!" shuddered a third.

But Torbert reassured the youngsters.

"They're just eating mosquitoes," he said. "In my book, there aren't nearly enough bats."

The woods grew silent again, except for the trilling of the tree frogs and Torbert's animated conversation with his owl friends. Starlight trickled through the leafy canopy.

The fidgety kids' whispers gradually turned to re-hashes of "The Young and the Restless," and complaints about supper.

"That pizza was *gross*," somebody grumbled.

Time for a change.

Guided only by a few flashlights dulled with red cellophane, the campers followed the path back to a playing field, where an almost-full moon gave plenty of light for games with a 5-foot "earthball" and a parachute.

But the early morning chill and dewy grass — and bodies unaccustomed to 2 a.m. activity — soon took their toll. The youths were ready for quiet time, when each was assigned a "wild place" to meditate for half an hour. (Before the week was out, some even got brave enough to find a wild place under the stars, instead of in a cabin.)

For five nights, the youths explored the darkness. During "awe-stronomy," they saw Saturn's rings through a telescope.

"Ooo, cool!" shrieked one girl. "It's just like the CBS logo."

On a night hike, the youths were intrigued to hear – of all things – worms. Counselor Debbie McDonald explained that the flopping of leaves in the still woods was caused by earthworms crawling up through the forest duff.

Some of the night prowlers even heard the soft yelps of wild turkeys roosting in the trees along the trail.

One morning, the students kept 2 a.m. appointments in Ames to visit the police department, hospital and bakery to see how human workers adjust to graveyard shift hours.

Most days, the campers slept in cabins, but one evening they hiked to a wooded campsite, had a 1 a.m. cookout and went to sleep under the stars at 4 a.m.

The "invaders" also spied on night insects and small animals, dusting a pile of birdseed with fluorescent powder, then using a black light to follow the tracks of creatures that stepped in the glow-in-the-dark potion. The youths learned that nature's world is alive with activity, even after dark.

Of course, even teen-agers can't sleep *all* day, so the camp included daylight fun, such as swimming, archery, rifle shooting, wading a creek, rappelling and scavenger hunts.

Throughout it all, the youth's reactions were just what you'd expect from 12- to 15-year-olds.

"Oh, neat!"

"Yuucchh!"

"Gross!"

"I'm hungry."

"I'm tired."

"I want to sleep."

The kids giggled through games, complained about the food, shivered at the cool night, grumbled about going to bed and relished the time away from parents and siblings.

As they re-set their biological clocks, fatigue occasionally tempered – but never killed – their adolescent exuberance. Just this once, there was no midnight curfew.

"Awesome!"

July 19, 1987

Biology students find idyllic setting
at *real* university at Okoboji

MILFORD, IA – Tucked beside Miller's Bay on West Okoboji Lake, with a view of blue waters, plush lakefront homes and hordes of boaters, lies Iowa's most unique college campus.

It's a classroom without parallel; a priceless natural area flanked by expensive real estate; the legacy of a pioneer Iowa naturalist.

At Iowa Lakeside Laboratory, operated by Iowa's three state universities, the "classroom" is the outdoors. Each summer, several dozen students and researchers spend up to 10 weeks at the field station, studying the rich marshes, lakes, prairies and scattered woodlands of northwest Iowa.

". . . The proper and reverent place for the study of natural objects is in their natural surroundings," wrote University of Iowa botany professor Thomas H. Macbride when he founded the lab in 1909.

"The Real World"

"Natural history work in all our schools . . . is too formal, too artificial, too much based upon material . . . laid up in herbaria, or conserved in cases and bottles. [But] the lakeside laboratory shall afford . . . a chance to see the real world, nature alive, accomplishing her miracles in their own silent splendor."

That's still the philosophy of those who run the lab, said University of Iowa biology professor Richard V. Bovbjerg, who's directed the facility for 22 years.

"We are keenly dedicated to that ideal . . . regardless of the fads of biology that come and go," he said.

The current interest in biotechnology may overshadow field biology, and lure some students away from the Lakeside Lab, Bovbjerg said. "But those students who want to see how biology really is, come here," he said.

Bovbjerg attracts students with a staff of scientists who he said are tops in their fields.

"We don't have the big, fancy equipment," he said, "we've got the big, fancy minds – and that makes a difference."

Diversification

Instructors this year included 11 professors from Iowa's three state universities – the University of Iowa, Iowa State and the University of Northern Iowa – and four other schools.

There is field work in botany, aquatic ecology, plant classification, mycology (the study of fungi), fish ecology and prairie ecology. Researchers have tracked radio-equipped fish, mapped snail populations and described sexual reproduction in flowers.

The lab is open to anybody, Bovbjerg said. Iowans predominate, but students have come from all over the United States and several other countries.

A seven-member board from the three state universities governs the facility; the Ames-Iowa City-Cedar Falls rivalries are forgotten. "One of the nice things here is that we drop all reference to institution," Bovbjerg said. "We have a new loyalty."

Much of the lab's equipment is leftovers from the three universities. For example, Bovbjerg said, stacks in a newly remodeled library building were liberated from the University of Iowa

Law School, the building is recycled from a one-room school and some lab tables were rescued from the dump after the ISU chemistry department discarded them.

"This place does that kind of scrounging," Bovbjerg said. "It's a low-budget operation, I'm kind of proud of that."

That austere approach also is a carryover from Macbride's era. When he conceived the facility, Macbride cajoled the University of Iowa Alumni Association into buying a five-acre tract for the lab.

Students originally stayed in tents, hauled water from a well, cut firewood for cooking and ate vegetables from their garden.

For a time, Macbride used his own money to pay staff salaries.

In the 1930s, an old barn was moved in for a lodge and dining hall. It's still used, complete with pegged beams. The Civilian Conservation Corps, a Depression-era federal agency, built several stone buildings for laboratories and living quarters.

Enthusiastic Students

In the 1920s, the lab grew after Macbride, then retired, campaigned for money to buy an adjoining 90 acres. Another purchase in the 1970s increased the campus to 140 acres.

Bovbjerg declined to estimate the value of the land, except to call it priceless as an academic and natural resource.

"What we do here is so right," said Bovbjerg who described the students as a dedicated, intense, wholesome bunch filled with a happiness that comes with working out of doors.

Macbride would be pleased.

"We sought . . . to rouse the common people, to awaken in them interest in the natural world, and persuade them, if possible, to use it sensibly and rightly," Macbride wrote of the lab's beginning.

"We taught our pupils anything they wanted to know; showed them something of the natural world, its richness and meaning; its moral purity and grandeur."

August 24, 1986

218

Farm creek teaches a valuable lesson

Muddy clothes, wet feet and the freedom to roam may be the best conservation education a kid can ever have.

That thought occurred to me recently, when I took my two youngsters, Andy, 6, and Emily, 2, for a romp at a small creek near our home. The kids hesitated only briefly before plunging in to the knee-deep stream to make mud balls, throw rocks, build dams and just plain splash. We *all* had a delightful outing.

I was reminded of my own childhood, when a hot afternoon often as not would find me, perhaps with a friend or two, sneaking off through the pasture to play in the "crick." (Yup, I still pronounce it that way.)

We frolicked and splashed and loafed and waded – and usually came home soggy-shoed and mud-caked. Mom, bless her, tolerated the grime. She must have known that we were learning as well as playing.

There was the class in engineering, where we constructed huge, two-foot high dams of mud and rocks and sticks. Then we'd grandly "bomb" our creations and watch as the resulting torrent swept down the stream bed.

We studied geology, carefully searching out the flattest, smoothest rocks for skipping across the big hole just below the road culvert.

Math consisted of counting the number of skips from each rock, or in calculating the trajectory of missiles we hurled off the bank.

Art was on the curriculum, as well. With great flourishes, we painted mud murals on the concrete walls of the culvert. And with our bare toes or sticks or fingers, we drew masterpieces in the mud flats along the bottom.

Biology class was nearly always in session, as we chased leopard frogs in the grass beside the water or shivered at the sight of the mossy-backed snapping turtle in a secluded pool or marveled at the occasional great blue heron that stopped to feed on the darting minnows. Sometimes we would catch a crawdad to take home in a glass jar, or scoop up tadpoles to stock in the cattle tank.

We also wondered at the water striders that skimmed magically across the water's surface, and shuddered at the tiny leeches that latched onto our ankles as we waded.

That creek got me started fishing, too. Grandpa took me there on one of my first angling adventures, and I caught a six-inch chub. After that lunker, I was hooked. We spent many hours pursuing the little bullheads and green sunfish and chubs that lurked in the pool.

There also were lessons in conservation. Where the creek curled through the pasture, we'd look for undercut banks to break off with our feet, creating miniature landslides. We not only *saw* soil erosion, we were a part of it.

Much later, more subtle messages about soil erosion began to sink in. Gradually we realized that the deep pool near the road wasn't so deep any more, due to siltation from road repairs and intensified farming by the upstream neighbors.

Was the creek polluted? We didn't know the word – but we did know enough not to drink the water that cattle and hogs had been wading in.

Were those happy hours in the "crick" mud just a routine part of growing up on a farm – or did they shape my whole life? Who can guess?

But creeks taught me at least one thing: "Conservation" means preserving the creek – and a kid's right to play in it.

July 22, 1984

CHAPTER 17

EPILOGUE

Outdoor ethics: Still a difficult issue

It was the height of irony: Three hundred conservationists, educators and journalists meeting in a garish motel overlooking a reservoir that had drowned a once-wild river.

For three days the group lamented the decline in outdoor ethics.

We wondered, while visiting the tourist town of souvenir shops, snack stands, flashy cigarette signs and tacky resort cottages, why our natural resources suffer such abuse.

But that's not to belittle participants in the Izaak Walton League of America's recent outdoor ethics conference at Lake of the Ozarks, Mo. The conferees came from across the U. S. and several foreign countries to face an issue that some say threatens not only our natural resources, but the future of outdoor recreation.

Need Land Ethic

Aldo Leopold, the Iowa-born conservationist and philosopher, recognized the problem a generation ago. He argued the need for a land ethic, whereby people develop a sense of belonging, and therefore respect, for their environment.

The ethics conference addressed blatant examples of that lack of respect. Uncontrolled off-road vehicles, trespassing hunters and litterers topped the list of sins.

A knee-jerk response to such offenses is to pass more laws. But laws address only the symptoms: a person puts his garbage in the trash can because he'll have to pay a fine if he doesn't.

Some conservation groups at the conference suggested codes of ethics. Code adherents, supposedly, would be well-mannered; they'd dispose of their trash properly out of courtesy to their neighbors.

But that still begs the question of ethics. A truly ethical person might strive to produce less garbage, then recycle his waste, knowing that was the right thing to do.

But even we purist, non-motorized, non-consumptive, non-littering recreationists are not without fault.

Hikers may seek out the wildest corners of the woods. But their very presence disturbs the solitude they seek – and their paths may bring other explorers.

Conscientious fishermen gently release trout or bass after the thrill of the fight. But what if the fish dies anyway, and floats downstream to rot on a gravel bar?

As a photographer, I like to get close to wildlife. But if I approach *too* close, I may flush the bird or animal and hurt its chances for survival.

Do we in the media foster unhealthy attitudes about outdoor recreation and resources? When we print a photograph of someone with a big fish or trophy animal, do we send a subtle message that the success of a hunting or fishing trip depends on game in the bag or fish on the stringer?

Do we over-emphasize the kill, at the expense of the experience?

221

"Frontier Mentality"

Some at the ethics conference lamented Americans' "frontier mentality." We still feel a need to conquer the wilderness. And we seldom take time to develop any lasting relationship, much less a tie to the land.

But weren't things better back in the pre-urbanized good old days, when people were closer to the soil?

Oh?

What about cut-and-run loggers of the 19th century? Or consider some farmers who, even today, think first of the size of their crop, and second (if at all) of how much soil they'll leave for their children?

Education can help set us right again, many of the conference participants concluded.

Aldo Leopold would have agreed, but with a caution: education must be deeper than a mere list of dos and don'ts.

"Obligations have no meaning without conscience," Leopold wrote.

"No important change in ethics was ever accomplished without an internal change in our intellectual emphasis, loyalties, affections and convictions," he added.

"In our attempt to make conservation easy," Leopold concluded, "we have made it trivial."

Decision-making, Too

Outdoor ethics education, therefore, must embrace not just rules, but decision-making, said Peter Greer, an official of the U. S. Department of Education.

Teachers should discuss "moral literacy," he said: character, respect, integrity, compassion, responsibility, courage, friendship.

If restoration of those values sounds like a simplistic cure for a host of society's ills, so be it.

But in the outdoor ethics puzzle, as in most social problems, there's not always a bad guy.

We're the ones who – in our rush to enjoy the great outdoors – trample natural areas, trespass, and disregard the rights of others.

Pogo, the philosophical cartoon-strip 'possum, put it best.

"We have met the enemy," mused Pogo, "and they is us."

December 13, 1987

25 years – long time for human, short for nature

Troubles, encouragement can be found along the way

Maybe 25 years seems like a long time because I'm human.

But on nature's scale, it's hardly a heart beat.

That's why there's hope.

Granted, people have fouled our planet and destroyed much of our natural heritage. But maybe we *can* learn to change our ways.

As I look back at my 25 years as an outdoor writer, I find some encouraging examples:

• Many Iowa counties now practice "integrated roadside management" instead of drenching their road ditches with herbicides.

• Catch-and-release fishing is surging in popularity, as anglers seek to enjoy – not exploit – the resource.

• Hunters, too, have become more conscious of "ethics." Most work harder to get along with their non-hunting neighbors.

• Prairie restorations – from backyard plots to the thousands of acres at Walnut Creek National Wildlife Refuge – have seized our imagination.

• Pesticide restrictions, plus reintroduction programs, have brought back bald eagles, peregrine falcons and other wildlife.

Will the lessons remain learned?

Good question.

• The agriculture pendulum keeps swinging. From fencerow-to-fencerow farming in the 1970s, we went to the heyday of the Conservation Reserve Program, with its enormous wildlife and soil-saving benefits. Now former CRP acres are returning to row crops. How quickly we forget . . .

• Roads continue to threaten our natural areas. It's sad to tick off the list: Bloody Run Creek, near Marquette; the Iowa River Greenbelt; several projects in the Loess Hills; Engeldinger Marsh, near Des Moines; the Eddyville Dunes, near Eddyville; the Wapsipinicon River at U.S. Highway 61; the Marion Bypass, in Linn County; the Mines of Spain entrance road, near Dubuque.

Our society is addicted to cars and trucks – and the land pays for the addiction.

• We're sometimes bent on competition with nature, rather than enjoying outdoor wonders for their own sake. May we hope that participants in fishing tournaments, canoe races, trophy hunts and birdathons never lose sight of their *real* roots?

• Gadgets have captured our fancy. John Muir set off into the Sierras with little besides the clothes on his back. But modern adventurers need a four-wheel-drive truck, cell phone, miracle-fiber sleeping bag, Global Positioning System, head-to-toe Gore-Tex and a month's supply of freeze-dried food and Gatorade.

The future?

We can take heart in the growing awareness of the need for a clean environment, open spaces, wildlife and natural areas.

But let's hope those concerns are more than superficial.

• Can we manage our public lands for the long-term good of the natural resource, rather than the ever-changing demands of vocal user-groups?

• Can people begin to see wildlife as integral parts of an ecosystem, instead of only from their own biased point of view? A deer *can* be at once a creature of beauty, a crop destroyer, a hunter's quarry, a photographer's dream, a motorist's nightmare and a coyote's next meal.

• Will government leaders ever see conservation as a *priority,* rather than just another minor issue waving in the political winds?

Let's be optimistic. We Iowans – with our instincts to tinker with our rich land – can have the satisfaction of putting back some of what we've lost. And we can yet save some of those remnants that have escaped 150 years of plow, cow and bulldozer.

But it's not a task to be undertaken lightly.

Burlington native Aldo Leopold, in his conservation classic "A Sand County Almanac," mused that the best definition of a conservationist is written not with a pen, but with an ax.

"It is a matter of what a man thinks about while chopping, or deciding what to chop," Leopold said.

"A conservationist is one who is humbly aware that with each stroke he is writing his signature on the face of the land."

June 22, 1997

224

BIOGRAPHY

Larry Stone has never outgrown his boyhood fascination with playing in creeks and exploring woodlots on the Warren County farm where he grew up. Those passions live on in the form of canoeing, bird-watching, hunting, fishing and nature hikes.

After majoring in biology at Coe College in Cedar Rapids, Larry obtained a master's degree in journalism from the University of Michigan.

During 25 years as outdoor writer and photographer for The Des Moines Register, Larry traveled throughout Iowa, developing a deep appreciation for the state's rich natural resources and dedicated people. Since leaving The Register in 1997, he has continued freelance writing and photography, with an emphasis on protecting our natural heritage.

Larry's work has received awards from the Iowa Wildlife Federation, the Iowa Chapter of the Sierra Club, the Iowa Division of the Izaak Walton League of America, the Association of Earth Science Editors, the International Regional Magazine Association and the Outdoor Writers Association of America.

Larry's wife, Margaret, who grew up on a farm near Traer, shares his outdoor interests.

The Stones now manage woodlands, native prairie and reconstructed prairie on a farm along the Turkey River, near Elkader. They have two adult children.